SOUTHERN APPALACHIAN POETRY

CONTRIBUTIONS TO SOUTHERN APPALACHIAN STUDIES

1. *Memoirs of Grassy Creek: Growing Up in the Mountains on the Virginia–North Carolina Line.* Zetta Barker Hamby. 1998

2. *The Pond Mountain Chronicle: Self-Portrait of a Southern Appalachian Community.* Leland R. Cooper and Mary Lee Cooper. 1998

3. *Traditional Musicians of the Central Blue Ridge: Old Time, Early Country, Folk and Bluegrass Label Recording Artists, with Discographies.* Marty McGee. 2000

4. *W.R. Trivett, Appalachian Pictureman: Photographs of a Bygone Time.* Ralph E. Lentz, II. 2001

5. *The People of the New River: Oral Histories from the Ashe, Alleghany and Watauga Counties of North Carolina.* Leland R. Cooper and Mary Lee Cooper. 2001

6. *John Fox, Jr., Appalachian Author.* Bill York. 2003

7. *The Thistle and the Brier: Historical Links and Cultural Parallels Between Scotland and Appalachia.* Richard Blaustein. 2003

8. *Tales from Sacred Wind: Coming of Age in Appalachia. The Cratis Williams Chronicles.* Cratis D. Williams. Edited by David Cratis Williams and Patricia D. Beaver. 2003

9. *Willard Gayheart, Appalachian Artist.* Willard Gayheart and Donia S. Eley. 2003

10. *The Forest City Lynching of 1900: Populism, Racism, and White Supremacy in Rutherford County, North Carolina.* J. Timothy Cole. 2003

11. *The Brevard Rosenwald School: Black Education and Community Building in a Southern Appalachian Town, 1920–1966.* Betty Jamerson Reed. 2004

12. *The Bristol Sessions: Writings About the Big Bang of Country Music.* Edited by Charles K. Wolfe and Ted Olson. 2005

13. *Community and Change in the North Carolina Mountains: Oral Histories and Profiles of People from Western Watauga County.* Compiled by Nannie Greene and Catherine Stokes Sheppard. 2006

14. *Ashe County: A History.* Arthur Lloyd Fletcher (1963). New edition, 2006

15. *The New River Controversy.* Thomas J. Schoenbaum (1979). New edition, 2007

16. *The Blue Ridge Parkway by Foot: A Park Ranger's Memoir.* Tim Pegram. 2007

17. *James Still: Critical Essays on the Dean of Appalachian Literature.* Edited by Ted Olson and Kathy H. Olson. 2007

18. *Owsley County, Kentucky, and the Perpetuation of Poverty.* John R. Burch, Jr. 2007

19. *Asheville: A History.* Nan K. Chase. 2007

20. *Southern Appalachian Poetry: An Anthology of Works by 37 Poets.* Edited by Marita Garin. 2008

21. *Ball, Bat and Bitumen: A History of Coalfield Baseball in the Appalachian South.* L.M. Sutter. 2008

22. *The Frontier Nursing Service: America's First Rural Nurse-Midwife Service and School.* Marie Bartlett. 2008

SOUTHERN APPALACHIAN POETRY

An Anthology of Works by 37 Poets

Edited by Marita Garin

CONTRIBUTIONS TO SOUTHERN APPALACHIAN STUDIES, 20

McFarland & Company, Inc., Publishers
Jefferson, North Carolina, and London

With gratitude to John E. Schrader (1935–1993),
whose work in documenting the culture of Appalachia
through film and photography
has been immeasurably instructive.

All photographs are courtesy of the respective poets unless otherwise noted

LIBRARY OF CONGRESS CATALOGUING-IN-PUBLICATION DATA

Southern Appalachian poetry : an anthology of works
by 37 poets / edited by Marita Garin.
p.   cm. — (Contributions to southern Appalachian studies ; 20)
Includes index.

ISBN 978-0-7864-3429-9
softcover : 50# alkaline paper ∞

1. American poetry — Appalachian Region, Southern.   2. Appalachian Region, Southern — Poetry.   3. Mountain life — Poetry.
I. Garin, Marita, 1936–
PS554.S68   2008   811'.00803275 — dc22   2008010237

British Library cataloguing data are available

©2008 Marita Garin. All rights reserved

*No part of this book may be reproduced or transmitted in any form
or by any means, electronic or mechanical, including photocopying
or recording, or by any information storage and retrieval system,
without permission in writing from the publisher.*

On the cover: The Blue Ridge Mountains near Carver's
Gap, Roan Mountain State Park; *inset* mountain stream in
Pisgah National Forest (photography by Sue McLeod)

Manufactured in the United States of America

McFarland & Company, Inc., Publishers
Box 611, Jefferson, North Carolina 28640
www.mcfarlandpub.com

For Byron Herbert Reece
(1917–1958)

"O Joy, be a bird
On a broken wing."

A Song of Joy and Other Poems

Contents

Acknowledgments xi
Preface 1
Introduction 3

Bob Henry Baber	11	Irene McKinney	136
Joseph Barrett	18	Louise McNeill	142
Kathryn Stripling Byer	24	Jim Wayne Miller	148
Fred Chappell	31	Robert Morgan	156
Mark DeFoe	40	Valerie Nieman	165
Charles B. Dickson	46	Lee Pennington	170
Hilda Downer	50	Ron Rash	177
Gregory Dykes	56	George Scarbrough	183
Marita Garin	62	Bettie Sellers	190
Richard Hague	68	Vivian Shipley	195
Marc Harshman	77	Nancy Simpson	200
Don Johnson	84	R.T. Smith	206
Stephen Knauth	92	Bob Snyder	213
Mary Kratt	99	Katherine Soniat	218
P.J. Laska	104	James Still	222
George Ella Lyon	110	John Foster West	228
Jeff Daniel Marion	116	Charles Wright	234
Michael McFee	124	Isabel Zuber	241
Llewellyn McKernan	130		

Glossary 249
Notes on the Poets 251
Index of Poems and Poets 259

Acknowledgments

Bob Henry Baber: "Poem for James Collins" (from *Now and Then: The Appalachian Magazine*, used with permission), "Trail of the Lonesome Pine" (from *Pine Mountain Sand and Gravel*), "Richwood" (from *Appalachian Journal*, used with permission), "Vandalia," and "The Inheritance" are copyright © by Bob Henry Baber. Reprinted by permission of the author. Autobiographical essay is copyright © by Bob Henry Baber, used with permission.

Joseph Barrett: "Woman Playing a Juke Box" (from *The Laurel Review*), "A Winter Baptism," and "Senryu" from *Old Martins, New Strings* (The Soupbean Press). Copyright © 1990 by Joseph Barrett. "An April Exultation" from *The Mason-Dixon Sutra* (Igneus Press). Copyright © 1999 by P.J. Laska and the Estates of Joseph Barrett and Bob Snyder. "Still Life" (from *Wonderful West Virginia*), "Homeward," and "The Strikers" (both from *Now and Then: The Appalachian Magazine*, used with permission). "Detour" and two "Haiku" are copyright © by Joseph Barrett. Reprinted from the Estate of Joseph Barrett by permission of Joanie McAnany, Literary Executor. Biographical essay is copyright © by P.J. Laska, used with permission.

Kathryn Stripling Byer: "Snowbird," "Diamonds," "Bittersweet," "Trillium," "Ivory Combs," "River Bed," and "Afterwards, Far from the Church" from *Wildwood Flower*. Copyright © 1992 by Kathryn Stripling Byer. Reprinted by permission of Louisiana State University Press. "Jericho's" (from *Southern Poetry Review*) is copyright © by Kathryn Stripling Byer. Reprinted by permission of the author. Autobiographical essay is copyright © by Kathryn Stripling Byer, used with permission.

Fred Chappell: "Remembering Wind Mountain at Sunset" from *Midquest*. Copyright © 1981 by Fred Chappell. "A Prayer for the Mountains," "A Prayer for Slowness," and "Here" from *Source*. Copyright © 1985 by Fred Chappell. "Remodeling the Hermit's Cabin" from *First and Last Words*. Copyright © 1989 by Fred Chappell. Reprinted by permission of Louisiana State University Press. Autobiographical essay is copyright © by Fred Chappell, used with permission.

Mark DeFoe: "The Former Miner Returns from His First Day as a Service Worker" from *Air*. Copyright © 1998 by Mark DeFoe. Reprinted by permission of Green Tower Press. "Opossum Spring" (first appeared in *The Yale Review*, used with permission) from *Mark DeFoe's Greatest Hits* (Pudding House). Copyright © 2004 by Mark DeFoe. "Street Dance: West Virginia" from *Bringing Home Breakfast* (Black Willow Press). Copyright © 1982 by Mark DeFoe. "The Farm Tender" (from *Adena*) and "Emergency Re-pairs" (from *Malahat Review*) are copyright © by Mark DeFoe. Reprinted by permission of the author. Autobiographical essay is copyright © by Mark DeFoe, used with permission.

Charles B. Dickson: "Magnet" from *A Touch of Wholeness* (Skyefield Press). Copyright © 1986 by Charles B. Dickson. "No More Hard Times" (from *Pembroke Magazine*), "Appalachian Parthenon" (from *Georgia State Review*), and "Blue Ridge Moments: Nine Haiku" (from *Modern Haiku* and *Canada Sheet: Appalachian Twilight, 1986–87*) are copyright © by Charles B. Dickson. Reprinted from the Estate of Charles B. Dickson by permission of Virginia Dickson, Literary Executor. Autobiographical essay is copyright © by Charles B. Dickson, used with the permission of Virginia Dickson.

Hilda Downer: "Hills so beautiful, they sting," "Rain polka dots the sidewalk," and "Bus perched on top of a mountain like a skull on a wedding cake" from *Bandana Creek* (Red Clay Books). Copyright © 1979 by Hilda Downer. "So much has come and gone that the Appalachians never existed" (from *Appalachian Journal*, used with permission) and "Back to Bandana in Brown Season" (from *Katúah*) are copyright © by Hilda Downer. Reprinted by permission of the author. Autobiographical essay is copyright © by Hilda Downer, used with permission.

Gregory Dykes: "Reflections During a Country Funeral" (from *The Lyricist*), "It Is...," "You Must Teach the Student," and "What I Have Learned" are copyright © by Gregory Dykes. Reprinted by permission of the author. Autobiographical essay is copyright © by Gregory Dykes, used with permission.

Marita Garin: "Blood of the Lamb" (from *Southern Exposure*), "A Yard Near Elizabethton, Tennessee" (from *Kenyon Review*), "From a Ridge in Eastern Kentucky" (from *Cumberland Poetry Review*), "Crab Orchard Prediction" (from *Arts Journal*), "15-Year-Old Mother Killed..." (from *Old Hickory Review*), "Weather Diviner" (from *Small Farm*), and "Picnic in Cherokee National Forest" are copyright © by Marita Garin. Reprinted by permission of the author. Autobiographical essay is copyright © by Marita Garin, used with permission.

Richard Hague: "Going Back the Hard Way," "Mary Daugherty," "In the Woods Beyond the Coal Fields," "Greenbrier Portraits," "October," and "Sometimes I Am Looking" from *Ripening* (Ohio State University Press). Copyright © 1984 by Richard Hague. Reprinted by permission of the author. Autobiographical essay is copyright © by Richard Hague, used with permission.

Marc Harshman: "The Barn" (first appeared in *Quarterly West*), "Primer," and "Setting the Hook" from *Turning Out the Stones* (State Street Press). Copyright © 1983 by Marc Harshman. "Beyond the Two of Us" from *Three Poems* (Costmary Press). Copyright © 1987 by Marc Harshman. "Almost" (from *The Laurel Review)* is copyright © by Marc Harshman. Reprinted by permission of the author. Autobiographical essay is copyright © by Marc Harshman, used with permission.

Don Johnson: "Going Home" from *The Importance of Visible Scars* (Wampeter Press). Copyright 1983 by Don Johnson. "And the River Gathered Around Us," "Baptism: Watauga River," "1946," "Raymond Pierce's Vietnamese Wife" (first appeared in *Appalachian Journal*, used with permission), and "Sailin' on to Hawaii" from *Watauga Drawdown* (Overmountain Press). Copyright © 1990 by Don Johnson. Reprinted by permission of the author. Autobiographical essay is copyright © by Don Johnson, used with permission.

Stephen Knauth: "Night-Fishing on Irish Buffalo Creek," "From the Cherokee," and "1836: In the Cherokee Overhills" from *Night-Fishing On Irish Buffalo Creek* (Ithaca House). Copyright © 1984 by Stephen Knauth. "Cumulonimbus," "Impossible Creek," and "The Pine Figures" from *The Pine Figures* (Dooryard Press). Copyright © 1986 by Stephen Knauth. "Driving the Great Craggy Mountains" (from *Arts Journal*) is copyright © by Stephen Knauth. Reprinted by permission of the author. Autobiographical essay is copyright © by Stephen Knauth, used with permission.

Mary Kratt: "On the Steep Side," "I'd Have Waited a Lifetime for You, Greer Garson," "The 1940s," and "Coming Back to West Virginia" from *On the Steep Side* (Briarpatch Press). Copyright © 1993 by Mary Kratt. Reprinted by permission of the author. Autobiographical essay is copyright © by Mary Kratt, used with permission.

P.J. Laska: "The Hillbilly Odyssey" from *SOUPBEAN an anthology of contemporary appalachian literature* (Mountain Union Books). Copyright © 1977 by P.J. Laska. "Ancestorial" and "Mystistry" (from *Appalachian Journal*, used with permission) from *Old Martins, New Strings* (The Soupbean Press). Copyright © 1990 by P.J. Laska. "Widow Horvath on Coal Run Then and Now," "The Widow McDowell on Her Granddaughter's Divorce," and "Asa Gray on Cheat Mountain" from *The Day the Eighties Began* (Mountain Union Books). Copyright © 1991 by P.J. Laska. "Outmigration Time Again" (from *Venue*) is copyright © by P.J. Laska. Reprinted by permission of the author. Autobiographical essay is copyright © by P.J. Laska, used with permission.

George Ella Lyon: "A Testimony," "Elopement," "Her Words," "How the Letters Bloom Like a Catalpa Tree," and "Looking at a Photograph of My Mother, Age 3" from *Catalpa*. Copyright © 1993 by George Ella Lyon. Reprinted by permission of Wind Publications. Autobiographical essay is copyright © by George Ella Lyon, used with permission.

Jeff Daniel Marion: "Ebbing & Flowing Spring," "Panther," "Rambling Rose," "Fall," and "Winter Watch" from *Vigils: New and Selected Poems* (Appalachian Consortium Press). Copyright © 1990 by Jeff Daniel Marion. "Panther" and "Fall" first appeared in *Appalachian Journal*, used with permission. "The Last Man on Devil's Nose" and "A Mountain Fable of a Sort" from *Out in the Country, Back Home* (Jackpine Press). Copyright © 1976 by Jeff Daniel Marion. "Hand-Me-Down Days" from *Lost and Found* (Sow's Ear Press). Copyright © 1994 by Jeff Daniel Marion. Reprinted by permission of the author. Autobiographical essay is copyright © by Jeff Daniel Marion, used with permission.

Michael McFee: "Plain Air" and "Shenandoah" from *Plain Air* (University Presses of Florida). Copyright © 1983 by Michael McFee. Reprinted by permission of the author. "Family Reunion Near Grape Creek Church, Four Miles West of Murphy, N.C., 1880" and "Cold Quilt" from *Vanishing Acts*. Copyright © 1989 by Michael McFee. Reprinted by permission of Gnomon Press. "Cold Quilt" originally appeared in *Poetry*. "Reclamation," copyright © by Michael McFee from *New North Carolina Poets: The Eighties* (Green River Press, 1983), edited by Stephen Smith. Reprinted by permission. "Tinted Pictures" from *Sad Girl Sitting on a Running Board*. Copyright © 1991 by Michael McFee. Reprinted by permission of Gnomon Press. Autobiographical essay is copyright © by Michael McFee, used with permission.

Llewellyn McKernan: "The Strike: A Bird's Eye View" and "The Shaker" from *Short and Simple Annals*,

Poems About Appalachia (Perfect Printing, Inc.). Copyright © 1979 by Llewellyn McKernan. "At the Edge of Town" from *Many Waters: Poems from West Virginia* (Edwin Mellen Poetry Press). Copyright © 1993 by Llewellyn McKernan. Reprinted by permission of the author. Quotation used in the *Notes* from *Short and Simple Annals, Poems About Appalachia* is used with permission of the author. Autobiographical essay is copyright © by Llewellyn McKernan, used with permission.

Irene McKinney: "Deep Mining," "Visiting My Gravesite: Talbott Churchyard, West Virginia," and "Twilight in West Virginia: Six O'Clock Mine Report" from *Six O'Clock Mine Report*. Copyright © 1989 by Irene McKinney. Reprinted by permission of University of Pittsburgh Press. "The Anguish Lessons" and "For Women Who Have Been Patient All Their Lives" from *Quick Fire and Slow Fire*. Copyright © 1988 by Irene McKinney. Reprinted by permission of North Atlantic Books. Autobiographical essay is copyright © by Irene McKinney, used with permission.

Louise McNeill: "Hill Daughter," "Blizzard," "Mayapple Hill," and "The Roads" are reprinted with permission from the West Virginia University Press, Morgantown, West Virginia, from *Paradox Hill: From Appalachia to Lunar Shore* by Louise McNeill, copyright © 1972 West Virginia University Foundation, Morgantown, West Virginia, on behalf of the West Virginia University Libraries. All rights reserved. "Moonshiner" and "Timber Boom" from *Gauley Mountain* (Harcourt, Brace). Copyright © 1939 by Louise McNeill. Reprinted by permission of Pocahontas Communications Cooperative. Autobiographical essay is copyright © by Louise McNeill, used with the permission of Douglas McNeill Pease.

Jim Wayne Miller: "Fencepost" from *Dialogue with a Dead Man*. Copyright © 1992 by Jim Wayne Miller. Reprinted by permission of the Jim Wayne Miller Literary Estate, Mary Ellen Miller, Literary Executor. "A Turning," "How America Came to the Mountains," "The Brier Losing Touch with His Traditions," "On the Wings of a Dove," "The Brier Breathing," and "Abandoned" from *The Brier Poems*. Copyright © 1997 by the Estate of Jim Wayne Miller. Reprinted by permission of Gnomon Press. "The Brier Losing Touch with His Traditions" and "Abandoned" first appeared in *Appalachian Journal*, used with permission. Autobiographical essay is copyright © by Jim Wayne Miller, used with the permission of Mary Ellen Miller.

Robert Morgan: "The Hollow," "The Flying Snake," "Lost Flower," and "Death Crown" from *Groundwork*. Copyright © 1979 by Robert Morgan. Reprinted by permission of Gnomon Press. "Broomsedge," "The Body of Elisha Mitchell," "Whiskey Tree," and "New Organ" from *Sigodlin* (Wesleyan University Press). Copyright © 1990 by Robert Morgan. "Nail Bag" and "The Gift of Tongues" from *At the Edge of the Orchard Country* (Wesleyan University Press). Copyright © 1987 by Robert Morgan. Reprinted by permission of the author. "Nail Bag" and "Lost Flower" originally appeared in *Poetry*. Autobiographical essay is copyright © by Robert Morgan, used with permission.

Valerie Nieman: "At the Union Picnic" (from *The Laurel Review*) and "Reclamation: Washing Machine" (from *Sing, Heavenly Muse!*) are copyright © by Valerie Nieman. Reprinted by permission of the author. "Expedition" from *Wake, Wake, Wake*. Copyright © 2006 by Valerie Nieman. Reprinted by permission of Press 53. (These poems first appeared under the name "Valerie Nieman Colander.") Autobiographical essay is copyright © by Valerie Nieman, used with permission.

Lee Pennington: "We Came" from *I Knew a Woman* (Love Street Books). Copyright © 1977 by Lee Pennington. "Billy Edd Wheeler" and "Poet of the Soil" from *Scenes from a Southern Road* (JRD Publishing Co.). Copyright © 1969 by Lee Pennington. "Dark Smell" from *Poems from the Hills* (Morris Harvey Press). Copyright © 1971 by Lee Pennington. "Return" (from *Mountain Review*), "Kentucky Lucky" (from *Red Clay Reader*), "The Hounds Are Restless," "Lady Sewing Songs," and "To Be" are copyright © by Lee Pennington. Reprinted by permission of the author. Quotation used in the *Introduction* from Lee Pennington's unpublished manuscript, *Appalachian Newground*, is used with permission. Autobiographical essay is copyright © by Lee Pennington, used with permission.

Ron Rash: "July, 1947" from *Eureka Mill*. Copyright © 1996 by Ron Rash. Reprinted by permission of Hub City Press. "A Preacher Who Takes Up Serpents Laments the Presence of Skeptics in His Church," "Sunday Evening at Middlefork Creek Pentecostal Church," and "Good Friday, 1995, Driving Westward" from *Among the Believers*. Copyright © 2000 by Ron Rash. Reprinted by permission of Iris Press. "My Grandmother Speaks of the Early Years" (from *Special Report*), "Having Foreseen the Deaths of Others, the Old Mountain Woman Awaits Her Own" (from *James Dickey Newsletter* Vol. 7, No. 2, Spring 1991, used with permission), "Having Recovered His Sight After Being Struck by Lightning, the Old Farmer Quiets Those Who Would Question Him" (from *Tar River Poetry*, used with permission), "Raising the Dead" (from *Kennesaw Review*, used with permission), and "In a Children's Graveyard North of Newry" are copyright © by Ron Rash. Reprinted by permission of the author. Autobiographical essay is copyright © by Ron Rash, used with permission.

George Scarbrough: "Tenantry," "Winter Bread," and "Hiwassee River" from *Invitation to Kim*. Copyright © 1989 by George Scarbrough. Reprinted by permission of Iris Press. Autobiographical essay is copyright © by George Scarbrough, used with the permission of Margaret Bates Rogers, Power of Attorney for George Scarbrough.

Bettie Sellers: "And All the Princes Are Gone," "Naomi's Nerve," "Pink," "Miracle at Raven Gap," and "Liza's Monday" from *Liza's Monday and Other Poems* (Appalachian Consortium Press). Copyright © 1986 by Bettie Sellers. Reprinted by permission of the author. Autobiographical essay is copyright © by Bettie Sellers, used with permission.

Vivian Shipley: "Worms," "Horse Breath Winter," "White Chickens," and "Outside Cecelia, Kentucky" from *Poems Out of Harlan County* (Greenfield Press). Copyright © 1989 by Vivian Shipley. Reprinted by permission of the author. Autobiographical essay is copyright © by Vivian Shipley, used with permission.

Nancy Simpson: "Night Student," "Crowded House," "White Lie," "Lives in One Lifetime," "The Wreck" (from *Tar River Poetry*, used with permission), "Leaving in the Dead of Winter" and "Bridge on the River Kwai" from *Night Student* (State Street Press). Copyright © 1985 by Nancy Simpson. Reprinted by permission of the author. Autobiographical essay is copyright © by Nancy Simpson, used with permission.

R.T. Smith: "The Bird Carver" and "Beneath the Mound" from *Banish Misfortune* (Livingston University Press). Copyright © 1988 by R.T. Smith. "Yonosa House" and "Weave" from *From the High Dive* (Water Mark Press). Copyright © 1983 by R.T. Smith. "After an Image in Faulkner" from *Rural Route* (Tamarack Editions). Copyright © 1981 by R.T. Smith. "The Call" from *Beasts Did Leap* (Tamarack Editions). Copyright © 1982 by R.T. Smith. "Hill Woman" (from *Xanadu*) is copyright © by R.T. Smith. All the above reprinted by permission of the author. Autobiographical essay is copyright © by R.T. Smith, used with permission.

Bob Snyder: "Comfort Me with Hyssop" and "Hiding" from *The Mason-Dixon Sutra* (Igneus Press). Copyright © 1999 by P.J. Laska and the Estates of Joseph Barrett and Bob Snyder. "Guard Duty" from *We'll See Who's a Peasant Now* (Mountain Union Press). Copyright © 1977 by Bob Snyder (under the pen name of Billy Greenhorn). "Pilgrim Number One" (from *The Laurel Review*), "Merle" (from *Pine Mountain Sand and Gravel*), "Dogwood Farmstead" (from *Stone Country*), and "The Shoenatural Prophet" are copyright © by Bob Snyder. Published from the Estate of Bob Snyder by permission of Peg Snyder, Literary Executor. "Comfort Me with Hyssop" first appeared in *Appalachian Journal*, used with permission. Autobiographical essay is copyright © by Bob Snyder, used with the permission of Peg Snyder.

Katherine Soniat: "Summer Tea" from *Cracking Eggs* (University Presses of Florida). Copyright © 1990 by Katherine Soniat. "Truck at the Top of the Field" (from *Pennsylvania Review*) is copyright © by Katherine Soniat. Reprinted by permission of the author. "A Shared Life" (first appeared in *The Ohio Review*, used with permission) from *A Shared Life*. Copyright © 1993 by Katherine Soniat. Reprinted by permission of University of Iowa Press. Autobiographical essay is copyright © by Katherine Soniat, used with permission.

James Still: "Spring," "Drought," "Pattern for Death," "Passenger Pigeons," "A Man Singing to Himself," "Dulcimer," "Banjo Bill Cornett," "Night in the Coal Camps," "Earth-Bread," "White Highways," and "Wolfpen Creek" from *From the Mountain, From the Valley: New and Collected Poems* by James Still, edited by Ted Olson. Copyright © 2001 by The University Press of Kentucky. Reprinted by permission of The University Press of Kentucky. Autobiographical essay material was excerpted from *Foxfire*, Fall 1988. Copyrighted © by Foxfire, Inc., used with permission.

John Foster West: "Aunt Orlena," "Pink Washborn," and "MacKenzie Gap's Namesake" from *This Proud Land* (Loftin & Co.). Copyright © 1974 by John Foster West. "Appalachian Nativity," "Dark Lake," "Winterfolk," and "Bull's Branch Revisited" from *Wry Wine* (John F. Blair). Copyright © 1977 by John Foster West. Reprinted by permission of the author. Autobiographical essay is copyright © by John Foster West, used with permission.

Charles Wright: "Blackwater Mountain," "Dog Creek Mainline," and "Firstborn" from *Country Music: Selected Early Poems*. Copyright © 1982 by Charles Wright. Reprinted by permission of Wesleyan University Press. "Homecoming" from *The Grave of the Right Hand* (Wesleyan University Press). Copyright © 1970 by Charles Wright. Reprinted by permission of the author. "Blackwater Mountain" and "Dog Creek Mainline" originally appeared in *Poetry*. "Homecoming" originally appeared in *The New Yorker*. Autobiographical essay material was excerpted from *Contemporary Authors, Autobiography Series* Vol. 7, Gale Research Inc., Detroit, Michigan. Copyright © by Charles Wright, reprinted with the author's permission.

Isabel Zuber: "Your Old Ways" and "Another Misty Morning" from *Oriflamb* (A North Carolina Writers' Network Publication). Copyright © 1987 by Isabel Zuber. "Solstice" from *Winter's Exile* (Scots Plaid Press) where it appeared in a slightly different version. Copyright © 1997 by Isabel Zuber. "Our Lands and Fields, Mother" (from *No Business Poems*), "The Decrease of the Tribe" (from *Whetstone*), "Before the Preacher Went Blind" (from *The Laurel Review*), "What the Hunter Brings Home" (from *Arts Journal*), "Made," "Thriving to Fail," and "Offerings of Light" are copyright © by Isabel Zuber. All the above reprinted by permission of the author. Autobiographical essay is copyright © by Isabel Zuber, used with permission.

Epigraph used for the dedication is from the poem "A Song of Joy" appearing in *A Song of Joy and Other Poems* by Byron Herbert Reece. Copyright © 1952 by E.P. Dutton & Co., Inc. Reprint published by Cherokee Publishing Co., 1985 by arrangements with E.P. Dutton. Used with permission.

Preface

This anthology grew out of a series of lectures, "Appalachian Culture and Poetry," prepared for an Elderhostel program held at The Mountain Camp and Conference Center near Highlands, North Carolina, where I was an instructor during spring sessions from 1987 to 1992. I wanted to focus attention on a region that has undergone a time line of development different from that of the rest of the country, its way of life and traditions having existed almost unchanged for much of its history. The "hillbilly" stereotype has been around in entertainment venues for many years, but what is less well-known are the circumstances basic to survival in the mountains through generations of hardship that have produced particular strengths of character and an identity rooted in place and family that are unique to its culture. As participants in the class reacted with interest and enthusiasm to the material, I began to think about putting together a collection of poems that could be shared with the wider public. Such an anthology would also document and preserve details of a way of life in the Southern Appalachian region that is beginning to disappear but still exists in areas that are out of the mainstream.

I started work on the project in 1989 and 1990, choosing poems from what was then available, looking not so much at the publishing record of the poets as at the poems themselves. I was searching for work that resonated on a human level, written with passion and caring by poets who felt compelled to write the sketches, stories, portraits, memories, and history that embody the mountain experience. Besides a degree of craft, I was looking for individuality of expression, depth of feeling, and a sensitivity to the landscape and the flow of generations — writing that could never be mistaken for originating anywhere else. Selections were not limited to poets whose family origins are Appalachian. Many had moved here from other parts of the United States, found themselves immensely inspired by the area, and wrote from their response to it. There was vitality in the poems that crossed my desk as well as variety: mostly free verse ranging from lyric and narrative to the experimental, a few formal poems, and some surprising haiku and senryu.

I especially wanted this project to cross state boundaries. Thus it begins in the southernmost Appalachian mountains with the hill farms located in north Georgia, moves up through western North Carolina and east Tennessee, passes through a small corner of southwest Virginia, continues into the coal mining areas of West Virginia and Kentucky, and finally reaches southeastern Ohio. Many anthologies have been devoted to a particular state's poets, but few have covered the entire Southern Appalachian mountains. And to my knowledge, there is no regional anthology that has included autobiographical essays by the poets to introduce themselves and their work. These provide interesting biographical and historical material as well as information about underlying impulses that led them to write the poems.

The mountain culture has a strong storytelling tradition, both oral and written, going back to the earliest settlers. Stories were their way to preserve family history and provide entertainment: a vehicle for imagination and humor as well as for the development of individual style throughout the many far-flung communities back in the coves and hollows, out-of-the-way areas where small mountain colleges emerged, eventually arriving in urban areas and universities. Mountain life distilled into words, shaped into art. How this particular anthology finally came to be published has its own story as well.

By 1993 poems had been selected, essays written and edited, the Introduction completed, and some futile attempts had been made to find a publisher. Then it all came to a halt. Everything was put away in boxes, sealed up, and there it lay in darkness for many years. Personal issues and family events needed my attention. Writing projects were on hold. With energy thus re-directed, it was a perplexing time that yielded no clear direction in regard to the anthology. Every once in a while the thought would surface: "I owe it to the poets to get this published."

One April day in 2004, following a sudden impulse to drive up to the Great Craggy Mountains, I found myself on the Blue Ridge Parkway northeast of Asheville. It was windy. By the time I reached the higher elevations, gale force blasts buffeted the car. Stopping at the Craggy Gardens Visitor's Center built on the edge of a steep ridge, I stepped inside and looked through large windows at the back to see the mountains stretching for hundreds of miles to the horizon and beyond. Wind whipped around the corners of the building, so fierce that it shrieked and howled, filling the place with a relentless wailing. As I gazed at the vast wilderness, I felt something moving through me, and thought: "This is the sound of Appalachia, this is the voice of all the hardship, struggle, heartache, hard work, and determination that comes from living in these mountains. This is the voice of Appalachia that needs to be heard. It is time to unpack the anthology and get it published."

Two years later the manuscript found its way to McFarland and was soon headed toward publication. It had been shortened, the Introduction revised, and a new section, Notes on the Poets, added where the careers and professional achievements of the poets were brought up-to-date. Later, at the suggestion of the publisher, photographs of most of the poets were added, including several who are now deceased. It's an interesting mix, vintage and current, that traces a zigzag line through the years, past and present, the living and the dead, leaving it to reader and scholar to sort through likenesses and elusive dates that belong with words, with a life. Yet they provide a visual presence that adds another dimension to one's engagement with the poet's work. These images take their place on the pages of this book along with the poetry and essays to become part of the history and culture of Appalachia, helping establish the region's identity. It has been a slow development, moving through the life cycles of many generations. What is most apparent is how deeply the heart remains connected to its roots and how others who have found their home here are similarly bound, not by birth or family, but by kinship with the land itself.

Marita Garin
Black Mountain, North Carolina

Introduction

To describe a region: that is my purpose in bringing these poems together. When I first undertook this project, I was certain the literature of the Southern Appalachians had evolved to the degree that the material *would* be available. The area was to include north Georgia, western North Carolina, east Tennessee, West Virginia, eastern Kentucky, and a corner of southwest Virginia, all of which share an historical and cultural identity apart from the rest of the Appalachian Mountains. The poets were to be native-born writers who still live in the region, those who have moved away yet for whom Appalachia still has a claim on their imagination and emotions, and newcomers whose sensibilities have been shaped by the region and who write about it with insight and sensitivity.

As poems arrived in my study, a collective voice began to emerge, so compelling in its variety, honesty, and intensity that I needed to let it speak on its own, to tell me what it wanted to say about Appalachia. I trusted what would take shape would be a balanced view of an extremely complex region yielding on close examination human qualities with much deeper roots and finer sensibilities than are usually attributed to it.

Although the work describes almost without exception life lived on hill farms, in coal mining camps and settlements, and in small towns or isolated communities, the authors are not just Appalachian poets. Many write of other places and people. Some are also essayists, short story writers, novelists, playwrights, and authors of children's books or science fiction. Some write their poetry in a classical tradition and style while others border on the experimental, pushing beyond traditional boundaries of language and imagination toward the avant-garde. However, all the poems document long-standing concerns of Appalachia and its people.

A few generalizations may be helpful for readers not well-acquainted with the area. Incorporated into the poems as naturally as any item in a familiar landscape, poverty has been (and still can be) a fact of life. Intimately known, it has at times been an exhaustion of the land — steep hillside farms that lose their good soil within a few years after the land is cleared — and of the people. The struggle to survive may involve the imposition of external regulations concerning land use and mineral rights or dealing with welfare and black lung disease benefits, coal mine owners, unions, and a volatile coal economy; or it can be a more personal conflict with neighbors or kinfolks (as in the notorious feuds of the past). Another way to talk about poverty in Appalachia is to mention the historic exploitation of natural resources by timber and coal interests and also of the people — their lifestyle, values, crafts, and music — by outsiders that can leave them feeling the poorer — vulnerable and defenseless.

One characteristic trait that has been a strength in dealing with hardship has been an awareness that is not so much an intellectual as it is a subconsciously integrated response to the environment, an intuitive relationship with the natural world reinforced by skills passed on for generations that has allowed them to survive in impoverished circumstances. Thus much of their creativity in meeting the challenges of daily life springs from their resourcefulness.

Isolation has been unmistakable in the region. Given the difficult terrain, enormous finances are needed to build roads and railroads. Until recently, these often did not exist for areas that could not yield an economic (or political) return for the investment. Isolation was a truth about early pioneer life all over the country, but in Appalachia it persisted through much of the 20th century and has shaped the inhabitants' sense of self, for some even becoming a necessity if they are to thrive. However, the pressures of isolation and poor economics can also result in extreme social behavior (as in Jeff Daniel Marion's "Rambling Rose").

How does one respond to problems that can overwhelm even the strongest? For one thing, the people do not give up. Although historically regarded by mainstream America as having a poor self-image—the hillbilly stereotype—they themselves have enormous pride and an intact sense of self. They are equal to the challenges because they know what they are capable of and what they value. Their identity comes from a deep sense of belonging to the land, such an intimate alliance that it is felt to be an extension of self, a bond that may persist long after one leaves the region. That sense of origin exerts a primal pull with all the power of the natural imagery in many of the poems. Given the intensity and psychological complexity of the emotions involved, the land at times is regarded as a trap from which one can never be free.

Family is another deeply rooted value in mountain life. Kinfolks, ancestors, one's immediate family—all contribute to who one is, but links with the past are especially strong. At times, past and family, along with the land, are inextricable in their grip on the individual and result in conflict—feelings of grief or disloyalty—when choices are made to discard the old ways or to sell land that has been in the family for generations.

Another characteristic of the region—it seems to be in the atmosphere itself but can only be subjectively verified—is that time flows differently here. That dreamy blue haze off in the distance where ridge upon mountain ridge becomes an endless ocean stretching to the horizon may account for a charged effect on mind and body, literally drawing the senses beyond physical limits. Whatever the reason, time has a way of moving into some other dimension where the world's concerns matter little (as suggested in Robert Morgan's "The Hollow").

Beyond these generalizations, much can be said about specific characteristics of the people. They possess a strong independence and desire to be self-determining and self-sufficient. Such is the basis for the social protest and political poems included here, many of which originate in the coal mining regions of Appalachia. That quality already mentioned of not giving up easily means the people draw on and develop enormous reserves of patience, resourcefulness, and endurance as described in George Ella Lyon's "Her Words" or Ron Rash's "My Grandmother Speaks of the Early Years." Sometimes the women show exceptional courage as in Bettie Sellers' "Naomi's Nerve."

Although mountain people care for their own and resist outside help or "interference," they can be irresponsible. Kathryn Stripling Byer's selections portray the wandering, restless spirit of a husband that finds its match in his wife's independent, defiant nature, her means of survival when she is left to live alone. Also the readiness to carry grudges, bitterness, and resentment can linger long in one's emotional life and may even be passed on to future generations as though it were a family heirloom as in Michael McFee's "Cold Quilt."

Religious traditions of the region include snake-handling services and speaking in tongues. Robert Morgan's "Death Crown" describes a rare and magical sign of saintliness among the believers. Faith healing and natural cures in times of sickness and other crises are resources originating not just from being distanced from medical care but also from the sharing and passing on from generation to generation of numerous herbal remedies and other cures, many of which were taught to them by Native Americans whose knowledge of local herbs and their healing properties were developed long before the first settlers arrived.

Physical violence at certain levels of anger, if not a way of life, is then a fact of life. Moonshine, a related topic, until recently still manufactured in these hills and hollows, was a commodity whose influence was complicated and difficult to sort through in trying to understand Appalachian concepts of justice in regard to individual rights as opposed to government regulations. Playing a hidden role in family and social problems and an obvious one in survival economics, it is referred to in many poems, as natural to the region's social and private landscape as are wildflowers and laurel thickets to its native environment.

A pervasive "good times" side to Appalachian life, especially evident in its storytelling tradition, appears in many poems: descriptions of unusual events such as Morgan's "The Flying Snake" or Marion's "A Mountain Fable of a Sort"; colorful sketches of backwoods, country characters in Richard Hague's "Greenbrier Portraits" and John Foster West's poems; an engaging account of one last ball game played as a valley slowly floods for a dam in Don Johnson's "And the River Gathered Around Us." These and numerous others that portray various aspects of ingenuity and humor are entertaining to read, at times exhibiting close attention to dialect, pronunciation, and the creativity of mountain speech.

Strong influences come from the region's English/Scotch-Irish ancestry, a heritage going back to the earliest settlers that includes the incorporation of medieval words and grammar into what is now referred to as "folk speech" or "mountain dialect." This "archaic speech" gives Elizabethan pronunciations to standard English words and uses old speech forms and grammar no longer found elsewhere. Although vanishing quickly, it can still be heard in remote locations, in remnants of how one's ancestors spoke, or in occasional idiosyncratic words, grammar, or phrases that attract attention because they sound out of place (many teachers have worked hard to eliminate mountain dialect, often to the dismay of some parents, proud of their heritage). Along with this influence came a ballad tradition, deeply embedded in Appalachian culture.

From 1914 to 1918 Cecil Sharp, a musicologist from England, made several trips to the Southern Appalachians in search of early English ballads and folk songs. He discovered versions more original than those in England, the area's isolation having promoted their preservation. Sharp managed to overcome an inherent shyness toward strangers, eventually collecting 274 songs in 968 variations, all passed down by oral tradition — a treasure trove of folk music that he believed needed to be documented before it became lost to history.

Ballads originated in medieval minstrel songs that focused on nobility, thus their references to lords and ladies. Basically a narrative poem, they involved dramatic action: death, romantic entanglements ending in tragedy, conflicts with their inevitable, doomed outcome, and elements of the supernatural. Bettie Sellers' poem "And All the Princes Are Gone" portrays a lingering, romanticized view of old-world nobility that comes from the ballad tradition. Isabel Zuber combines that heritage with contemporary concerns, notably feminist themes. Her poems, unlike any others in this anthology, evoke an unmistakably medieval atmosphere and a haunting, mystical quality with her use of tone and imagery.

I first learned of the Scottish word *hireath* from Robert Morgan that means "anguish" — that which comes from an intense longing for home. It may well explain the origin of the Appalachian highlander's capacity for nostalgia. In many poems, longing for a past time or home, for a place or one's family expresses this feeling of *hireath* (almost a heartache), a way of responding to life that has been handed down for generations. The reader may look at Morgan's poems as well as those by Jeff Daniel Marion, Jim Wayne Miller, and Fred Chappell for interesting variations on this theme.

Byron Herbert Reece (1917–1958), the north Georgia poet to whom this book is dedicated, gained early recognition for his skill in bringing the classical ballad tradition to a written level of metaphysical and artistic excellence. Discovered by Kentucky writer and teacher Jesse Stuart who had high praise for the brilliance of his poetic gifts, Reece was among the early writers of the 20th century who had the genius and ambition to bring to Appalachian poetry a modern voice and talent even though his subject matter was not always contemporary. Focused on folklore, deeply-felt Biblical themes, medieval characters, and 19th-century Romanticism treated in realistic ways, his brooding concern with death places him in the modern era (angst and depression), but his life also exhibits the fragile balance between a finely-tuned sensitivity and the harsh life of Appalachia. He received two Guggenheim Awards and other national acclaim, but his family background and lifestyle as a dirt farmer in a secluded area of the north Georgia mountains from which came his deepest sources of inspiration were at odds with his creative talent. Eventually, isolation from other writers, poor health, and alcoholism led to depression and suicide in the late spring of 1958.

Another influence on some of the region's writers has been the Native American culture, seen in the work of two poets represented here. Stephen Knauth picks up on that culture's mystical relationship with nature in his poems "From the Cherokee" and "1836: In the Cherokee Overhills." R.T. Smith writes from an actual Native American ancestry in his poems "Weave," "Beneath the Mound," and about his Tuscarora grandmother in "Yonosa House."

At the heart of many great works of literature one finds man facing his own nature, the most significant battle ever engaged in. (Two examples that come to mind most readily are Joseph Conrad's "Heart of Darkness" and Herman Melville's *Moby Dick*.) In Appalachia, given the isolation, its concentric energy that focuses — and thus intensifies — the self in place and time, there can be extreme situations in which a person has only the self to struggle with. The scene most likely to be repeated is that of a person alone, against the elements: nature, fate, God. There is an unavoidable element of truth or self-revelation involved. Isabel Zuber's poem "Made" even portrays God coming face to face with the inescapable darker side of what He has created. Fred Chappell's hermit in "Remodeling the Hermit's Cabin" is a powerful example of the struggle Appalachia can have with itself. A hermit has carved a figure of himself in wood along with other family members, but his is the only one without a face:

> a spindly figure
> Turned toward the ragged chinked log wall, unclothed,
> And set apart from the drama the other dolls
> Absorbed themselves in, deaf or contemptuous
> Of passions fierce for all their littleness,
> Fiercer perhaps because of littleness —
> A figure the world had cut no features on,
> Musing the figureless wall that was his mirror.

Self-revelation is well-suited to poetry, given the intensity, inner musical demands, focus, and brevity of the form. Certainly the act of centering one's consciousness invites any writer to work in areas beneath surface realities in a never-ending effort to discover truths. If life is to be regarded as an initiation into the higher mysteries of selfhood, then Appalachia might well be seen as one of its difficult testing grounds. In "Remembering Wind Mountain at Sunset" Chappell says, "Here is the place where pain is born." Response in these poems takes many different forms: protest against what nature is delivering; anger (for insight into how complex this issue can be for women, see Irene McKinney's "For Women Who Have Been Patient All Their Lives"); a crisis of self that can lead to a breakthrough in understanding (see Charles Wright's "Blackwater Mountain"); or a profound questioning of human life as in James Still's poetry. There are dark truths and influences (on a primal level as in Louise McNeill's poems). One may, as a last resort, decide to leave, as in Nancy Simpson's "Leaving in the Dead of Winter." And transformations occur by which one is drawn back into a primordial state of being (several poets who explore this possibility are Jim Wayne Miller, Valerie Nieman, R.T. Smith, and Stephen Knauth).

Arriving at a deeper sense of community with others is one hopeful outcome of crisis, the bridge out of the separated self being compassion. Some poets resolve the problem of self in ways that relate to Native American or Celtic mysticism. For them the natural world provides values which the intellect cannot and never will be able to provide. Nature is known to have its own consciousness. Not only is it a life-giving power, but it also can guide the fractured self toward a more integrated state of being, a grounded wholeness that opens a creative potential yet to be explored. Hilda Downer's poems show different ways of perceiving the natural world that are startling and highly original.

This anthology would be incomplete if it did not balance the portrayal of struggle, hardship, and conflicts in Appalachia with poems that celebrate the sublime experiences by which life is renewed. Some of these border on the visionary, establishing an invisible world paralleling the physical one as in Morgan's "Broomsedge." There are moments of felt oneness with the land (see Chappell's "Here"); a mystical communion with animals (as in Marc Harshman's "Beyond the Two of Us"); celebration in living a simple life and making a point *not* to think (as in Gregory Dykes' "What I Have Learned"); and renewal in the cycles of nature and its promise of a new beginning described in many poems in ways that are powerful and deeply felt. Not so unusual when one understands the intense closeness of the people to the land. And yet, as expressed by these poets, such experiences with their identifiable details and imagery are unique to the Southern Appalachians.

As in all cultures, the poetry of the region can be regarded as an extension or outgrowth of its music, that mountain music running through the lifeblood of the people with its singular rhythms, its characteristic twang, and emotional directness and which was there as an oral tradition in the ballads and folk songs long before it was written down. The originating impulse is the same for both art forms, but in Appalachia there is a driving need to sing the pain, to sing through the pain, and to let the singing become an expression of pain transformed into something that rises above the hardship and eases it, at least for a while. The tradition of pouring out one's soul in singing, playing musical instruments, and dancing goes as far back as the first settlers in the area. Indeed, mountain music and mountain clogging—a dance fascinating for its earthiness, high energy, and physical demands that blends the Scottish Highland fling, African buck dancing, and Native American tribal dancing—are so indigenous to the area that they have become a trademark of the culture. The need to express the self in music finds its voice in poetry and is tempered by the rigorous demands of the poetic art, not the least of which involves bringing an intellectual dimension to bear on musical and linguistic possibilities as well as rendering insight into complex human issues with emotional and imagistic integrity that place the completed work on a quite consciously evolved level.

With a degree of sophistication that is present in any significant literature, Appalachian poetry is finding its own literary voice while retaining its individuality in work that incorporates the area's own special rhythms, cultural nuances, private and communal struggles, and remarkable imagery. Morgan's poem "New Organ" can be seen as a studied approach to those parallel processes at work in music and poetry and, even more deeply, in all human life striving for levels of expression beyond the immediate demands of physical existence. A farmer works his land transforming it into food—sweet potatoes in this situation—then trades the harvest for a new organ for his family, physical substance thus being transformed into the non-physical, the earth literally changed into music with man as the instrument of that transformation:

> He picked each swollen
> root from the soil like a note
> and filled the basket eighty times,
> and then his wagon, thinking
> one hamper for each key, the milk
> becoming the strains of music

One gets the feeling here that working the land is a spiritual discipline with certain moral implications involved, "the heat of his labor / transmuted into a movement / of the air," the same discipline by which words are transformed into poems. It is a discipline in every instance connected with the natural world, one which instructs the poems in the beauty and grace inherent in the earth's forms even as it gives them form.

Lee Pennington writes that "Appalachia is a broken mirror," a metaphor that sees the region and its inhabitants as mutually reflecting a damaged image of themselves.* One can be so locked into this process that it is difficult to alter it. However, a new self-awareness is occurring that changes how the region perceives itself. Ecological attitudes are entering the consciousness of the area's people to the extent that they are re-evaluating what is already in fairly abundant supply—densely forested slopes, a wealth of wildlife and biological specimens, clear streams, and clear air—and taking measures to preserve it. Their position is one of not allowing these resources, of which they are the keepers, to be exploited again through their own failure to prevail against such influences. Pennington expresses this reversal of roles in the poem "Return" in which he states: "I battle now not against but with the wilderness."

Along with this there has been an awakening to values inherent in the culture, recognition and new respect for basic character strengths, and confidence in what Appalachia can contribute to society at large. Miller has been quite prolific in exploring the idea that the values the rest of America is searching for and needs for its salvation are right here in Appalachia. By simply honoring the lives of ancestors and various mountain folk in their poems, many poets not only commemorate them but also communicate a healing of human sorrows, of the land's wounds—a devotion both to the land and its people by way of affection and kinship that ultimately transcends the difficulties.

Life is being looked at from broader perspectives, from experiences outside the region brought to bear on local situations as in Don Johnson's "Raymond Pierce's Vietnamese Wife" or from the point of view of a newcomer as in Katherine Soniat's tragicomic rendering of a tense situation in "A Shared Life." In the poetry itself there have been changes from the ballad tradition, classical forms, and traditional rhyme and rhythm to a much freer form of

---

*Lee Pennington, unpublished manuscript, *Appalachian Newground.*

poetics. Two sonnets and at least one villanelle are included in this collection along with experimental pieces that vary language and syntax according to Appalachian speech, rhythms, sounds, and even "unlettered" spelling for highly original and unusual effects. The discipline of Eastern poetics can be seen in the haiku and senryu of Charles B. Dickson and Joseph Barrett (not to overlook the influence of oriental metaphysics in both Knauth's and Barrett's poetry), all of which heighten a literary tradition that is finding its own voice.

While working on this project, I was seriously questioned as to whether a truly regional literature is possible today given the mobility of the American population and the enormous technological changes reaching into every home and affecting life in even the most out-of-the-way places. I strongly believe regional literature is possible for Appalachia because Appalachia still exists in the mind, memory, imagination, and even the life of its writers in very powerful ways. Its social and historical past has been different from that of the rest of the country up to fairly recent times. Its unusual topography has created natural barriers and isolation. Its people have been regarded as an ethnic group — non-mobile until present times — distinct from the rest of the country. (For the most authoritative discussion of this, see Horace Kephart's *Our Southern Highlander*, a classic study of the area.)* It remains for the reader to answer the question of whether or not this is regional literature after reading the poems.

And yet the poetry is much greater than its regional distinction. It probes universal themes in ways that are convincing, profound, and always on an accessible, human level. There is intellectual and emotional brilliance here, sometimes quite subtle; sensitivity and music that stirs the senses at deep levels; compassion; generosity; pain and old or new wounds acknowledged; much beauty in the imagery; vulnerability and risks; delicacy of sentiment; humor and affection; passion and toughness. This is poetry that can enter one's being and remain there long after being read — powerful work that belongs between the covers of this book.

I thank all the poets who contributed to this collection: for their willingness to be part of the undertaking, their helpful suggestions, books sent to me on loan from their personal libraries, their autobiographical essays† that contribute yet another dimension to the ever-deepening portrait of Appalachia and its writers, and most of all for their poems and their belief in their poems. Special thanks to Robert Morgan who encouraged me to undertake this project and who remained a willing consultant on many issues. Thanks also to Black Mountain Library for locating books out-of-print or otherwise not readily available. Much gratitude to Jane Caris and Jerry Godard for their close reading of this Introduction and their offer of perceptive comments and suggestions. And thanks to all the readers who may look to these poems for a connection to the Southern Appalachians, be it by way of actual ancestry, by association, or by a coincidental emotional texture in the poetry. Given the way poetry resonates on a felt level of experience, it is likely they will be gratified by what they find here.

Marita Garin
Black Mountain, NC

---

*Horace Kephart, *Our Southern Highlander: A Narrative of Adventure in the Southern Appalachians and a Study of Life Among the Mountaineers* (University of Tennessee Press, Knoxville, 1981, reprinted from an earlier edition by arrangements with Macmillan Publishing Co.).

†The essays were written in the early 1990s, years before publication of the anthology. Many of the poets have since moved to locations or jobs other than those to which they refer. (Updates on their publications and awards are available in the Notes on the Poets.) What they chose to write then retains its significance in their insights into and documentation of many aspects of Appalachian culture, much of which was, even as they wrote, in flux, eventually to be altered by social forces intruding, bringing inevitable change.

Bob Henry Baber

There is no logic to love — which may explain why I was born in 1950 in Mineola, New York, to a Big Apple mother and a Hillbilly father. They met in a USO club. He was 22 and on his way to the South Pacific. She had not yet turned 15. But that's another story.

From the first I favored my father both in appearance and temperament. I have the characteristic Baber face, pointy and long, and I suffer from a nervous and artistic disposition that has been described in family parlance as "lacking a ground wire."

As a child I learned to appreciate Hank Williams, harmonicas, and homegrown green beans while at the same time connecting to city life with visits to maternal grandparents. I was raised primarily in Levittown, New York, the great granddaddy of subdivisions and a wonderful place to grow up in partly because one could put together a sandlot football or baseball team with just the kids on the street.

My father was a commercial artist for A & P and a painter. It was while sitting on a high stool and looking over his lean shoulder as he filled a primed canvas with images of Appalachia that I first developed the creative urge. I can honestly say I write because my father painted. Indeed his vision and voice have formed the bedrock upon which many of my mountain poems rest. From my mother I gained the confidence my father lacked.

My father's daddy, Henry Robinson Baber, settled in the Gold Knob district of Greenbriar County near Richwood where, after running a logging crew, he became a dairyman. It was hard and unprofitable work, often in inhospitable conditions, and so by the time I was old enough to remember visits to the farm, there were only a few cows and horses left on the 170-acre parcel set on top of the frigid highlands of eastern West Virginia. During my childhood I spent a number of summers with cousins in this idyllic and, later, idealized environment. And why not? There were forts to stake out, rocks to conquer, sod dams to be built and destroyed, trees to climb, weeds to pull, meals to be eaten, and most important of all, sumptuous stories to be heard. During this time, Appalachia became unalterably a part of my soul. It's hard to explain, but when I was in West Virginia, I felt as if I'd traveled back across time and terrain to reclaim the place that was mine. And when it came time to load up the Ford Galaxy and return to Long Island, I could never accept the fact that I was "going home."

Later, as I entered adulthood and explored America, I began to understand more fully the significance of tradition in a transient society. Like so many people around me, I was without roots. And so, even as I became immersed in the hippie counterculture and the anti-war movement, I also found myself being drawn, year by year and mile by mile, back to the old homeplace (although my grandparents had moved to town and the house had begun to run down and decay). And it was to West Virginia that I limped after being shot by the L.A.P.D. at an Easter "Love-In." Legal and financial considerations prevented me from staying, but during this time I made a conscious decision to live in the mountains, to restore my ancestral home, and to turn my pen toward Appalachian concerns. This decision came as naturally to me as topping off blackberry cobbler with homemade vanilla ice cream.

At that time I had no knowledge of "Appalachian culture" as such. I only knew there was an enormous gap between my idealized image of Appalachia and the political realities of mining and timbering, the debilitating effects of poverty, and the denigrating stereotyping of the region's people—*my people*—by the larger culture. What I desired to do was paint a positive portrait of the people and vent my anger over the destruction of the environment. As fate would have it, I stumbled onto a little branch of Antioch College in the unlikely place of Beckley, West Virginia. There a number of writers formed the Soupbean Poets, a collective that read together, published together, and generally shared cultural and political perspectives. From them I learned to appreciate the diversity and power of the region's varied literary voices. The Southern Appalachian Writers' Co-op also contributed substantially to my artistic growth. Since then, I have worked for the Southern Appalachian Labor School, the Pearl S. Buck Museum, Appalshop, and, of late, Southeast Community College here in Harlan County, Kentucky. To one extent or another, I have been able to integrate creative writing activities into my administrative and teaching duties. Above all, I've learned about life in the central Appalachian coalfields, the area to which I am most connected personally and culturally.

Bob Henry Baker (Jurgen Lorenzen)

By the time this book is published, I will be over forty years old and will have spent nearly half of my adult life in the region. Am I Appalachian? According to my birth certificate and upbringing, I'm not. Perhaps the phrase "a cultural hybrid" best describes my persona. Maybe the question itself is academic and irrelevant. I don't want to pretend to be anything that I'm not. I simply want to write with passion about this place that I love and hate — this place that *means* more to me than any place else on earth. If I can be one of the voices singing about the beauty and perseverance of the Appalachian landscape and the people it has spawned, then I am blessed indeed, and that's enough.

Richwood

Once I was a grape nehi
to the woodhicks standing on the porch of the Sportsmen
chewing mail pouch tobacco
and spitting into a Heinz pork and beans can...

Just a stripling really—
green and tender as a yearling—
all ears and crewcut and jughead
sent on a mission of milk
but waylaid by words
and stories of wildcats and blizzards,
skid roads and timber it took four tries
with a six foot cross cut
to lay down

on hot days when pulp swelled with puberty
I absorbed the woodgrain of men
who with horses stretched sinews in mud and work—
who dug brogan heels into mountains and shale
and grunted together like primal lovers in suffering sweat;
who filled their nostrils with fog and laurel thickets,
woodsmoke and fresh cut oak;
whose tongues grew fat with Karo syrup
thick as spring sap on biscuits;
who stripped naked and laid down in Laurel Crick,
bathed themselves inside and out with moonshine
and gathered pollen from the bodies of young women
sweeter than wild honeysuckle,
who scattered seeds over these hills
that sprouted and prospered safely beneath their canopy...

but now, with the stumps of ancient snags
rotting at my base,
I stand alone in sweetwater and sun
spiraling into an empty sky,
my roots sunk deep into humus, leafmold, and regrets,
richer, for what once thrived here, than death itself.

The Inheritance

Like soupbeans burned on a cookstove
it boiled down to a family brawl.
Aunt Ann, the executrix, was the frankest:
they would fight him tooth and nail.
Not that any of them wanted it—

scattered out across the continent
with their own lives and all —
they didn't, but it was a matter of cold hard cash:
the Old Homeplace up for the highest bidder
strip-miner or not.

Of course Tessie was caught in the middle
trying to ride out a storm that just wouldn't break:
trying to smooth over clouds
with her lean deft hands like she's always done before.
They wouldn't smooth.

All she wanted now was to work her quilts and plants,
refill her mason jars,
take her cares to the Lord and leave them.
They wouldn't leave.
They were like a dumb dog
that followed her into a tender garden
and wouldn't be shooed.

The family didn't see it but she was worn,
worn as a hoe handle left in the weather.
But she didn't break, she rocked.
And even as she rocked
blacksnakes claimed the attic
and bluegrass bounded over tombstones.

Bargain tarpaper went bald.
She rocked and she prayed.
"This too shall pass, shall pass, shall pass."

But it didn't.   She did.

Poem for James Collins

Now youse may not believe it, but it's the truth
I throwed lumps as big as I could lift
to get my Daddy his quota.
Why coal was so much a part of my life
I thought God made it before he made night,
but tell that to the Labor Board
and see what'll getcha —
a nock on the noggin' with that headache stick
the sheriff's got ahangin' on his hip

this ain't suppose to be a slavin' place
but we got widders out here
their husbands die
and they tell her autopsy autopsy

cut him open
see if he got blacklung
hold them lungs up to the light
listen to hear
iffin there's any air left to be wrung out

but this ain't suppose to be a slavin' place

tell 'em that
see if they stop pattin' their hair
and clicken their pens,
scream it in their ears
THIS AIN'T SUPPOSE TO BE A SLAVIN' PLACE
they'll say youse outa order
treat youse like youse a pop machine or something!

youse outa order, Mister, outa order

Well if this be order
give me a wheelbarruh of chaos
and a pop bottle full of shook up rattlesnakes

Trail of the Lonesome Pine

Restless
I come out into the night
to walk the Trail of the Lonesome Pine.

It is cold.
Naked trees shiver in the wind.
A dog barks in the distance.
And my shadow, as hard as the ground underfoot,
is revealed by the full moon straight overhead:

even in pain
there is joy; in separation, hope;
in darkness, light.

A shooting star falls for me.
It is love at first sight.

Daughter, it is your birthday.
You are seven years old.
Just as it did the day you were born,
snow lies deep in the crevices of the woods
where the tracks of the fawns traverse the hillside.

Tonight, when the moon is thick as cream in the woods,
when mountain laurel leaves huddle close to their stems—
when the surface of the stream ceases to move
and the milky way is a blizzard of stars
suspended in Canadian air—

tonight, when only the breath of the hoot-owl warms the dark
and every step down the country path remarks a painful report —
tonight, daughter, I miss you as spring misses thaw
when once again
I will bear true witness
                      to the awe
                                of your perfect bud and blossom.

Vandalia

West Virginia, what is it that draws me back to you?
What is your primal pull that holds me like metal to a magnet?
Is it laurel thickets riotous with blossoms;
deep mines and picket lines, rain that never ends?
Is it bear stories and wild strawberries,
the old homeplace, now overrun with blacksnakes, where pastoral
childhood summers slipped by
days of black-eyed susans and golden haystack?
What is it that draws me towards
your wicked winters, cruel greenbriars, and hard times?
Why return to your mountains, cursed by coal
and the caprices of slick operators — those who make you their whore
and pimp you for profit —
why come back to this Vandalia that was once almost heaven
but which now, with every gash of the blade, approaches hell-to-pay?
West Virginia, your hillsides cry milkjug tears, litter of resignation.
Your streams are floating landfills of grief;
your factories a script of minimum wage anguish;
your welfare offices a nightmare of republican eligibility workers.
West Virginia, your children have known hunger
and worse, the *shame* of hunger, in a land of plenty;
West Virginia, your miners have known pneumoconiosis
and worse, the inability to fight for benefits for dearth of breath;
and your dreams, so lately made of black squalor,
slide darkly into muddy hollers of pain.
West Virginia, this is your grimmest hour,
the hundred year flood of negative emotions,
the monsoon of your season in man-made hell.

Still, the means of your tormentors
will never be your end,
for you will thrive and survive;
will, with ample rain, sun and time,
heal yourself with dogwood saplings, locust, and sumac
sprouting miraculously from raw destruction.
West Virginia, wild cherry blossoms will shower your slag.
Native poets will honor you with haiku.

And balms of green, like Vaseline, will salve your reddog scars
masking the handiwork of your exploiters —
those whom I curse aloud with this poem!

West Virginia, your tolerance is too great,
your generosity too boundless, your forgiveness near complete;
you favor us too kindly with trees that strain the sky with leaves,
with rivers that, with the millennium, will purge themselves and us,
your progeny, grown to fruition in your moist shadows...

West Virginia, you are family
rocksalt and stone, blood kin and bone

that is why I come home to you
like a child to mother in crisis-time;
to lament your damned demise
and to sing the psalm of your praises
from the top of every folded ridge
to every person in every valley
                        who has ears to hear
                        and would do so

Joseph Barrett (1950–1990)

Editor's note: Joseph Barrett died unexpectedly before he had written his autobiographical essay. His was an accidental death, a shock to family, friends, followers, and the poetry community of West Virginia of which he was one of its most talented members, exploring new territory and bringing sensitivity and artistic genius to experiments with form and style. He was active in the "Soupbean" literary revival in West Virginia and collaborated with former Soupbean Poets Bob Snyder and P.J. Laska to form a group known as the Mason-Dixon Trio. Their book, *Old Martins, New Strings,* was being printed at the time of his death. He published three books of his own poetry, and his poems appeared in anthologies, magazines and many literary periodicals, some of which include *Southern Humanities Review, Poetry Kanto* (Japan), *Appalachian Journal, Southern Exposure, Modern Haiku,* and *Frank: An International Journal of Contemporary Writing & Art* (France). The following was written by P.J. Laska in consultation with Joanie Barrett (Joe's widow), Bob Snyder, and Terry Leffel.

Joseph Barrett was born in Montgomery, West Virginia, in 1950. He completed high school in Richwood, West Virginia, and attended Bethany College for two years. During this time he traveled to England as an exchange student at Oxford. He also studied for five months in the Middle East, in Israel and Turkey.

He found himself as a poet early and published his first book of poems, *Roots Deep in Sand,* in 1969. In 1975–76 he attended Antioch College/Appalachia in Beckley, West Virginia, and his poetry appeared in the *SOUPBEAN* anthology. In 1975 he published a second collection, *Periods of Lucidity,* with an epigraph from Frank O'Hara whose style was an influence on his work then.

In 1980 he moved to Lexington, Kentucky, and wrote that he had completed work on a third collection which included a number of poems that are experiments with a longer form in a style he called "peripheralist." His stated intent in them was "to render our evolving perceptions of our 'place' in much the same way that the cubist painters conquered space."

He was also studying Chinese and Japanese poets and exploring the haiku form. In the '80s his work was published in numerous literary periodicals, and he won an international haiku poetry competition. In 1988 he co-edited the anthology *Venue* and completed revisions of his third collection, writing that in his longer poems he was trying "to integrate the intrusive visions of obsession with conscious acts and thought. Like when you are buttering your breakfast toast and for reasons unknown you remember an airplane ride when you were a child or the smell of your grandmother's hair."

Joseph Barrett had a poet's vision of the transitory character of all things human and the poet's need to question that fate through the structures of language. The epigraph of his last collection, "Blue Planet Memoirs," is taken from the Japanese haiku poet Issa:

> The world of dew
> is the world of dew,
> and yet...
> and yet...
>
> — P.J. Laska

Homeward

entering west Virginia
the pavement shatters
and a whole family
leaving
hitches
along the highway;
mother, father,
a daughter in arms;
I pass a road sign
obscured by shotgun;
and so it seems,
forever in America,
home is in
the desperate going

The Strikers

arisen from the smoke
and anxiety
of their paydays
and nights
they bribe their children
with peanuts and candy
to leave;
and leaning against the bar
they stare into mid-space
nodding in low talk;

and limping men
circle the table
grimly shooting eight ball
with no bets down;

the storm blows open
the double doors,

cigarettes roll
still burning in sawdust;
and outside car horns blare
and men shout that it's time;
hands on hats they walk into rain

A Winter Baptism

I watch from a distance,
from the windy bridge,
as beneath a tree
split by lightning
the river ice is broken;
and sullen men
in floating robes
submerge a tearful boy
as the little flock
cries out, the hallelujahs
rising like timid spirits
into a brooding sky;
and perhaps it's so,
in delusion and in death,
only there and thus
our earthly reasons cross

Haiku

what hour is this?
    the squirrel barking
        on a dead limb

Senryu

a drunken night;
    one of leffel's new sandals
floats in the toilet

Haiku

they have wed;
the windy rainfall,
the cricket's voice

Detour

I tailed them up the mountain,
the old men
in the struggling pickup
and the boy sitting
in the corroded bed
facing me through
the blue smoke
of the broken exhaust,
the shadows of the trees
playing over
his petulant bearing,
and as our eyes
evasively met
I was startled within
by a bestial perception
of the boy and the men;
I then lit a cigarette
to help quell
the urge to pass
in the mean and endless turn,
realizing, he knows, he knows

Woman Playing a Juke Box

all evening she's danced
for three seedy men,
her ass a damp valentine
sagging in red slacks;
now only the broad feet
keep time,
baby blue sandals
tapping in sawdust
and spilled beer;

(O detroit city)

she must know
she is all the way home;
and turning from the machine
she carries her weight
through smoke
like a pregnancy
the slightest praise could father

Still Life

   the barn abstracts
      the hillside
         as locusts whirr
               in the heat
             of the rising field;
           a door slams,
         flies resettle
      on a torn screen;
    in the violet shade
     of the porch
    the rocking chair
rocks itself   to stillness

An April Exultation

against the lights
I'm crossing streets,
keeping in stride,
perfect timing
(some days are like that)
thinking
who can forget death
once they've read
its calling card,
say,
in a strange lesion
on the tongue
or the smart swelling
of a breast;
or who simply see it
falling so completely
over the next century?

today, though,
the world is working
in its resurrection
april way;
here, for example,
in lexington
I'm certain
the guardian spirits
are being born,
and for that matter,
in rangoon, boston

and richwood too;
and one day
they will tell us again
how to forget death
once and for all
and we will remember enough
to at times weep in the night
(and that's okay too)

this morning the world
is buying flowers
for all the right reasons
and duke willis,
fresh out of jail,
is back on little laurel
making baby dukies again,
and georgie is in heaven
with edgar bergen
(the world's worst ventriloquist)
and arthur rimbaud
(who no longer dreams of eden)
and hitler, next time around,
can only be a better boy,
and by intuition
our destinations
will change trains in aberdeen;

today, joanie is shopping,
buying gifts
for the sisters of saint joseph's
because she really loves them
and loves the world,
knowing love
more holy than logic;
crossing limestone
my tie blows wildly
and despite myself
                I find myself   whistling

Kathryn Stripling Byer

When I was growing up in southwest Georgia, I used to go walking in the wide fields near sunset. There I could sing as loud as I wanted and no one was likely to hear but the cows. I could look way beyond the border of oak trees and imagine the blue massing clouds were mountains, the Blue Ridge, the place my grandmother had wanted to be when she died. She had been born there and had spent most of her girlhood in another mountain range, the Black Hills, growing up as the daughter of an Irish miner and a German painter and schoolmarm turned, in later years, Presbyterian preacher. Mountains were where she belonged, though she lived out most of her adult life in the hot, mosquito-ridden flatlands of tropical Georgia.

Mountains were where I belonged, too, I decided during my sunset ramblings, and I began inching my way north, first to Macon, Georgia, where I took a degree in English at Wesleyan College, and then on up into North Carolina and the graduate writing program at UNC-Greensboro. There my teachers Fred Chappell and Robert Watson helped me realize poetry was what I wanted to write, not fiction. After completing my MFA degree and applying for every available job teaching college in western North Carolina, I was offered a position at Western Carolina University, and I have lived ever since in Cullowhee, a Cherokee name supposed to mean "valley of lilies."

Because my husband, a native of Tennessee, grew up hiking the Great Smokies and expected me to accompany him on his treks after our marriage, I soon found my imagination being stirred by those trails, the very leafmold and dirt of them, their shifting light, their windy sounds, their atmosphere of mystery and solitude. The music of the region, the old ballads and lyrics, began to work upon my imagination, too. And the sound of women's voices. Voices that ranged from Emma Bell Miles, whose *Spirit of the Mountains* was the first mountain woman's voice to catch me up in its world, to my friends Willa Mae Pressley and Linda Mathis, both Cullowhee valley natives whose sensitivity to the ambiguities of this region helped draw me into the human reality of the place. And then there was Lee Smith, whose Granny Younger in *Oral History* became a guide to the twists and turns of storytelling that was beginning to fascinate me. These women told me stories, stories of loss, cruelty, disappointments, bitter loves, and "blood on the moon." They taught me to sing Black Jack Davie and Shady Grove, to love the names of quilt patterns like "Heart's Seal" and "Winding Way," to relish the saying of particular flowers when I came upon them in the woods. Bloodroot. Gay wings. Trillium.

Wherever I went, I seemed to hear voices, and eventually out of all the voices grew the one with which I could write about these mountains, the voice of a woman named Alma, solitary, abandoned, strong yet susceptible to the shiftings of season and memory. Hers was the voice of a woman living within what Emma Bell Miles has called the "rift that is set between the sexes at birth and widens with the passage of the years." Her voice became for me the crystallization of those female spirits that haunt these mountains still. It was also, in some personal, ancestral sense, my grandmother's voice, yearning for the high places, all too familiar with the low.

These poems, Alma's poems, began in the middle of my work on a first book filled with south Georgia imagery. When Alma's poems began speaking, I had no idea who was speaking them, only that the voice had somehow originated on a hike up the Kanati Fork trail when I happened upon a deserted homesite, hidden away in the dark, overhanging vines and brush. What sort of woman could live up here, I wondered. How could she stand it? For a long time afterward, I was obsessed by those questions.

Meanwhile my first book, *The Girl in the Midst of the Harvest*, was one of the winners of the 1985 Associated Writing Programs competition and published by Texas Tech Press in the AWP Award Series in 1986. Around that time, many of the poems from *Wildwood Flower*, Alma's book, began appearing in magazines and journals. In 1988 I received a writing fellowship from the National Endowment for the Arts on the strength of Alma's voice, her determined singing, which refuses to give up despite years of being trapped in the competition racket, her poems coming up finalists again and again in every book competition in the country. In 1983 I published a chapbook of 14 poems entitled *Alma*, and I will do the same for all of these poems if I must.

Kathryn Stripling Byer

The voice of Alma has shown me how to wait. "Solitude is deep water," Emma Bell Miles wrote. Like Alma, you stay afloat on it, you sometimes sail away on it. You talk back to it, you sing to it. If you are a poet, you make the waiting at the heart of it *listen*.

Trillium

April, and I have come far as the trail's
fork to whisper it, watery sound
like the swollen creek running beside us
the morning we left church and walked till

he threw down his coat on the grass.
How the ridges were rife with that word's blooming

multitudes, sprung out of nothing
and overnight, as if the souls of all creatures

with wings buried under the leafmold had risen
and, but for our presence, might take to the sky
singing praise! Nothing moved.
Neither wind, nor the scurry of mice

in the underbrush. Far away I heard the bluejays
rejoicing. And then his breath filling my ear
with my name. Soul of Sweet Mercy,
I should have covered my head with my shawl

and kept silent! Though we spoke of love,
I know now it means little
but loneliness. Better if he had said, "Trillium,
trillium!" I might have known what

he meant: Flood tide.
Both of us well-nigh to drowning.

Ivory Combs

He sat on the porch every morning
and dreamed he would someday go wandering farther
than all he could see beyond Burning Wing Gap.
"Hear the wind," he sighed.
"Just like a woman she never stops calling me."

"What does she say?" I teased.
"That you're a cold-hearted man who cares more
for his rambling than for any wife?"

How he laughed!
Then he straightened his hat
and tried hard to look solemn.
"That song you sing when you turn sad,
Oh, it's down, down went her ivory combs,
sing it now," he said,
pulling me onto his lap.

I untangled his hands from my waist
and stood up again, smoothing my apron,
for I had grown tired of the old songs,
their garlands of rue and their thorny vines.
So many winding sheets.

I walked away to the edge of the apple trees,
watching him over my shoulder.
I let down my hair,

and he took off his hat,
tossed it far as he could in the sunlight.
The shady grass lay like a promise between us,
concealing the first of its gay wings
and meadow-sweet. "Gypsy girl,"
I heard him calling.
I watched him come after me,
crushing the wildflowers under his feet.

Diamonds

This, he said, giving the hickory leaf
to me. *Because I am poor.*
And he lifted my hand to his lips,
kissed the fingers that might have worn
gold rings if he had inherited

bottomland, not this
impossible rock where the eagles soared
after the long rains were over. He stood
in the wet grass, his open hands empty,
his pockets turned inside out.

Queen of the Meadow, he teased me
and bowed like a gentleman.
I licked the diamonds off the green
tongue of the leaf, wanting only
that he fill his hands with my hair.

Jericho's

walls shone not half so bright
under Jehovah's moon as he sees this mountain
stand to the west of his idle fields,
daring him climb it for what
reason he's never told me straight
out, though I know he dreams deer

by the multitude wander
my sleepless nights, safe within Jericho's
unexplored shadows he tells me not even the Cherokee
ever tracked. When he gets hungry
for wild meat, he disappears,
firing a parting shot into the chicken coop.

Soon enough he brings the same story
home to my empty pot, how he was led

by a golden buck, into the clouds
where it bolted clear over the edge of the world
and he found himself suddenly light
headed, cursing his luck and the creatures

that roam as he would, with no reason
to turn back the way he had struggled
up, clinging to rocks
breaking loose from his hold on what
little by little comes
tumbling down into the valley.

Snowbird

At midday you steadied our boat on the riverbank,
pointing your rifle to some snowy height.
"I will build you a house there," you promised.
I thought I saw sun on my windows,
the flash of a silver bird's wing. Can a bird
sing like ice melting? I never heard him.

Perhaps even now in the darkness he glows
like the lamp I left burning
the night your bay mare wandered
up the hill, dragging your saddle.

Sometimes he flies over me scrubbing
the hearthstone or threading my loom with the drabbest
of homespun. I never look up
into sky when I walk through the woods

for it's ginseng and bloodroot
a woman must take home, not feathers
to melt in her hands, little more
than the sweat after labor.

Someday I will not think again about lace
on the cuffs of a blouse
nor the earrings you fondled with cold fingers.
I will forget water
under our boat, how the rocks sang
like birds heading south.

Bittersweet

Under the thin flannel nightgown,
my daughter's ribs: frail
harp I stroke

as if I might make some lovely sound
of those bones. At my breast

she would cling to the nipple,
my milk like a sudden thaw straining
the downspout let down, oh
the stony earth blossomed, I saw
my pots brimming, my skirts full
of apples. I rocked her to sleep
singing, "Little bird,
little bird under my wing." Hear

my voice crack! I cough
and keep silent. Now she is the one
in this house who sings, crooning
like wind in the chimney. My sweet songs
have all blown away,
one by one, down the mountain.

Afterwards, Far from the Church

bells, my way back through balsam
seems darker than when I set out
for the grassy cove. Sundays a storm
always threatens by afternoon,
woods full of churchgoers singing
their leave-taking, *Over, our meeting
is over,* as I urge the mule to climb

faster, lest I hear you years ago
shuffle your feet at my side, meaning *Come
with me.* Almost your wife, who's to care,
I thought, turning to you at the last
chorus, hands all around us clasped tight
against parting. As we rode toward
Mossy Creek, I could hear voices still

singing, as now, when it seems many miles
till the women no longer wail mournfully
over the men's droning: *Save us!*
The Promised Land they yearn to see,
not an earthly creek, late-blooming columbine,
bed of wet maple leaves we made
beyond any singing but that of the ravens.

River Bed

And so I lie down
and let water throw quilt after

quilt on me, each of them older than any I know
how to piece and called endless
names none of us knows how to utter,
beginning with rain wearing down the gray rock
of these mountains where all night the wind
among sycamores scatters dry leaves like a lifetime
of scraps from an old woman's sewing box.
They cling to current like calico Hands
All Around or a True Lover's Knot
flowing downhill forever.
The trout enters this one,
and kingfisher snips golden thread
from the selvage of that one. A thousand,

thousand cater-cornered remnants
of dawn dally over me. Crazy quilt up to my chin
in this morning, I settle my body in silt
like a snake shedding, season by season, its stocking
of skin. Surely nobody knows where to find me
but you, though by now you've forgotten
my promise to sail away someday
on sunlight, your promise to follow me
far as the ocean itself. What you followed was sky
standing open through chestnut and beech as you rode
away, leaving me nothing but time
to remember you, day unto
day stitched, the thread knotted. Let me cut free
all my memories, each one a Heart's
Seal of light on the surface! If you should come home
from your long journey, calling me
far down the valley, my name on your lips close
to singing, I'll shiver
and hide myself under the laurel leaves.
Step from the thicket
and whistle, I'll run away into the green
silence, into the empty air. Lose
you. But Love, look around. See that
lone strand of silver hair carried downriver?

Fred Chappell

I was born in 1936 in Canton, North Carolina, a tiny paper mill town 20 miles west of Thomas Wolfe's Altamont. My family, for as far back as anyone cared to remember, comprised on my mother's side a line of farmers and schoolteachers. They held two occupations because either one of them paid insufficiently to thrive. In the mid–1940s my father moved into the retail furniture business, finding that he could no longer support the expense of farming with a teacher's salary.

Canton serves almost too neatly as a symbolic situation for the history of the Appalachian dilemma. The Pigeon River, tumbling down the bouldery gorges from Beech Gap through Sunburst, comes to the town swift and, if not pure, at least clean. Once past the Champion Paper and Fiber factory, it rolls on toward Tennessee, tar-black and tattered with chemical foam, malodorous with something that smells a little like creosote. That, surely, is how our mountain history ran free and clean until it met the Industrial Age, paying for its physical well-being with some of the health of its soul.

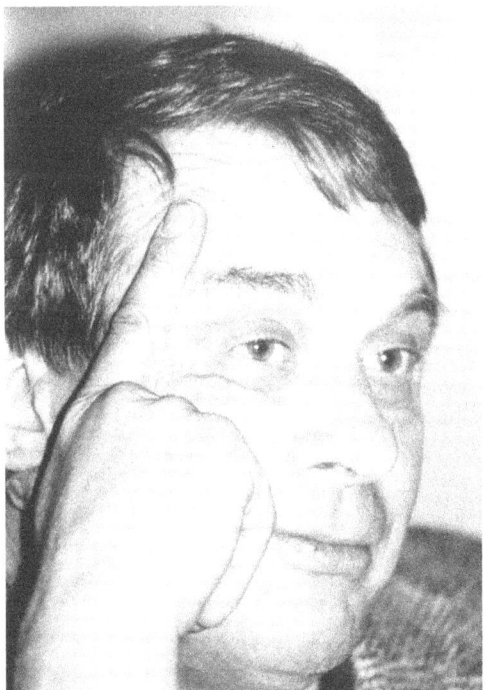

Fred Chappell (Robert Gingher)

It is impossible to fault anyone who must earn his living for desiring and working hard to live as well as he can. But if only there could have been another way!

There was not nor is like to be. We use up the resources of the world that supports us. It is not necessary to do so in the most efficient — i.e., the most barbaric way; but as of now we have not learned any other. We are advised to try to do so.

I married my high school sweetheart, Susan Nicholls, and we moved to the Piedmont area of the state, some 250 miles from our home, so that I might teach in a university. But we return to the mountains often and feel that there we breathe easier and more deeply and with larger assurance. This is only a feeling, but it is one of the kinds of feeling a person lives in order to enjoy.

A Prayer for the Mountains

Let these peaks have happened.

The hawk-haunted knobs and hollers,
The blind coves, blind as meditation, the white
Rock-face, the laurel hells, the terraced pasture ridge
With its broom sedge combed back by wind:
Let these have taken place, let them be place.

And where Rich Fork drops uprushing against
Its tabled stones, let the gray trout
Idle below, its dim plectrum a shadow
That marks the stone's clear shadow.

In the slow glade where sunlight comes through
In circlets and moves from leaf to fallen leaf
Like a tribe of shining bees, let
The milk-flecked fawn lie unseen, unfearing.

Let me lie there too and share the sleep
Of the cool ground's mildest children.

Remembering Wind Mountain at Sunset

Off Hurricane Creek where
the heady rattlers even the loggers
abash, out of Sandy
Mush and Big Laurel and
Greasy Branch, off the hacksaw edge of Freeze Land,
those winds huddle in the notch
atop Wind Mountain, where counties Madison
and Buncombe meet but never join.
Hardscrabble Aeolus,
that stir of zephyrs is the sigh of poor
folk screwed in between the rocks up
Meadow Fork and Sugar Camp and Trust, Luck,
Sliding Knob, and Bluff.
A lean wind and a meat-snatcher. Wind
full of hopeless bones.

High on Wind Mountain I heard
from the valley below
the wearied-to-silence lamentation of busted hands,
busted spines, galled mules and horses, last breeze
rubbing the raw board-edge of the corncrib,
whimper of cold green beans in a cube of fat,
the breathing of clay-colored feet unhooked

from iron brogans.
A glinty small miasma
rises off the rocks in the cornfield.
The cowbell dwindles
toward dusk.

I went walking up Chunky Gal
To watch the blackbird whup the owl.

Friend, you who sit where some money is,
I tell you, Sometimes the poor are
poor in spirit, the wind is robbing
them of breath
of life, wind from always Somewhere Else,
directionless unfocused desire,
but driving the young ones like thistle seed
toward Pontiac, Detroit, Cincinnati,
Somewhere, wherever is money,
out of the hills.
Can't make a go
in bloody Madison, too much the rocks
and thickety briars suck the breath of the hand.
Suck the womenfolk to twig-and-twine
limberjacks, suck the puckered houses sad,
tumbly shack by blackberry wilderness
fills to the ridgepole with copperhead
and sawbriar. The abandoned smokehouse
droops, springhouse hoards dead leaves.

I see blackbird fighting the crow
But I know something he don't know.

Over Hunger Cove
the rain-crow keeps conjuring rain
till Shitbritches Creek is flooded, tobacco
drowned this year one more year,
the township of Marshall bets half its poke
and the French Broad takes it
with a murmur of thunder.
Lord, let these sawtooth tops
let me breathe, give me one good stand
of anything but elderbush and milkweed,
I'll keep Mama's Bible dusted off,
I'll try not to murder
for spite nor even for money,
just let that wind hush
its bones a little and not fly so hard
at the barn roof and the
halfbuilt haystack, I'll go to the Singing

on the Mountain with Luramae this
time I swear I will.

Fished up Bear Creek till I was half dead.
Caught a pound of weeds and a hornyhead.

Where you're from's
Hanging Dog, ain't it, boy I knowed
your daddy years back, that was your Uncle
Lige wasn't it lost his arm at
the old Caldwell sawmill, they called him Sawmill
after, took to hunting sang
and medicine root, heard old Lige had died,
is that the truth, I disremember, he
was how old? Hundred and forty-nine
counting nights and hard knocks.
that's what he told me, I'll never forget.
Standing right there by that stove he said it.

If you could eat the wind,
if you could chew it and swallow
it for strength like a windmill.
If anything could be made of this wind in
winter with its scythes of ice when it comes dragging
blue snow over the ridgetops and down
the mountainsides here to the house, finds any
little cranny, wind squirms through the holes
like an army of squirrels.
Go over and sit by the fire, won't
be long till your fingers turn blue again
anyhow. Somehow
I don't have my proper strength
a-winters, been to the doc how many times,
it's a poser to him says he, I told him
Doc I just get down weak as rag soup and
he says, Maybe you need a rest, By God
rest I says, reckon maybe I do,
why don't I lay up here for a while.

I saw blackbird fighting the hawk,
He whupped his hiney with a pokeweed stalk.

And then he says, Now how you
going to pay me? I says, Pay you doc, you'll just
have to garnisheer them Rest Wages.

Two women fighting over a box of snuff,
Lost three tits before they had enough.

First snow like a sulphate powder, bluish,
and up-top the trees like frozen lace, crystal white

against the crystal blue of morning north,
look fragile as tinsel, no wind yet much,
only down the back of your neck now and again to
remind you how long about milking
time it'll come on.
It'll come, everything hurtful will come on.
Here is the place where pain is born.
No salve or balm.
Ever you notice how deep cold the rocks get?
No I mean it, you hoeing round in the field
summertime, hit rocks, sparks
jumping every whichway, come winter
you can beat all day on a rock with a crowbar,
never see spark one, rocks
get froze up deep in the heart is why, told
my oldest boy, No wonder our raggedy
ass is cold, even the goddam rocks
have done give up.

                                      And if you was to get
a little warm, go in by the cookstove there,
just makes it worse, wind when
you go out peels the feeling-warm right
off, you'll think you've fell
in Spring Creek River, way it goes over you
ice water, but the funny part is, come summer
same wind out of the same place,
feels like its pouring out of a coalstove,
ain't a breath of soothe in it. Now that's funny.

Maybe the wind like that gets me so low.
Hateful to think of it stepping on my grave
when I'm took off, and then still clawing
you know the apple tree
and the hayfield and the roof of this house,
still clawing
at my young ones after I'm laid safe
out of it. What's the relief in that?
Under the sod you know here'll
come that Freeze Land wind crawling my joints.

Turkey buzzard took old blackbird flying
Like a pissant riding on a dandelion.

Youngish preacherman, heard him
say there ain't no bad without some good
in it somewhere, wanted
to ask him, What's the good in poison oak,
tell me because I can raise twenty solid acres

right in a jiffy, sawbriar too, didn't think
what was the good of this Freeze Land wind, you
know it gets so much inside you, never think
about it being anything, I mean
nothing, just there is all, not anything.
Something you can't see like that you never think.
Like that War in Europe, what'd I know
back here in the stump roots, but they stuck
me over there in the mud
till wild rose and ragweed took my bottom land.

For fighting niggers and hauling loads,
Pulled fifteen months on the county roads.

Friend, you who sit
in the vale of comfort,
consider if you will that there are corners
in this flab land where shale edge
of hunger is chipping out
hearts for weapons, man don't
look from year to year but day by day
alone, suffering of flesh
is whetting the knife edge of spirit in
lower Appalachia, margins
where no one thinks you're his buddy,
don't come driving that big-ass Lincoln
up Hogback Ridge if you like your paint job,
they's some old
bushy boys in here kill a man for
a quarter, eyegod, you seen about that feller
in the papers? I'm not saying
what I've heard about them Henson brothers,
you knowed old man Henson or your daddy did,
him that burned the sheriff
out, had two boys nigh
as lowdown as ever he was, I
don't know what-all I've heard tell.

Up on Wind Mountain there ain't no help.
Blackbird went and killed hisself.

Friend, sit tight on your money,
what you've got, there's a man
on a mountain thinks he needs it worse.

All this I heard in the stir
of wind-quarrel in Wind Mountain notch,
rich tatters of speech
of poor folk drifting like bright Monarchs.

And then on the breeze a cowbell,
and the kitchen lights went on in the valley below,
and a lonesome churchbell
calling
home, home, home, home
till I could bear it no more.
Turned my back
Walked down the mountain's other side.

They hauled old blackbird's carcass away,
Buried him head-down-deep in red clay.

Here comes the preacher to say the last word:
"It's a fitten end for old blackbird."

Remodeling the Hermit's Cabin

an epilogue to the Constitution of the United States

Not what we expected. And dark in there,
The one little window not a proper window —
A chopped-out off-square page of cloud and treetop
That let a grayness in. No pin-up girls
Leggy in froth panties, but recipes
On the walls, head-heavy crayons of hawks,
Torn-out leaves of Bibles, pictures of flowers.
"This old feller was a different kind of lonesome,"
Reade said. We didn't understand. The bed
Was rusty and narrow. The floor was bare.

We found his handiwork. A carved and sanded
Walking stick with a twice-twined rattlesnake
Leaned in the corner. Ferrule and knob smeared silvery,
The snake was blotched unlikely black and orange.
Reade hefted it for balance. "I've seen worse,"
He said. "This old-time whittling, you always wonder
Where they got the hours. I bet I've started
A dozen, and never finished one I'd carry."

In a corner shelf we found his Little People,
Whittled men and women and children hand-sized,
Naked, or dressed in closely twisted cornshuck,
Disposed in attitudes forlorn and studied,
Each inhabiting a single space
That set it well apart from all the others,
Even in the narrow shelf. "His family,
How he remembers the way it was," Reade said.
"You see they didn't get along too good,

But what the story is would be a puzzle.
This one here is him." The only doll
He didn't give a face, an oval of soft
White pine blank as a thumbnail, a spindly figure
Turned toward the ragged chinked log wall, unclothed,
And set apart from the drama the other dolls
Absorbed themselves in, deaf or contemptuous
Of passions fierce for all their littleness,
Fiercer perhaps because of littleness —
A figure the world had cut no features on,
Musing the figureless wall that was his mirror.

We swept them all into a cardboard box.

Outside we gathered our courage. "That Florida buyer
Wants us to raise the roof," Reade said, "and lower
The floor. Might be we'll do the roof pretty easy,
Just loosen the nails and shim it up with blocks
Wedged in under the joists. But would you look
At them foundation beams? That main one there
Must be two-and-a-half foot square, and dug in
Solid where it's set two hundred years."
"Whose cabin was it before the hermit came?"
"Old hunting club from maybe nineteen hundred.
Before that I don't know — Daniel Boone's,
I reckon. Don't see logs like this no more."
He measured it with his tape. "What'd I tell you?
Thirty inches, and lodged into the hill
Since the flood of Noah."

      "Well, what'll we do?"

"Rassle it," he said, "unless you've got
A better notion."

     We wrestled it. And broke
The handles of two twelve-pound sledges, and bent
His faithful old black crowbar into a U.
We stopped for a cup of water from the s-
shaped runlet below the spring. "Takes a grade-A
Fool to take this ruinous job," Reade said.
"They could've paid us to cut a window or two
And left it like it was. There ain't no way
To get the foundation as stout as it used to be."

"What do you reckon it cost to build this cabin?"

"Twenty-eight dollars and twelve and one-half cents,
In pure cash money. Then you've got your labor,
And the brains it took to think the construction out,

And whatever it's worth to stand out independent
And be thought wild or crazy or just plain dumb."

"It looks kind of sad and busted, what we've done,"
I said.

"That Florida feller will tack up plastic,"
He said, "and put him in an ice machine,
And have him a radar carport and a poodle
He's trained to count his money. These modern days
We're all a bunch of cowbirds, you know that?"

A Prayer for Slowness

Let the deep valley take me over
with its sundown shadow a little at a time,
by little and little, as if the hourglass
lay on its side and the grains leaked through
one by one into the cloud of infinite separate
moments. I shall enter that cloud

when once I am become as slow as the brindle
cow who walks the molded path along the hill
to shadow of the barn darker than hill shadow,
not lifting her broad head to watch the climb of
spade-edge shadow on the other mountain, but
steadily imprinting the dust with her divided name,

going into the barn where her rich welcome
is taken from her, to lie down grateful and eased.

Here

Burdened with diadem, the
Queen Anne's lace overhangs the ditch.
The lace is full of eyes, cold eyes
That draw a cold sky into their spheres.
The ditch twinkles now the rain has stopped.
And the ground begins to puff and suck
With little holes. A man could live down here forever,
Where his blood is.

Mark DeFoe

I'm a flatlander originally, born in Enid, Oklahoma, who grew up in Texas, Kansas, Oklahoma, and Colorado. As an Air Force brat, I lived in small towns and large cities and spent a year and a half in Japan. I served in the Army National Guard during the Viet Nam years and plodded through my B.A. and M.A. in English at Oklahoma State with little distinction before I captured a Ph.D. from the University of Denver. Now I chair the English Department and teach writing and literature at West Virginia Wesleyan College.

After I left the Southwest, I began to understand how the land is a presence there, as it is in Appalachia. And the weather. And the people are not that different, many coming from that same Scotch-Irish, German, English stock who settled much of Appalachia. Not a few of the settlers who came into the Southwest, as my relatives did, migrated from Kentucky, Tennessee, West Virginia, and those often unrecognized outposts of Appalachia, southern Ohio and southern Indiana.

West Virginia has been my home since 1975, longer than I've lived anywhere — I've brought up my children here, given them a place to come back to. That's important in this part of the country, and it's something that many Americans have lost — a sense of belonging, a sense of family. And I've come to admire the people of Appalachia, their resourcefulness, their toughness, their loyalty, their independence, their humor, their devotion to kin. Making a go of it has never been easy in much of the Mountain East, and I respect those who have built a good life in this beautiful part of America. But I can't be sentimental about Appalachia, either. Even in my short stay here I've seen it spoiled. One would have to be blind not to see the ugliness and squalor in parts of these hills. Nor can I close my eyes to the ignorance, the rotten politics, the fear of education, the oppressive social structures that sometimes gain control here, even though I might know their historical roots, understand the conditions which sustain them, and sympathize with the fears that energize them. Many Appalachian scholars damn Jack Weller's book, but it has its seed of truth, although nowadays it might be a blessing to be counted as one of "Yesterday's People."

I can't deny that many of the natives who live here today are among the first to sell it out, always ready to give the land away to outsiders to be ravaged. Many of their parents and grandparents were only too willing to do the same. Then it was coal and timber; today it's out-of-state garbage, toxic waste, land developers, and yes, still more coal. West Virginia remains in thrall to the coal companies. I doubt if this state can save itself until it breaks the political and economic death grip of the energy conglomerates. It's still the same story, whether it's coal stripped out or garbage trucked in: those who live here, who stay behind — who can't or won't escape to Boca Raton or Hilton Head or D.C. or take the

Hillbilly Highway to North Carolina — have too little control over the fate of the land they live on, and die on, and love.

My own poetry has focused on present day Appalachia, this contemporary life I see around me. Since I didn't grow up here, I don't wax nostalgic about the past, a weakness I see in much writing about Appalachia, at least among those who seem to have raised their status as Appalachian writers to a profession. I've seen a few folks come down out of the hills of West Virginia on a mule; now they come ripping down in mud-splattered Broncos or Cherokees with cassette decks blastin' out a cheatin' song. Of course, that's just another stereotype in itself. Robert Penn Warren had some good advice years ago in an essay entitled "Do's and Dont's for Literary Regionalists." Maybe we should all re-read it.

At least for me, I resist becoming a trumpet for either the "pastoral" or the "political" camp in Appalachian letters; but I think when I write poems, I write with an eye for my surroundings and what is important — and what is important extends beyond my own petty,

Mark DeFoe

personal concerns. I live on a street, in a small town, in a state, on the land, in the mountains, of a region. And though I'm an independent cuss, like many of my neighbors, I do belong. What happens here matters to me and my family.

Though I write about Appalachia, I consider myself a poet first and leave it to others to attach the nametags. I have purposely tried to publish my work widely. My poems have appeared in Great Britain, France, Canada, and the U.S. in such magazines as *Paris Review, Poetry Ireland Review, Poetry Durham, Sewanee Review, Malahat Review, Antigonish Review, North American Review, Poetry, Commonweal, Kenyon Review,* and many others.

And the truth of it all is I couldn't escape the hills if I tried. My two little books of poetry, *Bringing Home Breakfast* (Black Willow, 1982) and *Palmate* (Pringle Tree Press, 1988) are full of poems about Appalachia. Some of my very best ones, I hope.

The Former Miner Returns from His First Day as a Service Worker

(at McDonald's — somewhere in Appalachia)

All day he crushed the spongy buns, pawed at
The lids of burger boxes and kiddie pacs
As if they were Chinese puzzles.

All day his hands ticked, ready to latch on
Or heave or curl around a tool
Heavier than a spatula.

All day he rubbed his eyes in the crisp light.
All day the blue tile, the polished chrome, said
Be nimble, be jolly, be quick,

All day he grinned while the public, with bland
Or befuddled faces, scowled over his head
And mumbled, whispered, snarled and snapped.

All day his co-workers, pink and scrubbed,
Prattled and glided and skipped while he,
All bulk and balk, rumbled and banged.

Near shift's end he daydreamed — of the clang
Of rock on steel, the skreel
Of a conveyor belt, the rattling whine
Of the man trip, the miner's growl of gears
As it gnarled, toothing at the seam.

He makes his slow way home, shadow among
Roadside shadows, groping back in himself
For that deep sheltering dark.
He has never been so tired.
His hands have never been so clean.

Street Dance: West Virginia

Girl with a patch on her pert rear
bumps a trucker in a REO hat.
Swing stomp hoe-down, chugalug beer.

Two women in their granny gear
allemande left their down-home fat,
right by that patch on her pert rear.

The crowd goes clapping, stands to cheer,
whoops at a clogger — "Stamp that rat!"
Swing stomp hoe-down, chugalug beer.

Lean dude with a mutton-chop leer
sure doe-see-does and tries to pat
girl with a patch on her pert rear.

Fiddle and banjo hone the ear
of a mountaineer aristocrat.
Swing stomp hoe-down, chugalug beer.

Hey, promenade! You city cat!
Ain't she a foxy pioneer,
girl with a patch on her pert rear?
Swing stomp hoe-down, chugalug beer.

Emergency Re-pairs

BLANG, BLANG — WHACKA-WHUNK! Point blank in the middle
of the discount mart lot this hoop is beatin'

the be-jesus out of a pumpkin-orange
Ford flatbed, "Farm Use Only" scrawled on the door.

A sign surely perpetrated by a one-armed
cousin using the tail of his wife's house cat.

The letters angle off strange and slant-ass,
as if cousin or cat had a serious twitch.

He humps under the differential, boots bouncing.
Sudden quiet. A pink foot pokes from the cab,

tapping to the twang of a cheatin' song.
Redheaded, freckled, she tugs at her halter top,

anoints skinny legs — the sudden nutty reek
of coconut oil. A baby, his sucker

like a cigar, gives me a gooey leer
out the cab's back glass. The mechanic rises,

pot belly and beard, his hat on backwards. It reads
"Zeb" because there's a gob of mud on the "co."

He swipes at his palm-printed T-shirt, ambles
toward the store's glass façade. "More parts," he grins.

In my Izod shorts with my sack of tennis balls
I return and find him supine once more,

hammerlock on a new muffler, wrestling it
like a silver anaconda. WHANG WHANG

THUNKA THUNKA WHANG THUNKA WANG! "Da-gone
contrary son bitch," he growls. Then he sighs,

falls back, staring up into his metal heaven.
I pull out. His bumper announces "DISCO SUCKS."

Opossum Spring

This season of birth they seem to celebrate
self-slaughter. They squander on the berm,

in ditches, splatter the concrete
like the gray shreds of a retreating army,

repeating the same slow-brained blunder
across the path where the man things hurtle.

I bend over one, brush the flies away, and touch
the whorls of grizzled fur, fur that kept it

warmer than dinosaur or mastodon.
Here the habitual curled lip, always

the toothy leer, as if at last it got the joke.
And yes, as always, the thickish, scaly tail,

curled in perpetual question mark.
What vision echoed in your tiny skull?

What scrap worth clutching in those paws (so like
a child's spread fingers) made you start across

the asphalt in your shambling, nose-down way.
No time this time to feign death, but turn, face it

with your sort of addled courage. And then
the exploding glare, what must have seemed a sun

come down. And surviving all those eons,
here it comes again — one millisecond to gape,

grin your possum grin, and blink, and
wonder at this final rush of radiance.

The Farm Tender

Some say she came from Jersey. Now she goes
from farm to farm, keeping things up
when the owners die or move to town.

No one claims to have seen her work, but
geraniums in coffee cans row the sill,
three clean boards close that hole in the barn,
coils of barbed wire lean on the shed wall —
her arms bear not a scar.

They say she finds the little forked men of the woods,
that she makes goat cheese and blackberry jam,

applesauce and bread-and-butter pickles.
That in the glow of tallow candles
she quilts comforters of stars and moons.

If you come up her hill, her voice from the garden
will slip around you, a nodding sing-song,
like a hymn measured, shaped to
the snick, snick, snick of her old thick-handled hoe.

She might be in a faded, tie-dyed skirt, naked
to the waist, her small breasts nutmeg brown,
bending to the heart-shaped bean leaves,
in the green fountains of new corn.

If you come, she may feed you mushrooms.
If you stay, you may beneath the skin
on her wrist as she milks,
see the play of tendon, bone and sinew.
She may take you on slim hips. The scent
of her hair will be cedar,
her arms will be mint, her belly dill.
She will give you spiced tea and rough bread,
send you down the road looking back.

Then she will call to the others — the stock, the dog,
the cat, weaving home in the shafts of light
that spill through the sumac beyond the garden.

She brushes down the bed and her day opens,
smooth as the grass on the far field.
What time she tells will be by birdcall —
crow and hawk and swallow, sparrow and jay,
mockingbird and meadowlark, dove and owl.

She pauses to note your trail, wiggles
her toes in the dew-chill grass. She takes up the hoe.
She does not care who owns this farm.

Charles B. Dickson (1915–1991)

I was born in Marietta, Georgia, in the foothills of the Appalachians. Among my earliest memories are many trips in the family touring car to the North Georgia mountains to visit my mother's relatives, some of whom lived in log homes handed down by their pioneer forebears.

How well I remember the breezy dogtrots and wide, wraparound verandas with rocking chairs and screens of leafy vines for shade. And the food from wood-burning ranges in the kitchen! Huge fluffy biscuits buttered with gold straight from the churn by the hearth and dipped in sourwood honey from a bee tree. Pies, multi-layered cakes, fruit cobblers, tea cakes! Chicken, fried or in pies or cooked with dumplings! Sausage, bacon and hams from the smokehouse! Milk, flecked with cream and cool from the springhouse! Do I romanticize?

Not the cooking, certainly. And I believe it is fair to say that my kinspeople, although scattered across the upper breadth of the state, were typical of the mountain population — hardworking owners of small farms, self-reliant, deeply religious, honest, hospitable after an initial reticence with strangers.

It is a matter of deep regret to me that survivors from the early 1900s and their descendants are increasingly in retreat before bulldozers which razor mountain slopes and valleys for sprawling developments of summer and retirement homes, golf courses, and ski resorts. I shudder to see once-quiet hamlets converted into pseudo–Alpine tourist traps. It is true that vast areas of wilderness beauty remain but equally true that destruction continues with irreplaceable loss to environment and mountain culture.

Although we live near Atlanta, my wife Virginia and I spend considerable time in the

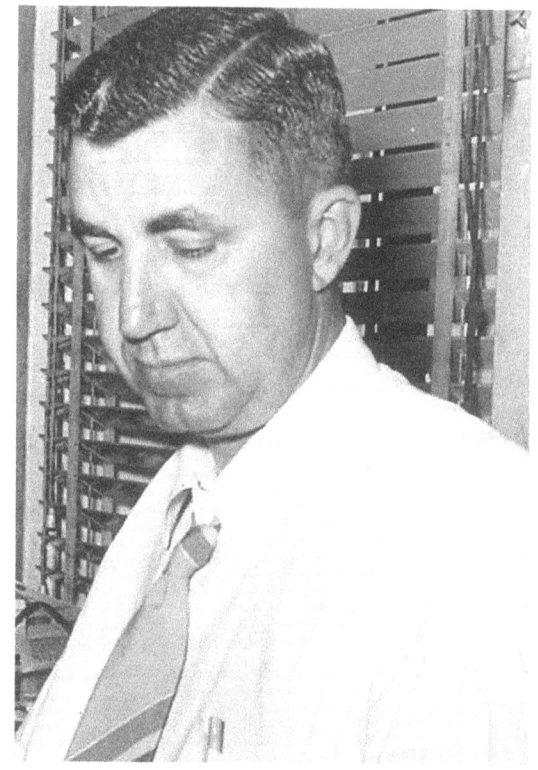

Charles B. Dickson

highlands of North Georgia, Western North Carolina, and East Tennessee. I am a graduate of the University of Georgia and have worked as editor and feature writer for *The Atlanta Constitution, The Florida Times-Union* in Jacksonville, *The Nashville Tennessean,* and *The New Orleans States-Item.* Over the years I have written widely for magazines—fiction, non-fiction, poetry.

My first published poem appeared in 1935 in *Bozart,* the literary journal of Oglethorpe University. My poetic output was sporadic for many years because of career and family demands but has increased vastly over the past decade. Poems have been published throughout the country in such literary magazines as *Pembroke, Chattahoochee Review, Georgia State University Review, California Quarterly, The Lyric, Black Bear Review, Dog River Review, Piedmont Literary Review,* and others. They have also appeared in a number of anthologies and have received numerous awards in national and international competitions, including the annual Lyric Memorial Award for 1988, 1989, and 1990.

I began writing haiku and related Japanese-derived forms six years ago, and my work in this genre has been used by journals throughout the United States, Canada, and Japan. My haiku have received many awards, including those from the Museum of Haiku Literature (Tokyo) and *The Mainichi Daily News,* an English-language newspaper in Tokyo.

I am the author of three books: *A Touch of Wholeness,* consisting of English-tradition poetry, and *fragrance of frost grapes* and *Out of Cassiopeia,* both haiku chapbooks. All were published by Skyefield Press of Deer Isle, Maine.

No More Hard Times

He parks his pickup under a pignut hickory,
clambers down the rocky mountainside, letting
his mind ramble back more than sixty years—
to the hardscrabble days when he hunted possums
and squirrels for the table, searched these
Appalachian slopes for ginseng roots to make
a little pocket money, helped his dad smooth
chestnut logs for the cabin. He thinks
of the thirty years he worked in the textile mill.
"No more hard times for me," he tells himself.

Today, as in other summers, the pink, drooping,
heart-shaped blossoms of wild bleeding heart
sway under the beeches and yellow-poplars below
Crippled Turkey Knob. White butterfly-winged
petals of Dutchman's Breeches assuage
the slight mountain chill with fragrance.
He sits on a granite outcrop, listens
to the melancholy trill of a pine warbler.

He frowns, remembering his dad's refusal
until his final breath at ninety-two to sell
the family's high, steep slopes and fertile
valley bottoms to land developers. He sticks

his hand into the pocket of his overalls
to finger the folded sales contract signed
two hours ago. He wonders why, with all that money
in the bank, he feels empty, why he drove directly here.

Magnet

Sunday afternoons for almost forty years
he whistled up a hound or two, lifted
his scarred oak walking stick from a nail
in the smokehouse wall and tramped
the valley's length, checking fences,
cattle, terraces, crops in season,
listening to summer tanagers
rattle *chick-tucky*–TUCK and watching
white-tailed deer arch up the mountainside.
Sometimes, if he had heard the bream
were bedding, he carried a jar
of crickets and paddled up the west fork
of Limping Warrior River with his fishing pole.

Today he rows slowly upstream from the new
power dam. He often wonders what magnet
still pulls him here on Sunday afternoons,
with his fields, his fences, his terraces,
his locked, empty house fifty feet below
the shimmering sunset surface of the lake.

Appalachian Parthenon

I climb the trail again. As always on the final mile,
my weary feet begin to feel as if they walk
on springy depths of mountain flowers,
not on stony earth. Late-afternoon shadows,
blue and luminous, blur a steep ascent of fern.
Great white whorls of snow trillium flicker
under hemlocks, birches.
                          I step into the clearing's
gentle light. A thicket of Catawba rhododendron
masses lilac-purple blossoms beyond the cabin.
Weathered gray as granite, the cabin thrusts
out of the mountain. My great-great-grandfather built
it of chestnut, the wood pioneers claimed would last
forever — chestnut for wall logs, door planks
and sills, puncheon floors, rafters and joists.

The fieldstone chimney has crumbled, the red-oak
shingles long ago whirled away on gusting winds.
The hand-hewn timbers remain, resting as solidly
in their dovetail notches as the columns
of the Parthenon stand on their pedestals.

I drop my backpack on my customary camping site
beside the pink-veined waxy white glisten
of lady's slipper. I hear the brook's faint splash.
The sky's translucency softens toward night.

Blue Ridge Moments: Nine Haiku

morning mist—
evening primrose petals close
around dewdrops

        callused fingers
        on a Blue Ridge dulcimer...
        wind in the cedars

outcrops of granite
across the mountain field
crooked furrows

        acid rain
        growth rings thinner and thinner
        on the new-felled pine

still trapped
in tangled barbed wire
antlers and bones

        white laurel blossoms—
        from the mountain's deep darkness
        bright water gushing

sandstone outcrop—
a yellow butterfly clings
to the fossil fern

        mountain twilight—
        the lake's darkening blueness
        slap-slaps the canoe

midnight campfire—
from the dark thicket, fragrance
of frost-grape blooms

Hilda Downer

Perhaps the most important element of my poetry is place—what place and childhood I came from. Much of my life is trying to realize all that I knew as a child, such a sensory overload that I still cull certain smells, sounds, and images from that deep spiritual well. Even now, in the observance of my son's childhood, I map that unchartered frontier in silence and amazement. Childhood is the secret of ourselves that we continually unravel or knit back together. If I can dive deeply enough into its well to rise again clutching a few pebbles, then I have gone to the depth that exists in us all—a common ground or place—and through these pebbles we can understand one another.

The reason I think the place I come from is the center of the world is because I continue to collect pebbles from its granite foundation and its mountains just happened to be the ones I could think to. Their shadows never lay as though they had turned their backs to me but always embraced me. The name of the place, Bandana, derived from the Clinchfield Railroad's use of a bandana tied to a laurel limb to denote the train station. The idea of a real train stopping at a pretend station to me epitomizes childlike imagination and the "real frogs in imaginary gardens."

In Bandana, my cousins and I pretended a cinder block was a doll's refrigerator. Long river rocks served as toy cars, and two bobby pins held up by a third one danced in their high heels. I am not so amazed at our imagination as children as I am by the imagination and figurative language of the adults we knew—for they were the ones receiving and delivering items at a pretend station. I often think of my relatives as being silly, though they also appeared rigid and stern, held in by the book ends of poverty of the Appalachians.

It was in the richness of the land that the people were rich. Thick laurel formed abundant rooms, and moss furnished them with couches and smell. Bandana soil brimmed with enough garden vegetables to last until the next summer. Pink lady slippers and flame azalea startled me in the woods. I knew where various flowers grew again and again. Eggs 'n' Butter framed what we called "the cat trail" in its narrowness down the hill. Virginia Blue Bells leaped out around one curve of road. I have tasted of every color of apple that apple trees could imagine to grow in Bandana. On our walks we would eat an apple until we tabulated to the next kind of tree where we would throw away the last apple and start on a new one. I believe the specific minerals in home-grown food call us back with a physical need for the very soil.

Even beneath the soil breathed a richness. The woods are filled with sinkholes indicating an underground network of caverns. Some Indian caves were bulldozed over when the strip mining began next to my grandfather's woods. Many mines were rich with aquamarines, emeralds, garnet, feldspar, kyanite, and mica. Walking down the road was an experience of the sparkling of tiny flecks of mica on the road and banks — stars, stars everywhere. I remember a whole field of daisies, as far as one could see, until the Lower Sink Hole Mine stripped us of that wealth. I am not even bitter about the mines for they, too, are a part of my solitude.

One of the most beautiful images from my childhood was that of huge clusters of quartz displayed at Dave Gibson's store. The post office took up a corner of the building, and when Dave Gibson died several years ago, people voted to go on route. The idea that a letter can no longer be mailed to Bandana alarms me in the same way that poems seem to be like letters mailed to no address. Poems attempt to explain something indefinable, and they are going to a place that one can't get to from here. They are like messages in floating bottles, lost to the sender, found by someone else. Much is lost to Bandana now. Even the ginseng and galax sold to Dave Gibson have become rare. If the place is lost to me now, a new catalyst is eternal homesickness.

Hilda Downer (Jan Hensley)

There once was an old house down from Bandana store in which a staircase led to a wall. I relate to this house since there is the person I am who faces the world, who cooks, works as a psychiatric nurse, teaches English at the local university, sews clothes and dolls, and serves as a "Room Mother" at my kindergartener's school. And there is the second floor that has been sealed off. There is much that I keep up there to draw from. If my poetry does not seem accessible to everyone, then it is because I do not speak to everyone, only those who choose to understand it in an attempt to understand themselves.

People ask sometimes how I began writing or how I come up with all those metaphors. The beginning was Bandana, and then there was my beginning. I never began writing. I began thinking. I've never "had to come up with a metaphor." It is simply the way I think and have always thought. Writing is such a part of me that I cannot discern if it was there in the womb or if it waits in the soil for me.

My first book of poetry, *Bandana Creek,* was published in 1979 by Red Clay Press. I've published in various journals, but not much. I'd rather spend the time writing.

I now live in a place much like Bandana, complete with caves, a river, fields, and distant waves of blue mountains. I'm thrilled to have the privilege to be a mother, and I love my home and family life. I'm working hard now so I can devote more time to writing. Meanwhile, I am watching in wonderment.

So much has come and gone that the Appalachians never existed

There are people living now
fading in and out of composition classes
who have no memories
and no childhood
recorded in black and white.
Those of us who do, come from another planet.
We are like the souls that bodies do not accept.
We are the chant of old Bandana
with its quilt in variegated grey
airing familiarity across porch banisters.
Against weathered clapboard
the wringer washing machine,
like the space ship that brought us,
protrudes too modern white for the dark ages.
Summer takes over the edges with excess,
leaves springing from nowhere.
No one is on the porch.
Only a four-year-old me, my brother stark as a tooth,
Paw in a dismal hat, and cousin Jaybird —
we are looking into the camera with all that we are
until the click stuns us with what the world was then.
When I was a child, the world was a child
climbing in with the green of my own eyes.
Times, my fingers could feel themselves being thin grass
as much as feeling themselves being fingers.
I was humming soft among the naming flowers,
the cage of speculation.
Now, half-buried and half-dust at the very site,
the clothespins caught haphazard through the jaws
grin at their foreknowledge nearly camouflaged in black and white.
Even more awkward growths amid the creeping foliage,
we caused too much light in our astonishment.
We were too easy to kill and already extinct.

Hills so beautiful, they sting

The Johnson boys
were headed up Conley Ridge
when the least 'un got copperhead bit.
Arching like a pitcher handle
against his thigh,
the snake shuddered there.
Breaking off in a scream,

the oldest 'un spurted
back up the hill,
losing himself in the creek,
finding himself on the opposite bank,
slapping through woods.
Trees seemed to swat back.
Distance erased all but one hill
before home.
Clutching breath,
his back measured up to an apple tree,
he slunk to somniferous ground
where snakes might think he was one of them.
Eyes patted closed.
Respiration heaved like tractor wheels,
heavy as thighs after running.
Feeling like cornbread softening in milk,
or the gathered top of gravy stagnant in a bowl,
his mind snapped stringbean alert,
pricked like ears of distant grass,
heart almost leaping over the darkening hill.
Twenty years would find a lot of people dead.
Slithering over the blind of hill,
he tasted the wet kerosene smell of light,
slid through the back screen door,
and seeing his brother lying safe on a tick,
his face narrowed into a grin.

Rain polka dots the sidewalk

Weather guesses how I feel,
resembles a day I would have been with you.
Fog moistens windshield,
an eye about to spill.

Quiet to enjoy our own minds,
we would cull levels of sound —
footsteps
backed up by creek,
backed up by rain,
or we might practice situations,
biting bullets at the mention of people
who think they have us memorized.
Cupped spring water
would dribble chins like watermelon.
Flowers bending into showers,
you would pick me a weed.

We would remember a road unpaved,
apples floating on gentle dirt,
brown-spotted like old woman skin.
Talk would finish
as though a hard rain had fallen,
as though volumes of poetry
looked upon from the floor,
sunshined gold lettering.

Bus perched on top of a mountain like a skull on a wedding cake

My city walks are secrets with the moon,
tongue tipped with fox-desire
of gliding beneath budded trees.
Poncho drags lizard tail behind me
until thrown into a blanket on concrete,
hamburger and coke before me.
Lights dot darkness
like dandelions in a field.
Cars drone constant as a creek.
I am a secret to the city,
but I can kick a building and watch it crumble.
I can change poems into frogs.

Back to Bandana in Brown Season

The old people are calling me back,
back to a linty road that chides dusty stamens,
back to the deep of rocks that reflect river sound.
The old people are calling me back.
Back to a somnambulant blade of grass smoothing water,
to submerged yellow quartz that thinks holding light is life,
to the meandering flag of a salamander's tail,
back to the stubs of a tobacco field open as a notebook,
to a spot in my grandfather's yard that is my heart,
to the stillness a screech owl conducts,
to the rain that has watched where its cold is going,
back to the Roan, Mt. Mitchell and the Black Brothers—
to the shape of mountains I can think to,
the old people are calling me back.
I was among the unborn to whom someone spoke.
The old people are pulling me back,
back to excavate old papery dreams,
faded lines varicose with ideas for novels,

the Woodchopper emitted from a shaft of light,
antique baby clothing stacked into a pillow quiet,
back to those who blinked the mica glittering of a Bandana book,
who met in loneliness and sent me beyond myself—
Whitman, Wordsworth, Yeats, Pound, and ole Fred.
The old people are calling me back.
I collect my bones in such a way
as to move with amnesia of flesh.
Earth, think nothing of the shattered web of hair.
Let it drift from you like Bandana Creek.
Winter my skull for a lost cricket bath.
Instruct an appleseed to root the umbilicus
and to always love the burden sky.
Earth, do not consider the broken vanilla bottle
that posed a woman's body.
At times, I translated vision,
my words easily and finally dust.
Bandana, no matter who comes to see you,
never let go of your laurel or fern.
The old people are calling me back.
They speak past summers, this field always corn.
Sag and bent of gender,
stalks wave or clap short wisp arms,
overjoyed to have me back.
Edging the parchment of their dry chime,
they clatter from a stick like a picket fence.

Gregory Dykes

I was born in Washington County, Tennessee, on August 14, 1952 — my ancestors (on both sides of the family) came to East Tennessee, probably in the 1790s, and settled the rolling, fertile valley and ridge country between the Blue Ridge and the Cumberland Plateau. Jonesboro (now incorrectly spelled Jonesborough) is my hometown, and I went through the local school system in a quiet and undistinguished manner.

I was graduated from East Tennessee State University with both a bachelor's and a master's degree in English (my thesis consisted of a volume of poetry) and have since worked at a plethora of jobs including newspaper reporter, wire editor, editor's assistant on a magazine, college Public Relations Director, English and journalism instructor at three different colleges, and a few others I would prefer not to remember.

I am married to Gwen Jenny, weaver, spinner, painter, and descendent of some of Buncombe County, North Carolina's original settlers (not to mention a paternal grandmother from County Cork, Ireland). Much of Gwen's mother's family still lives in and around Burnsville in Yancey County, Western North Carolina.

Gwen and I have been gypsies within the region. During our time together we have lived in Jonesboro, Johnson City and Greeneville in East Tennessee; and Asheville, Cullowhee and Hendersonville in Western North Carolina, which means we have been located from valley to mountains and back again several times. In the spirit of Thoreau, we are well-traveled in Concord.

I must, with some hesitation, admit that I have trouble with the concept of a distinctly "Appalachian" poetry. The settings, nomenclature, personae, and many "particulars" in my poems are most certainly Southern Appalachian, but the themes of love, loss, remembrance, death, order, meaning, faith, striving, and joy are universal. If a Southern Appalachian theme does exist — inasmuch as I am capable of detecting

Gregory Dykes

it — it is the telescoping of cultural change within the region in the 20th century and the confusion, irony, and, more often than not, trauma which come with it.

My grandfather has become a symbol of this telescoping in my writing and figures prominently in my most recent poems. He was born four years after Custer's Last Stand and lived to see Alan Shepherd go into space, but he never personally entered the industrial era. He was a 19th-century agrarian with a television in his living room: a plower with mules, a rider of wagons and sleds, and a living dichotomy. Yet he lived in a world I distinctly remember. It is to him and my grandmother I dedicate "It Is..." which is included in this volume.

My father's was the first generation to leave the farm — literally forced out by World War II — and go to the factories and to the Northern cities. Sitting in front of a word processor writing this, I span the industrial era and find myself, like it or not, in the information age. I find this to be a constant source of amazement and try to translate this sense of wonder and continuity into my writing.

Yes, sense of wonder will do nicely.

"I trip in the wake of my grandfather's furrows."

Gwen, my stepson Jason, and I live in Hendersonville, North Carolina, and I teach at nearby Brevard College.

It Is...

(in memory of George and Maggie Dykes)

It is cleaning a plow with the shank of his heel,
the same motion used when he stomped the dog
to death for howling into no full moon —
a young man's wound an old heart cannot heal.
His boots are more of earth than leather,

cuffs afull with clods and brown dust,
small stones to fall and tumble across
the kitchen floor with its linoleum
curling in its dotage like brown birch bark.
Then, it is the clucking of his wife,

pretty still in faded flowers, stouting smartly
through seasons lean and bless'd of birth
and canning and beheading chickens;
face and hands of a creamy suede with dusty pearls
inlaid upon her serrate palm, polished hard

by hoe and teat and paring knife with a
splendid grip for birthing, baking, and cutting
all that must be cut in a life of knives and thread:
a hand to smooth the ruffles of the world.
It is old pants faded that blue of denim

on the knee and much-used thigh like the sky
paling around the edges of noon. It is two

hands, a face, inseparable, cracked alike
beyond blister or hurt — too much old leather
to be spoken of prettily. But it must be beauty

when five generations of plowing can be found
in the squareness of a thumbnail pared like
an apple-peel with a knife or the jagged grooves
cleft from eye to chin that mark the eyes'
defense in sun–cut summer fields. It is two

hats in perpetual cycle, one for field, the other
for hymns and prayers and courtly wagon rides,
dancing from church to barn and around in end-
less turning to mark the passing of the days.
It is making life on eight acres — one per child —

stumbling 'round to fall and landing feet
firm, legs spread to meet two furrows
in the plow's wake; returning to the plow,
the mule, the wagon, the sledge — growing
the face you have earned. It is taking

the luxury of shade and knowing the
foreignness of money — shoes for eight
and two are bad to drink. It is knowing
nothing else and wanting less, caring
little beyond the meat, the garden,

the field, the flesh on the bones and
the song. It is living so long no one
is left to call your given name, so
mister goes, now, before it all, it all —
mister. It is burial by none who knew

your birth or the child you once pretended
to be. It is gravestones worn smooth by
corn-making rain and sun. It is the end
of all whose memories held a place for
you. It is. It is.

        It is.

You Must Teach the Student

    about song
    something in the brain-stem
    ear must oscillate
    reverb-
        arate

make the skin move
across the bone
  those of intellect
must pluck at the feet
  and the groin
must stamp around fires
  by moonlight
must make their songs
  dance like
faceless silhouettes
about a fire   must mimic
deer & bear & buffalo
exactly in replica
like heartbeats striking
behind the iguana's eyes
'tis song   belay the gray brain
& dance & stalk & lay
amongst the riverbank foliage
  with men & women &
strike that early brazen forge —
hot copper flecks to speckle long-scarred
arms (a pain long-known
familiar as a mauling wound)

"No garden   no song"
plants and songs
grow the same   not speed
but unfolding
moves the world
  and the soul
empty bellies gave us no song
"no game   no song"
no mimic   no long-necked bird
drought brings silence when
rhythm is void and the cycles
rest   with rhythm comes
the music amplified
for it was there
all along.

Reflections During a Country Funeral

(for Miss Kathleen Smith, 1901–1987)

What we remember of ourselves
cannot stem the tide of forgetfulness
which slips in certainly

as one generation ends
and peels itself away from
the leading edge of time, exposed
is another and yet another
and so forth from the beginning
to the end of what we shall ever know.

I think I am the only one who knows
    now
that one day long, long before my birth
two greatuncles, one by marriage,
the other by blood,
shot my grandfather's blind and crippled mule
and cried
for having ended a life
so large and so long—
when I am gone
   that moment will end.

At country funerals
the pallbearers sit
to the front and left and lift
the coffin from its rest
to its rest
   and touch mud.
We cannot separate ourselves or hide
from the realness of earth,
it fills our nostrils
wafting from the open grave,
no subtle reminder of why we are here.
Its purpose abounds
around us.
Cattle watch across the fence
chewing new grass, earth-rooted,
they who are made of grass,
this same grass, this sod.
The old stand watch as the coffin
goes in — they wait their turn
to be lowered beneath the farmland,
one by one,
but go now to homemade pies,
hot coffee, and, later, milking.
Tomorrow, spring plowing,
back in a month to see if the sod
has taken hold, if the stone is set,
to reminisce.
To them who must plant
there is no season well-defined,

only doing and planting and birthing
        and burying.

What I Have Learned

is not what I promised
I would learn. Odd,
These dancings about the
Point of it all. Following
Behind the bearded ones,
Long dead — books, scriptures,
Laws on crumbling scrolls.
What I have learned
Is not what I promised
I would learn.

What have I learned?
To keep a woman, smiling,
Warm, in a candle-lit bed;
To build a fire, steady, slow,
Hot, on a rain-soaked hearth;
to think myself
A man in the company of men
And women; to wrench loose bolts
Long frozen, red with rust,
With glove-clad hands;
To split poplar, oak, ash and
Stack it neat against the rain;
To drive a truck, too far,
And leave it empty
Beside my new home; to
Cut a chicken into nine parts
And fry it crisp;
To mind my neighbor's boundary
And make it mine;
To walk ten miles and drink
Black coffee in cold winter air;
To sit; to wait; to think
  Not at all.

Marita Garin

I was born in Missoula, Montana, not far from Dixon where my mother, Mary Ann Neffner (German extraction, as well as English and Scotch-Irish), was raised on a ranch homesteaded by three women in the late 1800s — my grandmother, her sister, and their mother. Their father had died along the way as the family traveled from Michigan to Nebraska by covered wagon; the rest of the trip was by train. My father, George James Illichevsky, came from the other side of the world, southern Russia, at a time when that country was in great upheaval. His family lost their land and possessions when my grandfather was killed by Communists in 1918, a year after the outbreak of the Russian Revolution. Eventually my father came to the United States in 1923 as an immigrant, worked at various jobs along the East Coast, then entered the University of Idaho forestry program. Along the way he changed his last name to "Garin," easier for Americans to spell and pronounce. Employed with the U.S. Forest Service, he met and married my mother in Montana. Within a few years, he was back East, having borrowed enough money to take my mother and three small children to New Haven, Connecticut, where he would earn his Ph.D. at Yale. There would be five children in my family, of which I was the second of four girls.

My childhood was spent living in the west: Montana, Oregon, Utah, and Arizona, the latter being the most formative period of my life. Living on the Navajo Indian Reservation, my sisters and I went to school with Navajo children, explored canyons, climbed sandstone cliffs. During those years nature became a tremendously nurturing force that has stayed with me from that time on.

At the end of World War II we moved to Alabama (my father took a job in the Forestry School at Auburn University) where I attended high school and college. Married shortly after graduation, I moved to Beaumont, Texas, earned an M.A., then my husband and I moved to Johnson City, Tennessee, where both our children were born.

I lived in East Tennessee longer than anywhere else — raised my family, started a long process of learning about Appalachia, and began to write poetry. In 1979 I earned my MFA from Goddard College in Vermont. In 1984, with both children grown, I left my marriage, moved to Hendersonville, North Carolina, found a place to live close to a small lake, and began to re-structure my life. I wrote a lot of poetry, the ever-changing, reflective surface of the water just beyond the window where I had my writing desk. Among other odd teaching jobs, I began lecturing on Appalachian culture and poetry for an Elderhostel program. Wanting to see the poems I was using in these lectures gathered into one volume became the impetus behind my putting together the present collection.

As I began to describe the region to visitors, I discovered an Appalachia I had not realized

I knew that much about — not from books, but from having lived in the area for years. My husband had made many documentary films, with help from students and other faculty at East Tennessee State University, on mountain crafts and culture, filming interesting mountaineers in out-of-the-way locations. Ray Hicks of Beech Mountain, North Carolina, was one of his most endearing and valued acquaintances — teller of Jack Tales, an extraordinary example of what it meant to "live off the land" in Appalachia even into the late 1900s. The photographs, films, and stories that came from this work meant I had many opportunities to learn what the life of the mountain people was like, and I absorbed it all. ("Blood of the Lamb" was written in response to one of these films.)

Marita Garin (Perrin Todd)

Back then East Tennessee was not much different from other areas of Appalachia which have resisted outside influences. Finding it at times a difficult environment, I was often thrown back on my own resources. I'm not a regional writer in the sense that deep cultural roots and an Appalachian heritage are the subject matter of my poetry. But I lived there long enough to feel located in the landscape and use its imagery in many poems.

In 1988 I moved to Black Mountain, east of Asheville, North Carolina, where I now live, surrounded by those mysterious, towering, and inspiring presences — as I learned from one of the poets in this collection, called by the Cherokee Indians *Sahkanaga,* the "Great Blue Hills of God." I have a deep appreciation for the strengths the area draws on and develops in its people.

Support for my writing has come from an Artist's Fellowship for Writers from the Tennessee Arts Commission and a North Carolina Arts Council Fellowship. Publication in periodicals includes poems in *The Kenyon Review, Southern Humanities Review, Cumberland Poetry Review, Indiana Review, The Hudson Review,* and others.

Blood of the Lamb

Lester took the serpent from the box
before I was ready.

Praise the Lord

Hung there loose like a rope,
then turned stiff.
Lester handed it over.

Praise God

It jerked. I held on,
but I didn't have the spirit yet, Lord.

Hallelujah to Glory

Lester was speaking in tongues,
but nothing flowed through my hands.
They were still cold.

Oh Lord, up out of sin

It struck. I held on as long
as I could. Blood ran down my cheek.

Praise be to God

I knew what was meant.
But I wasn't ready yet, Lord.

"15-Year-Old Mother Killed..."

Wind rocks between the hills.
In a hollow of twisted metal, the child
beside her is trying to breathe —
the tiny mouth laboring
the way she strained three months ago
for air. The radio still plays —
country music, faint as a heartbeat.
Small stray lives are busy in the field.

From a Ridge in Eastern Kentucky

A man is standing alone
looking down into the Cumberland Valley
where the land folds in
on the thin gash
of a road. He watches a woman
carrying a child, her husband
has the baby. They climb
to a stray clump of daffodils,
too far for him
to see her face as she bends
to flowers, color rising in her hands
like music plucked
from a dulcimer, one bloom

given to the father, one
to each child. Then
they are gone, past
the desolate car rusting
in weeds, the scraps
of coal, the mud yard. Night begins
its claim on the valley
the way absolute grief absorbs
the living beside a grave.
Above them, the man thinks
there is nothing here
he could want, not this interval
binding them, returning
him to himself.

Picnic in Cherokee National Forest

My sister sits on a log
in the middle of some poison oak.
She talks of Martin Buber,
I-Thou shapes her mouth.
Why does she ignore the mountain kids
slipping in the stream?
Doesn't she see the bruised back
of the little girl, the brother
loosening his pants downstream?
My sister is explaining
"the anxiety of becoming."
Sunlight bites through leaves.
She turns away, the father turns
and rages at his boy,
his thick gut shaking, the split
lip of his fly opening.

Weather Diviner

When the hawk's shadow floats
larger and blacker,
corn husks grow thick as scars,
spiders weave their last breath deeper
into summer grass,
then the old Indian syllables for *hard winter*
rise from her bones,
tremble like dry leaves in her throat.

Crab Orchard Prediction

1

Six snows will drift
over the Cumberland Plateau
this winter...

    because wind presses
    against the trees and leaves its shape
    like a memory

    because fog invading the hollows
    on six early August mornings
    will be released from that memory

2

The first killing frost
will come
on October 29...

    when the katydid's call
    first broke
    through late August air
    it found the wind's shadow
    circling the slope and silence
    that would descend later
    onto fields

A Yard Near Elizabethton, Tennessee

Where Tin Can Hollow Road crosses Minton Road
and runs back into the hills,
where joe-pye weed guards the established
trash, a mound with its dog,
its bottles, its cracked, prominent sink,
five birds in flight fold into one
fugitive shape and I want to ask why
we who do not love
these hills, drive the blind
violent curves past Harmony Baptist Church,
past the starved look of bare-wood
porches, back into the hollow
where the hill's flank
is cold, protective, the yard

isolated in which a retarded boy, fastened
to a wheelchair, his hands
held like broken
wings, talks to air, to insects pulling bright
strands of light between the trees
and grass, repairing
something torn, the boy
instructing them, then raising the perfect
fabric in his arms to catch
nothing we could see
plummeting toward earth
without weight, without wings.

Richard Hague

We lived in an isolated ridge-top neighborhood in Steubenville, Ohio, accessible only by a steep, winding road cut into sandstone cliffs; the ball field I played on had been scraped out of the edge of an abandoned strip mine. My best friend's father, of Czechoslovakian descent, worked as a crane operator in the mill. He kept coon hounds down over the hill, collected ginseng, and ate rabbit, squirrel, and coon. A friend of my father's, Dutch Riesling, raised a copperhead in his basement. I was taught by nuns in high school who spoke Polish in their convent. I went to the same Irish Catholic grade school my great-grandmother Madigan had attended just after the Civil War.

And there was always the river. I spent days there in the summers, fishing and watching the men who gardened the rich river silt along the Pennsylvania railroad right-of-way. From my grandparents' porch, I saw carp the size of small boys dragged across the tracks, and once, way out in the river, the Sprague, the largest stern-wheeler ever built, on its way to Pittsburgh.

I listened to stories: train wrecks, cave-ins, immolations; character sketches of notables like Money O'Brien and Hambone McCarthy; fish stories, tall tales, intricately embroidered genealogies; and the unceasing cheery dirges of my Irish aunts recounting the latest deaths and disasters.

I lost friends and classmates: a girl I was in love with, drowned in the river at fourteen; a fellow I'd gone through school with, killed by a runaway gasoline tanker; a high school classmate, killed in Vietnam.

There were other friends, too: the beautiful, gentle daughter of a wealthy coal operator; sons of millworkers, railroaders, and lawyers; boys who were interested in war and girls who were interested in science; the fellow from Mingo Junction who played football for Yale; and the whole huge family of Coulters who lived far up Paddy Mudd Road in a trailer the size of a hen house.

Later, I lived in southeastern Ohio, in Monroe County, out on Greenbrier Ridge. I had a whole trailer to myself as well as the hills, woods, nights, blacksnakes, and creeks. And the local general store proprietor, Arnett Whitacre, who'd once kept a pet groundhog, and his buddy Jim Winland, from Martin's Ferry, who had retired to the county to fish and chew Red Man — I had them pretty much to myself, too.

For two summers I lived there, listening to stories again, fishing, soaking things up: the Daugherty family down the road with their garden on the knob and all their children and grandchildren living with them, Ralph himself too injured to work, and Edna hobbled but still putting in a couple of days a week into a job up in the county seat, all of them still managing to be strong and plain and kind; the local people who griped about the government buying up old homesteads for Wayne National Forest; fog drifting over the road at two in the morning as I drove back from a saloon twenty miles away; minnows nibbling at my

Richard Hague (Joe Enzweiler)

legs when I bathed in Clear Fork; the creek rising in bad weather and covering the bridge at Rinards Mills; certain fellows at the Malaga Crossroads Inn who hated to lose at eight-ball.

Once on the porch of the trailer there, my father, munching M&M's and drinking a beer, hazarded a definition of Appalachian literature: "Truths that are unbelievable, lies that are believable, and everything in between."

Later again, at the first Appalachian Writers Workshop in Hindman, Kentucky, I met lots of people and listened to stories: Cratis Williams, sipping George Dickel and telling Jack Tales on the back porch past midnight; Gurney Norman, remembering Palo Alto and Hazard; long talks with George Ella Lyon, Peggy Hall, and Pauletta Hansel; James Still, reading "A Ride On The Short Dog"; Jim Wayne Miller, reading from what would become *The Mountains Have Come Closer*; the energy and enthusiasm of Betty Payne James.

I had been set down, I finally realized, in the middle of a novel — no, not exactly a novel, but something larger and wilder and more impossible — whose beginning stretched unreachably far back in time, far before the settling of Appalachia, before the colonization of America, far before the beginnings of history itself. And I came to see that my own poems and stories were simply moments — passages — from that unruly, gargantuan, motley, and mostly-unwritten work whose author is not only everyone everywhere, but simultaneously the woman at work on a play in Morgantown, the young boy writing a poem in New Market, and the old man remembering his youth in Johnson City. I realized, too, that through all these people there flows into that work the knowledge of trees and animals, bulldozers, deeds, betrayals and triumphs, oceans and language and air.

Now I live and teach — as well as father, garden, write, husband, and loaf— in Cincinnati in a house almost as old as my great-grandmother would be if she were alive, on a piece of land that still remembers the glacier which stalled just a few miles north of here twelve thousand years ago, a piece of land drained by the Little Miami River, which is drained in turn by the Ohio, and so on and so on, amen.

Going Back the Hard Way

1

We stand in the center
of a field
whose edges are lost
in mist.
From the ghost of air
comes the sound of a man
driving long nails in a coffin.
Then it is gone.

Back on the road,
the world rebuilds
as sun burns off thick fog.
The Burma-Shave signs,
dim stations of the cross,
disappear around a bony ridge of skull.

2

The only crucifixion known of
in these parts
involved a black man
from Wellsburg, West Virginia.
They hoisted him kicking
up a skinned pole
on a morning much like this,
in 1892.
Fathers brought their sons,
as a lesson,
and made them touch the body
when they dumped it in a wagon.

3

The Sunday paper
scatters on the porch's spattered floor.
We are not likely to pick it up,
to rearrange its pages as we used to.

4

We close the door, feeling
splintery wood rasp at our spines,
the long tongue of paralysis.
All day, a numbness spreads in our brains,
like the instinct of a snagged fish drowning,
diving for the bottom,
where the deep mud darkness breathes
and waits to take us back.

Mary Daugherty

When she stands like this
in rain beside the road,
I remember all the iron
she's taken from
her father.
When the oil pipe broke his back,
a man from Antioch, Ohio
waved snakes above his bed
and Mary watched, believing.

From her mother, Mary has
the strength of clay,
and the power that is given
certain women by their gardens,
by their summers,
by their birthings and their mendings.

From her brothers, Mary has
the joy of talking back,
and the honor of
many fistfights, won and lost.

From her sisters, Mary has
the promise of early childbirth,
and a taste for
wildness:
berry,
beechnut,
and the rare
mayapple.

In the Woods Beyond the Coal Fields

I have come here to forget
the red god of my fathers

and the furnace of his meaning.
But the breeze is westerly today,
hauls Ohio's sin here.
Far across these Seven Ranges
float smoke and coalspill,
which to this summer's common wounds
upon the hillside, field,
and pond
apply no healing poultice.
The large, warm woman of the air
who once nursed blighted fox
and split-branched tree,
who once spilled health like splashed weeds
up and down these hollows,
hobbles now, hammered
in the darkness of old mines.
I will not find her here,
but I cannot go away.

In a dream that stalks me like my doom,
I fall through all the daylight
of these woods,
and stumble upstream toward the mine,
where the rotting bodies
of my fathers
slip like nightmares
from black slag.

Greenbrier Portraits

Uncle Buckley

On a porch in Ozark, Ohio
this man with water in his face:
clear eyes twin springs
beneath gray up-country hickories,
wet hollows in the dark of white oak slopes;
nose a flood-scoured prow of sandstone
outcropped from a creek bank's south exposure;
forehead broad, a furrowed
bald once wild with sumac thatch;
two downridge gullies running
to the corners of his mouth.

Under his smile
white stones gleam,
lucky quartzes

smooth as an Angus's grinders,
sweet with talk of greenness,
good to whistle through.

Old Man Mackey

Hat Mackey's skin
the color of old horseshoes,
rust of brakedrums, universals
off old Fords. Arms
lean as axles, he lifts
the young pig
from the worm-fenced pen,
sets it down,
claps the thick dust
from his palms,
muscles rippling, working—

cords of hardwood by the chimney,
fenceposts weathered forty years.

Mrs. Buell, Sunday

In her holy ghost smock
and bishopy hair,
she fishes by the Clear Fork,
singing, "To Sleep by Thee Oh Jesus."
In her shoes
the color of heavenly palominos,
she fishes by the Clear Fork,
singing, "The Lord Is My Rest and My Peace."
In her hat
like a clutch of white doves,
she fishes by the Clear Fork,
singing, "Safe in the Ark of Our Savior."

In her dark-fingered gloves
made of serpents,
in her shawl
like a fire made of vestments,
through her teeth that are older than Calvin,
she sings, "Nearer My God to Thee,"
and her Lord flashes bright,
like a bluegill at bait,
in the wild, pentecostal waters.

Drunk Jimmy Wetzel's Witty

A boy as small as a grackle.
Rides like Jesus on the dashboard.
Eyes flash red and green.
Hair like moss-whorls on an acorn.
Eyes flash red and green.
Talks back to the sheriff.
Tells lies to deaf old women.
Chews hickory sticks and needles.
Eyes flash red and green.

The pet of every pretty girl.
Sips whiskey from a thimble.
Eyes flash red and green, O
Eyes flash red and green.

Boy Fishing

Wild hair orange as broomsage
ripe in autumn, forehead
smeared with chrisms — pond mud,
slick juice off a catfish —
knees resurrecting through
his jeans
like fingers knuckled through
a dusty glove,
feet butt-tucked,
spine readied in its perfect curve,
he sits hunching
in the warm day's womb,
umbilicaled to greenness
rank with jumping things.

In the sudden tautness
of his line,
in a heave of
August waters,
comes each hour
his deliverance.

October

He has heaved his last hay
under roof. The cedar waxwings
disappear, one by one,

all day.
The hill road kills another drunk,
come sundown:
the wrecked car darkens
in the dust,
fills with flies.
A fox barks
in the dark field
where he spent his sweat
for hours.

He takes his whiskey
to the hilltop, where
night is never accomplished.
He can make out cows
like rocks along a windbreak
far below.
The creek runs through
its willowed tunnel
like a small girl
talking in her sleep.

Soon, the curse or spell is on him.
He lies, face down,
in a fume of whiskey,
arms thrown out,
his flesh like
fresh snow on old bones,
a century of cold.

In his yearly habit
he sleeps deep
where sometime in the night
the big wind
comes against the county
and his rich fields
fail, again,
toward winter.

Sometimes I Am Looking

Sometimes I am looking
for the rusty feather
of the vulture
near the path's edge
where it settled, dim and dry,
abandoned

in the downdraft of a dream.
Sometimes I am looking
for the snakeskin
crackling in the hickory branch,
where black-backed beetles
cut it scale by scale apart
into a kind of food,
transparent, weightless as an eye.
Sometimes I am looking
for the deer's fresh
birthing place,
the thin grass blue-red,
rising,
steaming still.
And sometimes I am looking
for the clearing
where a huge oak
wrestles up from
massive roots
to shade
a banked and mossy shed
in which
a man I never knew
cried once
into the darkness,
pulled the sheet
up to his chin,
and left, to tremble
always in the
halt arms of the leaves
and cobs and
husks,
that sound,
this sound,

our own.

Marc Harshman

I was born and raised in Randolph County, Indiana, on those flat uplands where rise the Mississinewa, Salamonie, Wabash, White, and Whitewater rivers, all draining to the far Appalachian Ohio. It is an Appalachian river, for where is it not surrounded by hills and old memories, this Oyo, this "la belle rivière." I now live in West Virginia, less than ten miles from where the great river forms the northern reaches of a long, twisted border with the state of Ohio. More precisely, I live in what was once a modest farmer's house, two rooms down then, and two up, and the outhouse, out. The 125-year-old dwelling sits in Marshall County on Bowman Ridge, the southern tail of which is called Sally's Backbone because bent old Sally Arnold, gentle cleptomaniac that she was, lived in the last inhabited cabin on that steep, switchbacked point above Lynn Camp on Fish Creek. I live near that story and a hundred others. And I might have lived here all my life. If the Indiana Company had had its way in 1768, the territory which was to become West Virginia might well have been named "Indiana" instead.

My people were Hoosiers, my father, a struggling farmer. As a boy, I knew the back forty as a very real place whose vistas were dominated by straight green rows of corn or soybeans, the view occasionally broken in the distance by a small woodlot. These humble vistas would remain unchanged as I grew up, but it would not be my father pulling the disc harrow between those emerald rows. The exodus from the American farm had already begun. An unforgiving economic order concerned only with itself would never see him or thousands like him in their seasonal rounds but only as ciphers in an eight-hour shift in much the same way as the coal miners were seen in the vicious boom and bust cycle that distinguishes their work.

Among family and friends I was to know a frequently frugal and rural existence there. When I came to West Virginia over twenty-two years ago, I recognized a way of life not dissimilar to what I had known. The accents were different, the steep and narrow hills a changed geography, the supplemental vocations different — mining and chemical plants and timbering — but the fervent attachment to place, knowing that where one is is important in knowing who one is, felt like home.

Living in Appalachia these many years has meant living where place impinges upon most aspects of daily life. But place yields its stories only when there is someone able and willing to remember them. If this is representative of Appalachia, I cannot say. It would seem that there are places elsewhere where also exists the same predilection for the storying of one's place. Perhaps the frequency of such neighborhoods persisting is greater here.

What is easier to assert is simply that I like it here. It's a rich atmosphere for a writer, that is to say, for myself as I perceive what's necessary for me to write. Here access to event

Marc Harshman

and experience is enhanced. Both are immediate to my life the way things should be when "at home."

It is just such immediacy that distinguishes this place for me, making it feel like home, similar to that one where Grandpa long ago in Indiana could nod toward the woods and say, "Back'n there is the edge of the old Dismal Swamp and it's your Great Grandad Andy Hartman shot the last bobcat in there." It feels like home now to see Lloyd Rine point to a particular portion of what appears to be a thousand acres of forest east of his barn and say that there stood the old Miller place, "right smart of an orchard he had there, too."

There is within even the most commonplace of conversations a pronounced sense of narrative. This storying of one's life not only by place but also by event and character becomes a way of thought. Things said are said within the context of things remembered. As I talk, I remember where I am standing, who owned this place before I did. I remember the blood ties of the subject of my story. Often what is said is within the context of certain larger, ongoing stories such as Biblical tales, the "old ways," or the "by hand and horse ways" background, each lacing perhaps different conversations.

When Lloyd comes to repair my garden tiller, I invoke the old Miller place in our conversations because I've become interested in apples, because I'm curious to discover if there are other tales clinging to the place, because it's the polite thing to do, to compliment Lloyd upon his storying by remembering it to him myself. And so the storying grows and becomes imbedded in the very moment of composition. I try to remember, as I go forward, how to tell what is told, to remember where I am and that I am surrounded by a company of listeners whose names stretch into a past we call tradition. I listen carefully, to remember just how to tell what is to be told, hearing Lloyd hearing me. He will be listening to see if I get it right:

that this place, which holds and begins to define even myself, has been told truly; that this moment "here" will describe the bank of trees out the west window, filled with piss elm and wild cherry; that the desk on which sits Miki's aging Olympia typewriter is simply a sheet of stained plywood straddling two two-drawer filing cabinets from Sears; that this very place, he once told me, where I sit and type, this section of flooring beneath me, covers the hole the Woods family opened one hard winter in order to slop the hogs which were allowed to enter the root cellar below to keep from freezing. The cellar is still there, but the floor is solid now, as I hope this telling has been.

The Barn

The chock out, and gravity rides the door open,
the changed air, a closed-in smoke of odors—
chaff dust, straw, animal heat and fur, oats and manure.
Slowly, the patchy, clerestoried ceiling
lets the light down; shadows grow into benches and beams,
cowstalls, mangers; the crib ripples stripes
in the quiltworked sun, its flintcorn flashing red
and orange through thin slats.
On the left a harrow tucks its blades into drifts of hay
beside a room walled with tools and belts,
harnesses and the single window.
I'd trailed the yellow rope of your cigar
all through this barn, to this place,
this room, the work shelf strewn with nails and twine,
coffee cans of screws and bolts and clamps webbed in shadows,
my name drawn quietly between the spit and chaw clatter of your voice.
And it is to this place I want to return,
that held the out-workings of our blood,
the made place of our single heart,
the place that is lost, that was made good with living,
the things at hand directly useful
to the life of the place and the men in it,
men once fathers and sons and grandsons
in one life, one land,
making it the breath of their hearts, giving it room,
their walking of it around
a graceful reasoning with the seasons.
And it was not size that gave them room,
something small was enough, a lifetime spent learning it,
forty acres remembered well could serve you,
the space in which you lived measuring itself by the cycles:
Holstein fathered by Guernsey to breed in another
more milk, the same butter; the corn followed by beans
followed by fallow; the family, too, returning,
year after year coming to table, to church, to visit.

Coming to table with the old ones: "and Bobby, how he related?"—
figuring out the cousins, remembering the dead, the places,
the snake in Hettie's well when she and Elmer ... this comes to
Grandpa's mind, his cousins so long gone now but living,
capable of life where there is time and place left to talk it out,
time to put words to their names and stories, where somewhere, too,
there is enough left of the landscape
to gather from it a language,
enough left of a room, a barn,
to keep what was worked of remembered life
holding flesh to the names,
life inside our living.

Primer

The blue suspenders had two lines of red
running the center of the fabric.
Their flat, tin snaps gripped your pant waist
and with you in your chair
I could look straight at them,
already six years into your history,
held to it now
by the glint of those snaps and the fabric they held.
This pulled me
up over your chest into your sight,
the run of that red through blue cotton.
I knew you by this, to be different
and kind, that you let me
follow you to your eyes.

Almost

I

The stack
stands stiff
and bright, brilliant,
towering, rolling its
narrow cloud
into the clear
night.

It's evening.
The lazy darkness
begins to separate

the oranging dusk
from the purple hills.

The town below
comes on
in diamonds.

Good for a few years yet,
this world
she wishes
no luck.

II

"Owned it is,
all of it, bought
and sold and nary
as much as a
please
or thank you ...
Wouldn't give em
time of day —
no manners, no
consideration.

Pa coughs
and wheezes, dying
in gasps
like a dozen others
I've known
in this valley.

And you think he was ever asked,
asked if he'd like to know
just what was what
when they put up these
God almight wonderful plants?

He loved to fish, he
liked quiet, he
believed in asking
every time
he went for grouse
on Joseph's, asked,
even though they's friends
these many years, asked
every time, asked,
believing, trusting ...

But now he knows,
now he knows, too late,
but he knows, and so do I:
the soil out of whack,
him going like this,
the babies with these tubes
in their ears ...

I can't sleep at night,
all them lights and
the whirr, but that's
o.k., it's the kids
worry me, hearing it
but with no mind to it,
comfortable with it almost,
almost, but now quite,
not quite yet ..."

III

But soon.

Setting the Hook

Larch & fir, green shadow & mist,
cold and the noise of the stream,
its push to sea hurried, constant,
and my work a silent rise & bend,
a flicking rapid toss
& then gentle the laying down,
a practiced repetition done again & again.
Edging down midstream slowly
the bright-tiny feathers gray
where they finally reach the water.
Impossible the patience, but come it does
and loved; it is the air and solitude
as much as the magic, liquid pull of the fish itself,
though it is there, somewhere, always,
the hope of surprise, the
swift silver & leap, the flash,
the lift of line & pull;
and the work is to get
the eye of the stream —
the possible map of the fight —
and the hands' feel of what's in him,

what the line reads to the fingers,
to become the fish, the stream,
to get the hook set in me as well
so that there's no getting free
of what it is here I love.

Beyond the Two of Us

The peach-skinned deer shivers to attention,
its ears stand like stilled moths,
legs stiffen, but the black heel of its nose
is working, I know it is, like a fine radar.
The long-dead cow I cut as steak for supper
pours its scented spirit from my pores and
should electrify my sudden partner into flight,
but the breeze holds my smell away
and the quiet we pull between us tightens —
any closer, my eyes finding hers,
and we could talk a lost language
filled with that prehistory
which surrounds us all,
all awe and always.

Don Johnson

I was born in South Charleston, West Virginia, in 1942, but I spent my earliest years in Poca, West Virginia, where my father ran a beer joint. He was only nineteen and not old enough to have a liquor license, but he was essentially the owner. He went to the war right after I was born and was gone most of the next three years during which time my mother and I moved back to South Charleston. One of my earliest memories (I must have been three) is being literally blown off the couch one night by an explosion at the nearby Union Carbide plant. After the war we moved back to Poca where I went to first grade twice: once when I was five, because all my friends were there, I didn't have anything else to do, and the teacher encouraged me; and again when I was six. I went to a four-room school which served eight grades.

Unlike most World War II fathers, mine remained in the army after the war, and his duty took us to Germany in 1951 when I was eight. The war was still recent enough that there was considerable evidence of the toll it had taken on the land and its people. I remember vividly the displaced persons who would pick through our garbage for food. But most of my memories of Germany were very happy ones. My father was only a second lieutenant after having been an enlisted man for ten years, and I had two sisters and a brother, so there was never much money. But the economy was in such disruption that Americans could live rather well, so we had babysitters, a housekeeper, and a yard man. The statue of the Grimm brothers that I refer to in "1946" stood in the marketplace in the small town of Hanau near the village of Lindenau where we lived. One of the brothers is seated while the other stands at his back. Legend has it that the two exchange places at midnight.

After four years in Germany we returned to West Virginia, Nitro this time, and then moved from there to northern Virginia, and then back to Nitro, and then back to northern Virginia. In all I lived in West Virginia a total of eleven years, but the memories of the place and its people have had a profound effect on my writing. Although I went on to get an undergraduate degree at the University of Hawaii and a graduate degree from the University of Wisconsin, when it came time to undertake the serious writing of poems, it was the land and the people of my native West Virginia that I wrote about.

The area of the state that I grew up in isn't noted for its scenic beauty. There are probably more chemical plants per square mile in the Kanawha River Valley than anywhere else in the country, and the area was much more polluted thirty years ago than it is now. Still I had fond memories of fishing, hunting, and berry picking, of listening to my father, my uncles, and my grandfather tell stories about their lives. I believe my paternal grandfather remembered every hunt he had ever been on, and all the stories began with a specific "fix" on time and place: "It was right after your Uncle Clarence had moved to Washington and I started to work at the Ford place.... We had to take the car through a big mud hole to get to the Humphries place over beyond Black Betsy, and we got the car stuck...." He remembered such small, specific details, right down to how many shells he had come home with after a day's hunt. I'm absolutely certain the narrative tendencies I have stem directly from listening to those stories.

Most of the poems I've written in the past five years have been Tennessee poems, but even the Tennessee landscape and the people I have put into it owe a great deal to the memories I have from West Virginia in the forties.

Many people have influenced my work. I think the first poem I read as an adult (about 19) that moved me was Archibald MacLeish's "Ars Poetica." The image of the moon releasing "twig by twig the night-entangled trees" just thrilled me. When I became serious about writing on my own, I was overwhelmed by James Dickey's work and also by James Wright. In some respects I had more in common with

Don Johnson (Carolyn Novak)

Wright's industrial Ohio than Dickey's Georgia, but Dickey's rhythms really grabbed me. Since those very early influences, there have been many other people who have helped me and from whom I have learned. Dave Smith has been of great help. Although we are exactly the same age, he's been a mentor of sorts, but then so have Fred Chappell and Jim Wayne Miller. Some poems were sent back recently from an editor who said he felt my poems sounded a lot like Elizabeth Bishop's! (He didn't take any.)

I like to think I've developed my own distinctive voice over the last ten years or so. I can certainly hear how my poems differ from other people's. No, I didn't say better, just different. And I believe I'm still growing, evolving. I don't feel I'll ever get to the point, however, when my poems won't be clearly identified as from these hills and rivers.

Baptism: Watauga River

She said I would have to go under,
that the Methodists' scattered drops
could not touch what I kept hidden,
that even the First Baptists' tank
would take just "the first inch"
of sin off the surface, like a bath
in a wash basin. But the river would jerk
out the sinner inside me, tumble it

downstream like a skinned mink
to the pool where the unclaimed drowned
eddy forever. At night I lay beneath
the tin roof's griddle listening.
The river flexed its cold, angelic arms.
If I waited too long, like my daddy,
they would reach over the bank willows
into our swept yard and take me.

"Sailin' On to Hawaii"

The first recording of an Hawaiian style guitar in country music was made in April, 1927, by a West Virginian singer, Frank Hutchinson.
—Tom and Mary Anne Evans, *The Guitar: From Renaissance to Rock*

A half mile underground, one of his pumps shudders,
coughs, shuts down. The foreman calls him away
from the coal camp's attempt at Christmas:
an orange for every child and enough
pick-handle liquor for the men to forget
the next day's digging.

     A band had walked in
from Clifton with the first Dobro
he had ever heard. They played a song
called "Sailin' On to Hawaii" that he whistles
entering the drift mouth.

       At a fair once
he had seen a woman dance on a flatbed truck.
Her hair was coal-black but lusterless,
her skin the color of a Melungeon's. He remembered
most her hands, how they tried to shape in air
the words the fat man beside her sang—"tradewinds,"
"tropical islands," "aloha."

       Now the air shapes
his breath in the light from the miner's lamp.
"Cold," it says. "Take another drink."

        Water drips
from the seam beside the short wall machine,
the mountain trying to clear its own black lung.
And he works for an hour up to his ankles
in an oily pool before giving up, his back fused
in the curve of the shored roof, fingers cut
and scraped but too cold to bleed.

The Dobro still rings in his ears,
and when he has another drink the liquor's warmth
forms in his mouth the words of the fat man
in the Florida shirt.

                      His body sways. His hands
float up from his sides, knocking the cap askew,
putting out the lamp. When he dances
the black walls come alive in the dark
with thick ferns, green vines curling up
out of swamp vapor, beyond dreams, beyond
imagining, toward a sun that he knows
hangs above the high canopy of trees —
warm, potent, bearing down.

1946

After Europe
he returned to a valley like the war,
a town of cellar holes and stumps
where yard trees, homeplace oaks and walnuts,
had been lumbered.
                      Farmhouses, jacked loose
from foundations, waited like dazed refugees
for trucks.
           He couldn't separate the tanks
and half-tracks that clanked and back-fired
in his dreams
               from the rumble and scrape
of bulldozers under arc lights at the dam site.

Roads were dust or mud.

Twice he dived in the ditch
when unscheduled charges went off on the bluff.

No one cleaned or planted.

The day his family moved, he sat on the front porch
chain-smoking Luckies, as he had the evening
he paced the Marktplatz in Hanau.

The only things left standing in the square
were one Grimm brother's statue
and a figure that hunched from the rubble
when his back was turned

to glean his discarded butts
that the moonlight made shine
like white pebbles on the dark cobblestones.

Raymond Pierce's Vietnamese Wife

couldn't understand milk gravy,
how her mother-in-law could brown
biscuits, keeping their insides white
and flaky, and her family transform
them into sodden lumps of dough
and warm liquid. She could not
fathom the distance and space
in her new life: vacant acres
of land between towns,
the squat brick ranches
shadowed by empty-windowed farmhouses
abandoned and allowed to fall.

Afternoons, she would cry
on the floor of the walk-in closet,
her husband's shirts crowded
along the wall like ghostly applicants
for visas. When he found her there
he couldn't understand her tears.
She had so much, now. In 'Nam
her people slept and ate in a room
no bigger than that closet.

When he drove her out to the lake,
he pointed at blank water, saying,
"I was born there, a hundred feet
down," thinking she would not
understand a valley flooded
so there would be no more floods.
But she did understand, as she
stared at the water's sheen
baring no hint of village, only sky
and the deep mountain of green.

And the River Gathered Around Us

After they wheeled away the town,
when the floodgates closed
and the river turned on itself,
we came back day after day
to watch the coves slowly fill up.

At the end of a week one road in
lay open. We drove it in three
Ford cars and a pickup towing

Wash Holt's rubber-tired wagon
that the boys from Mountain City rode.

It was not a Sunday. Most of us
had jobs, but we agreed to one more
game of ball before the smoothest
diamond in three counties
turned to lake bottom.

Water already lapped at the right field
fence where I killed a snake
before the first pitch, a fast ball
the batter himself called
a strike since we had no umpire.

Right went under with two out
in their half of the third
and we declared a ground ball
to that field an out. I played
barefoot and cheated toward

the infield, but it didn't matter.
Before the fifth was over,
water covered all but the mound
and the raked dirt at the plate.
By then, anything not a bunt

or fly ball was an out
and we were losing 6–2
when their pitcher called time
and said all three balls we had
were water-logged and that

he wouldn't ruin his arm
for no damn game in a lake,
so we brought him in half-way
where it was wet but close enough
to lob those melons in

with no pain. Then we lost
the bases, but ruled that running
in the right direction counted
if the runner didn't stop
until he made it home

or got out. We tied the score
on four straight hits to left
when a jon boat floated through
and blocked the fielder's way.
We called anything that hit

the boat a homer and it rained
that inning, the score tied
and water finally touching
the plate where both teams
congregated, soaked and up

to our knees in a field
without bounds, where everything
slowed and floated and nothing
sliding beneath the flood
would ever be forgotten.

Going Home

*My home's across the Smoky Mountains
And I'll never get to see you any more, more, more,
I'll never get to see you any more.*
             — Appalachian Folk Song

The last to arrive from farthest off,
I am given my grandfather's bed,
While he lies this first night beneath
The year's last snow to fall on West Virginia.
Gladys Craddock at the wake said,
"He is sleeping," and I craved
Silver dollars for his eyes,
Watchfires stoked at every hollow's mouth
From here to Gauley Bridge, finality
In crepe across the small town's
Fading railroad signs,

                    not sleep,

His or mine. I lock his door and windows,
Keep my vigil rocking in the dark
As wind whimpers in the sycamores'
White bones like unfed hounds after hunting.
These slow hours I nail my waking
To the walls in lists: odor of Old Golds,
Tincture of gun oil off the Ithaca,
Camphor, mentholyptus, dust,
The wind again in trees, beams tightening
Below me, the graveyard shift's uncoupling
Of tank cars in the Carbide yard.

In Carolina at the old homeplace,
We found the spring; he made a cup
From one broad leaf, a toothbrush

From a gum twig chewed to form
A soft white thistle. I drowse
Counting the times he put me down

In this same bed, a victim
Of the fight's last rounds
On Friday evenings after checkers.
Is he here in these clock-lighted quilts,
His spirit breathed out in the sparks
I release like bright quail
From the clean, starched sheets I now strip,
The flung linen floating like ghosts
To the floor?

          I lie out stiff
Along the edge on empty ticking, right hand
Wedged between the mattress and the frame,
Afraid of falling off to sleep.

But when, in the snow-quiet time
Before dawn, I submit and am drawn
In a slow, insensible assumption,
To his body hollows and his dreams,
I find him gone, escaped from this room
Of slow dying, already journeying home:
To dance to banjos on the cabin lawn,
To drink cool water, sweet from the beaded
Dipper, and taste the year's first
Sourwood honey, dripping from the comb.

Stephen Knauth

I was born in Milwaukee in 1950, but my real hometown is Pittsburgh where I spent most of my childhood. "Beautiful, filthy Pittsburgh," Gerald Stern called it. That landscape still smolders in my memory. Steel mills lighting the night sky, harrowing mountain tunnels, bridge after bridge stitching the rivers to their beds — all testament to man's dominion over nature. Even the beer was called Iron City.

When I moved to the south in 1972, I encountered an Appalachia different from the one I had known. The mountains of North Carolina, Georgia, and Tennessee seemed softer, lusher, more feminine, wilder — as though cast in a spell yet to be broken. The grim Lutheran doctrine of my youth hadn't prepared me for the kind of communion with nature I experienced on trips to the Snowbird Mountains, the Little Tennessee River, Wayah Bald, and other places. My armor melted. In those brief, indelible moments I discovered I was part of a great shimmering web of creation that included everything from chorus girls to crabgrass. Lines of Stevens I had learned in school began to come back to me, now more than mere words: "The pine-tree sweetens my body/The white iris beautifies me."

Stephen Knauth

Those mountains did something to me, threw a switch and opened a circuit through which strange new music flowed. A confirmed non-reader, I suddenly found myself leaving the Knoxville library with an A&P bag full of poetry books. Before long I was writing my own fledgling poems. A couple of mornings a week I'd drive back into the Smokies, find a good place to sit and wait for the words to come. When they did, it often felt as though I was taking some kind of muffled dictation, like a secretary to the trees.

For the last few years I've been living in Charlotte with my wife and kids and working as an educational and technical writer. The mountains are not too far, and I head that way when my spirit flags, a good tonic for urban distress. Though when

I see where developers have set their latest money trap, I wonder how long it will take them to pave and degrade what little remains of this paradise. I sadly envison the tourist of the not-so-distant future gazing out over a broad vista of Weyerhauser saplings, mechanical bears, and drive-through waterfalls, and exclaiming, "Ah, wilderness!"

My poetry has appeared in a number of national magazines and in two collections: *The Pine Figures* (Dooryard Press) and *Night-Fishing on Irish Buffalo Creek* (Ithaca House). I've been awarded fellowships from the National Endowment for the Arts and the North Carolina Arts Council.

Night-Fishing on Irish Buffalo Creek

Where does it go, the music of creeks
drifting up the slope all night?
To Heaven, I hope, through the starry Way
smelling of pine sap, roses
and gasoline.
My neighbors pity this creek
as though it were someone else's stricken child.
When I relax here for hours
among the tin cans and kudzu vines,
waving my cigarette in wide, rosy figure 8's,
they pity me more.
And if I love a woman I've never known
whose faded brassiere
floated this far, snagged a root tip
and filling with water has filled me with joy,
so what? So what if I tell my children
that the foam along the water's edge
is the spit
of some huge, luminous angel upstream?
This creek is a highway where both worlds are mixing,
shifting and pouring forward, full of darkness
and news.
A chicken head floats by, crowing,
though morning is breaking oceans away.

From the Cherokee

Rivers may flow easily northward
that were laid before the mountains broke.
The ancient Teays

was there, bubbling through the earth's hair.
A nation drank this water,
went away to die
in Oklahoma.

The new faces are different: strong
but vaguely wounded, kind of stabbed,
kind of bleeding...

"Water!" one of them cries out tonight.

A child brings the pitcher, & stands
the way any child stands
near the end of her father's life.

In so many years, all the words spoken
have not spoken the word
that tells where a man can live
& never die.

"Say it, daughter, with me —

Sah-ka-na-ga,

Sahkanaga,

The Great Blue Hills of God."

1836: In the Cherokee Overhills

In a pasture of the Milky Way
where the Little Pigeon glides down over the dark rocks
of Tennessee,
a man has landed on his belly,
drinking water from a cup made of hands,
wrinkled olive skin,
hair black as the soil of eternity,
swept back and tied with ryegrass,
listening down the mountain
for the dull heartbeat of troops, for miners
jingling through the trees toward the goldfields
of Dahlonega. As a child he could conceal
his body so easily behind a single stone,
behind even the petal of a cornflower!
He learned, *To be whole*
be each part of the whole.
In this way the body cannot suffer
in death, in the ocean-that-drinks-men,
but only grows more peaceful, like a sparrow
in the throat of a blacksnake,
wet and half-alive,
wings folded lightly against the breast,
flying downward through the rosy coils of home.

Cumulonimbus

A long while I rode that cloud last night,
past supper, the President's lies, past walnut
pie & peaches! That cloud was sweet & worth it.
My eyes climbed up like Hilary, ledge by ledge,
whale-gray to gold to a bride-white summit
where I stood & looked down on everything,
the broken-down rooftops of town, steeples
provoking the low September sky, that dirty
bootstrap of a river, Irish Buffalo Creek,
draining down through a dark stubble of pine
to the fields where our lives grew long &
stringy, to a clearing where a woman stood
knee-deep in deerflowers, calling my name,
her hair rising & falling like a pigeon
lost in a storm, a scene so sad & true that,
glimpsed from a cloud, was almost worth coming down.

Impossible Creek

I

Down on Impossible Creek
where the real world thrives
the weed they call *everlasting*
nods in the windless night
as if engaged in solemn correspondence
beyond our calls to order
beyond our mettle
or ken.

Above, in the strip of sky between pines,
the ancient text revolves,
illegible, clear.

My neighbor John keeps pigeons
names them well. *Hercules
& Corona,* the silver Rollers.
The Fantails, *Perseus & Hydra.*

Draco, the lone Blue King.

What a racket, every morning,
when all the heavens descend
to a few kernels of corn
shining in his dirty palm.

II

Impossibly,
the manuscript revolves,
illustration by illustration,
in which man is the mad apostrophe,
possessive, holding himself above the rest.

At our best we are like Impossible Creek —
relaxed, reflecting starlight,
irresponsible,
clear.

Yeats peeled a hazel wand
caught a little silver girl.

Buddha shone beneath the bo.

Prophets & poets of the boneyard
what golden bough or fleece
in these modern trees?

What sprites in the baobab?

III

Waking up on original ground
the world is irresistibly new, clear.
Music in the smoking trees!
Tew-Tew...

Purty-purty-purty...
The sleepy mind accepts but cannot place it.
Bird? Bird? Sparks
from the intricate lathe of morning.

Then language begins to yawn & bloom.
The trees become scrub pines, *Pinus virginiana*,
having the familiar red-brown, finger-stabbing cones.
The creek becomes Impossible Creek, Pisgah Forest,
North Carolina.

As it fills with knowledge, the scene contracts.
Birds fall silent, dismissed by their names.
The wilderness grows empty as it fills with me.

IV

The day goes by in thinking
about not-thinking, about not falling

on the pointed rocks of Impossible Creek
where a moment of sudden enlightenment
can mean a headwound like a mountain sunset.

Sometimes the sheer *hereness* of it all
can make a person downright lonesome
for a world we can't quite recall,
a world beyond birth, beyond the rubbery
womb of the mother,

as if death itself
were a home to be sick for,
a dark broth we'll slip into, face first,
singing as we swallow
each of its ten thousand dreamy hooks.

Let it all go by,
the loud water, the secret-keeping weeds,
the silver, white & blue specks
rising now above the pines
in a tangled ribbon of possibility —
Altair, Vega, Draco...

Let the real world roll,
incomprehensible, clear, & true.
Any God, glancing down, knows we didn't run.

Driving the Great Craggy Mountains

Gazing weakly off into the seems-blue beyond,
wondering if eternity's this clean and bright,
if God just keeps rolling by, one pine at a time.
Ahead, a hawk pulls a rabbit out of its world —
long ears, scarlet talons, stuck pedal of death.
Knowledge curls away. My Pinto sweats the grade.
Him or Hell some boulder says and maybe it's so.

The Pine Figures

Standing out on the planet,
light snow filling the sky,
thinking how pines excel in difficult weather,
how easy it is to love
that which cannot be embraced.
Last week a man disappeared on Roan Mountain.
They found his car, still running,
the radio blasting between stations.

In all the books of wonder, where is the word
for *dark cove lit by frost,*
a place that smokes and burns slowly in the mind,
where men are said to vanish
and reappear as pine, as loblolly
and she-balsam. Eternity, that's the music
of winter pine: another quiet stroke
on the vellum.

Mary Kratt

Because two Appalachian interstates now converge there, people these days may have heard of Beckley, West Virginia, but in the 1940s, Beckley was a remote coal mining town. My father was a newspaper editor there. He kept a coalminer's metal hat with its single battery-powered light ("that third eye") on top of the bookshelf. Occasionally he wore it into the mines on an emergency story. For ordinary, above-ground events I often followed along, carrying in my pockets the large flashbulbs for his Speed Graphic camera. Ours was snake handling and mine-strike country where entertainment consisted of ice skating on frozen lakes or a molasses-making gathering, or walking the train tracks past the mine's wind tunnel on Sunday afternoons. Each summer we came down the mountain in our Studebaker to visit relatives in piedmont North Carolina where the earth was red, the pastures flat, and folks thought such terrain was normal.

After the end of World War II, my father took a job with a Charlotte newspaper. So we left West Virginia for the rolling red dirt and sandy pine fields near Charlotte among coveys of kinfolk and quail, both of whom I learned were easily startled. Ever since then I have had one long leg and one short, one for climbing Appalachian slopes and the other for the conventional urban landscape. At certain times of the year I keep looking and heading west. The mountains are calling.

There are a lot of lawyers in Charlotte these days, and many I run into will tell me at social occasions that they are originally from a mountain place in western North Carolina named for a pioneer, a landmark, or most often for a swift, tumbling creek. I find that even Charlotte's wide Catawba River gathers its strength along Black Mountain. A lot of us got started up there somewhere. Some keep writing and talking about it.

Mary Kratt

From my desk which looks out onto pine and water oak woods I write regional stories, poems, and non-fiction books about real and imaginary people of the Virginias and Carolinas. It seems quite natural to wander back and forth between poetry and regional history. There are astonishing stories hereabouts.

Some of these stories appear in my books: poetry forthcoming *'Til After Freedom* (Carolina Wren Press). Published books include: poetry, *Spirit Going Barefoot* and *On The Steep Side* (Briarpatch); biography and history, *My Dear Miss Eva, Marney, Charlotte: Spirit of the New South, Legacy: The Myers Park Story*, and *The Imaginative Spirit*; and humor, *Southern Is...*

I attended public school in Beckley, West Virginia, and Charlotte, North Carolina; Agnes Scott College (B.A.); and am at this writing midway in course work toward a M.A. in English at the University of North Carolina at Charlotte.

Coming Back to West Virginia

Past Nitro, Ansted, Belle,
two days by car climbing to where I first came from.
Past Gauley's Bridge, the rock relics
of the old bridge stand like teeth in the river
where Confederates burned it. The mountains
close like my thighs around you.
Mountains are knees. Each town a woman's
crotch and sometimes there's a way
over them and sometimes not.

Years ago I climbed out to where land is generous,
not hard as a witch's tit as you would say, rocky
steep, yet with apples, corn, rhubarb
and I knew no other living.
I had never seen thoroughbred wealth of Kentucky,
horses running with morning, the long articulate fences
to all horizons, high black barns of tobacco curing.
I had never seen Shenandoah cattle roam the wide shoulders
of grassland easy under Allegheny's shadow. I knew
a dense wildness they never suspected.
If the mouths of women pinched, it was from
seeing too little sky, knowing children, like husbands,
may not make it out of the mines, and daughters
would marry too young, too soon, or not marry.

Now in the Hawk's Nest Park bathroom,
a woman wears shorts. Her legs are still good.
For a time, they, even more
than her face, told her fortune, she knew,
and on the cold, tile floor, she changes a naked baby,
her own arm blue-tattooed with a flower.
Outside I see which man is hers.

He stands by a rusted pickup
as children pile in back under tin roofing.
They ride down the road in the lane beside me,
and it's hard and soft, hard and dark, light
coming over the mountain, finally out past Rainelle
where towns start hoping. Coming back
down the switchbacks that make any car humble,
the mountain is more than anything.
I leave it, but here it's all I can think of,
larger than a river to drown in,
and only your arms can hold me
or this kind of mountain.

I'd Have Waited a Lifetime for You, Greer Garson

You had to grow up in a coal mine town
to know what it meant to have her come.
I was the age when a day took a lifetime
and that's what it meant waiting
for that red hair we knew we'd know
anywhere, here especially
in that ordinary square of a
mountain town in the war
with a bank on one corner,
five and dime on the other,
the two-story hotel and the shop where
they sold swell dresses we could only
stare at. It was a town
where white men wore black faces
coming home with raccoon eyes.
A spare town on a pinnacle with
half the buildings holding on for dear life.

I see it in black and white, like movies
were mostly, the crowd tramping grass
round the courthouse, the old cars dark
as they always were and sensible, then finally
"Here she comes," in a long sedan,
the door opens and a man
gets out and she's here suddenly
all in green, a suit and that rich
red hair. Selling war bonds.
We'd have bought anything she offered.
What does it matter now except
the color keeps,
in a nothing town halfway through a war,
Greer Garson in green and that sparkle hair.

On the Steep Side

Everything rolled down
in West Virginia.

Potatoes, dug in the garden, tumbled
to the back door. Houses clung
to inclines like cicada shells to tree bark.
Molasses vats filled deeper at one end,
cooked late by torchlight near the barn.
And our picnic watermelon, toppling from the car,
rolled like a cannonball to the lake,
split, floated like two pink islands.

Climbing to Mount Hope
one curve, walled with coal,
rose like a torn shoulder of that dark
nether giant who held our lives;
and everywhere men's faces blackened with dust,
lanterned miner's hats with the third eye.

Downhill to the mine's wind tunnel
we walked railroad ties on Sunday afternoons,
dug sassafras roots coming home.
We owned the land's crust for house, rhubarb,
potatoes. Underneath
belonged to the mine. Blasts jiggled
cups in the kitchen.

From Grand View I got the sense
that level was for common people.
When we moved down
to lowland Carolina where some thought
humps were hills and hills were mountains,
the steep eye stayed mine
and saved me from a level life.

The 1940s

In a picture above my mother's mantel
a woman in red played a grand piano.
Her back turned always to me. Dark hair
on bare shoulders. Her long dress
like Jennie Churchill or Scarlett O'Hara.

On the opposite wall above the mousehole,
a woman in blue by a lake.
Hair gold as her sandals. A letter beside her.

She gazed west of the picture frame
to London or Madagascar.

The pictures hung in a house closed in
by brown, stubbled mountains
which rubbed you daily like the war
and hard times. The thin woman next door
had a black dog named Otto.
We called her Mrs. Otto.
We moved away to a lowland house
in woods among kinfolk. Women
who wore hose and girdles every day,
told me to stand straight. They canned
squash, rhubarb, blackberry jam and
brought pies when somebody died. I used
to wish somebody would.

These pictures,
I still see them sometimes
in living rooms or flea markets —
the woman in red plays her piano,
the woman in blue with her letter. And others,
a sketch of a girl in a prairie dress,
gazing far out a window of infinite wishing.
All over America, women buy them.

P.J. Laska

I was born in Farmington, West Virginia, in 1938. My father was a coal miner, as was his father who emigrated from Poland in 1900 to escape the Tsar's draft. My mother's parents were peasants who left Russia just before World War I. They leased a farm in the hills above Buffalo Creek but lost it when my grandfather died from injuries received in a car wreck. At that time the town of Farmington was surrounded by coal camps that were microcosms of working class America — multi-ethnic, multi-religious, multi-racial. I grew up hearing a fascinating mix of languages spoken by old men on the steps of beer gardens and old women weaving rugs on their back porches. After high school graduation I became part of the fifties out-migration from Appalachia caused by massive layoffs in the coal industry as the country changed over to oil as its primary fuel. Trained in Russian, I did Cold War military duty in Japan as part of America's electronic spy network, then worked in Washington, D.C., and attended college.

I began reading and writing poetry while working for the D.C. Public Library. A major influence on my early approach to poetry was Rudd Fleming, a teacher at the University of Maryland who had been active in helping to free Ezra Pound from incarceration at St. Elizabeth's. Fleming led me to the discipline of imagism and the Whitman-Williams tradition in American poetry. During this period I got involved in the Civil Rights Movement, joined C.O.R.E., and participated in some sit-ins. Eventually, I got a Ph.D. in philosophy and began teaching.

My consciousness of Appalachian identity was influenced by Bob Snyder whom I had met in graduate school in Cincinnati. In 1974 I joined him on the faculty at Antioch-Appalachia and helped him start the poetry workshops from which the Soupbean Poets evolved. The following year my first book, *D.C. Images and Other Poems,* was a National Book Award Nominee. Since then I have pub-

P.J. Laska

lished in poetry magazines, edited a poetry annual, *The Unrealist,* and self-published two chapbooks of poetry.

In the past year I collaborated with Bob Snyder and Joseph Barrett on *Old Martins, New Strings,* a book of poems by three poets. Partly as a result of this collaboration, my work is evolving away from the linear anti-lyrics and folk-narratives of mine that appear in this anthology. I'm interested in exploring the paradigm shift to a new ecological earth story with less discursive, interlinear translations of the cosmic code.

I now live in Morgantown, West Virginia, and teach humanities at West Virginia University.

Widow Horvath on Coal Run Then and Now

This was always a pretty rough
place to live. Fightin gamblin
killin — you name it.
It was a boomin place
when the mines were workin.
There were sixty houses
up on the hill there and
a bunch more along the river.
Lord, it was a hard place
for a woman to be alone.
Course, it's different now.
Not much happens around here
that we have to worry about.
Just a pack of stray dogs
and a motorcycle gang.
Last night I woke up scared —
I thought a car ran into the house.
It was next door at Jiggs' —
his porch fell off.
He won't fix a thing,
just lets it fall to the ground.

Outmigration Time Again

At the Exxon station we talk
across the pumps. It's been
years, since high school.
A generation ago I went
to the Air Force,
he went to the Navy:
-Why the hell'd you come back,
there's no work here.
The mines are closed. My boys
went with a bunch to Florida

to pick the orange crop,
there's nothing for them here.

There was no time for reasoning
about a past that
has the advantage, and later,
as I studied the place
with elbows down on the hill,
I thought about places where
the past is past, and comes
to mind only on holidays.
Here it scabs on the present
like a thug, an old yellow dog
that keeps coming back
in violation of the contract
to lie quietly in the past
and leave us alone.

The Widow McDowell on Her Granddaughter's Divorce

The window she jumped from
that night was a portal to
reality, and I saw she was
one resourceful woman.
That clan she married into
owned all four corners of
Crossroads, Alabama,
and she left them
crying in their beer.
His mama must have choked
on her tobacco spit when
they forced the bedroom door
the next morning and found
her gone. By the time
they tracked her down
her lawyer had the papers
ready for that boy to sign.
He said he only slugged her
once and that was a lie,
but the worst thing was
his fat mama saying in her
house it was HER baby—
that was gasoline on
the smouldering coals of doubt.
She said she was leaving
right then, but they locked

her in, thinking she'd cool
off by morning. I say
that truck driver whoever
he was ought to get
a medal for stopping in
the middle of the night
on a backcountry road
to pick up a barefoot
woman with a bundle
tied to her chest.

Ancestorial

When I take him out
for a backroads drive
he shows me again
the swampy leafthicket
where the park pavilion
of his dancing days
burned to the ground
and where they sat
beneath the syggamoore
one Saturday night
paralyzed to the knees
unable to get up
for mustobeen whiskey
          hours.

Once more then
we drive the hillclimb
brick road to the camp
overlooking the creek,
row house number one's
shadowy fiddlehead ferns
older than immigrants
older than electricity,
only not like it is —
as it was then, as it
lives without evidence.
In memory nothing
absolutely nothing has
        changed.

Asa Gray on Cheat Mountain

The sun has long been alive
the sky has long been blue

when Asa takes the hermit trail
of a jigsaw stream
and climbs high into the past.
He has no quarrel with origin
or destiny — his is the true
path of science.
In leaf thickets
the light turns tricky,
the logic of the land
slows him down. All the while
he's thinking: ground fern,
wild iris, hempweed.

He stops for a smoke,
the tops of the beech trees
wave in the breeze.
Beneath his feet he feels
the ancient gatherers' steps.
That's when he sees her —
near the summit,
in the wildest place,
his old granny,
rocking her chair
in a grove of blueberries.

The Hillbilly Odyssey

In debt up to their necks
those Black Lung checks
came too late to save families
bustin' up. Some ran away
and joined the Army,
some went up to Akron and
Cleveland looking for jobs
while big city culture snickered
at those hillbilly white socks.

In those days nothing worked
but self-hypnosis
and Dale Carnegie speech lessons.
If they could stop stuttering
they figured they could talk,
and that would be a step
in the right direction. Then,
when the world turns round
and forward comes back,

they bend but don't crack —
they just keep on
beginning again.

Mstistry

The approach is west —
south — south — north
on the dark side.
Below ever vernal cuts
of ridge rock
signs of the leaf-canopied
speed zone
forewarn of enterprise
two turns past DIP,
and you peer off
through bone-white branches
of sycamore
across the bottomland's
still cool awakening mist,
and there it is —
house of your original face,
older no older
than immortal immigrants'
humble beginnings,
a puzzle that will always
have pieces missing.
You cross the bridge
to the mobius strip
of Main Street's
one way in one way out
and park beside the garage,
older no older
than the last time,
piecing it together still
from feeling and effect —
the unscried plot
within the word,
the always becoming
commonplace things.
And down the steps
to the still fell
silence at the door,
forgetting, remembering,
those living on...
those that are gone...

George Ella Lyon

I grew up in Harlan County, in the coalfields, and was in high school during the War on Poverty. I remember the television stereotypes — not just on "The Beverly Hillbillies" but on the news — of mountain people who were both materially and culturally deprived. So I thought, if I am going to write, the first thing I have to do is go somewhere and acquire a culture. During that process I would learn to sound like I was from somewhere else. I didn't know that that was like cutting your throat to remedy hunger.

In college I wrote poetry primarily, and my subjects were medieval music, Dutch painters, and love. The language was that of a person born in a book and majoring in Men's Studies. We called it English.

But I kept a journal, too, where I set down things that interested me. One was a sentence I'd seen printed in crayon on a young child's paper at Pine Mountain Settlement School: *I hope how soon Spring comes.* I loved the way the rising sap of spring, hope itself, lifted the words into a new order. Not standard, but rare, expressive. *How I hope Spring comes soon* is tired by comparison.

Another thing I took notes on was how my grandmother talked. "I feel like a stewed witch," she'd say. Or "I ain't seed you in a month of Sundays." I wrote down names of relatives she remembered: Honey-Eating Richard, Pie-Belly Miracle. I wrote down a story she told me of Old Aunt Martha Money who could cure the summer complaint. I didn't put this into poems. I just collected it. Poems, as far as I knew, didn't have stuff like that in them. But I valued the live language and elemental nature of her stories. Let not thy left brain know what thy right brain is doing.

After graduating from Centre College, I applied to writing programs across the country and was accepted by Indiana University. Since they required an M.A. for a teaching assistantship, I went to the University of Arkansas for that degree first and then to Indiana University where I studied with Samuel Yellen and Ruth Stone. It was exactly what I needed. Not just the workshop but the community of writers which it fostered. Among those friends, the most immediately important to me was Michael Allen, an Ohio poet who wrote about Sunday dinner at his grandmother's, about growing corn, about everyday things he knew as well as his face. I was astonished. Could I do that? Why not?

Ruth's class added to this realization the fact that it was not only possible, but crucial, to write out of my experience as a woman. Suddenly I had a wealth of material. In the sixteen years since then, I've been trying to learn how to be true to it.

Where you're from is not who you are, but it's an important ingredient, and I believe you must trust your first voice — the one tuned by the people and place who made you —

before you can speak your deepest truths. My education to this possibility was continued by discovering Jeff Daniel Marion's magazine *The Small Farm* in 1975 and *Appalachian Journal* the year after. Danny and I began corresponding, and I found out there was a whole passel of people out there writing down how their grandmother talked and why she talked that way and why her farm had been taken away from her. I found out there was an entire tradition of Appalachian writing; furthermore, some of the songs my daddy had sung to me were Child ballads.* In short, though it wasn't short — it took years — I found out I had a culture. I'd been to college and graduate school, London and Paris, the Smithsonian and the New York Public Library, and now I needed to go home. For while I found all sorts of necessary and wonderful things in those places, I couldn't find my voice.

George Ella Lyon

I was aided in this homecoming by getting to know Lee Howard (*The Last Unmined Vein*); Gurney Norman (*Divine Rights Trip*), who can walk into a group of strangers and leave a community; and Jo Carson (*Stories I Ain't Told Nobody Yet; Daytrips*). Like Danny Marion, these writers taught me things and started a conversation about writing and issues of the region which is still going on.

In 1983 my chapbook, *Mountain,* was published by Andrew Mountain Press. Since then I've published several books for children, including *Cecil's Story,* a picture book, and *Borrowed Children,* which won The Golden Kite Award for the best novel for young readers in 1989. I have also had two plays produced: *Braids* (1985) and *Looking Back for Words* (1989), on which I collaborated with my husband, composer Steve Lyon. We live in Lexington, Kentucky, with our two sons.

A Testimony

— for L.H.

My daddy baptized me
in the Red Bird River.
We waded into green water
— him in his preaching pants,

---

*Child ballads are those collected in England and Scotland and published in five volumes by Francis J. Child (*The English and Scottish Popular Ballads, 1882–1898*). Many of them were carried over and transformed in the Southern Mountains.

shirt sleeves rolled up high,
me in a white dress
that hung like a pillowslip.

You know my daddy
was no more holy
than that car up on blocks.
The middle of the night might find him
sneaking out of town
or a trespassed bed.
But all the same his baptizing
did me good.
           I liked the ache
of his voice when he prayed in the river,
how everyone sang, mournful and drenched
from the ooze of cattails and willows.
And his handkerchief over my nose
smelling of the iron in Mama's hand,
his palm cradling my neck
as he bent me back and under.

Through the arc
of green-fringed blue,
a world I knew I was leaving,
into the all of water, cold,
his hands bore me
down.

Elopement

The screen door bangs, shaking the flowers on the table,
zinnias Ella May put in a mayonnaise jar.
She's upstairs now, packing her cardboard suitcase —
nightgown, toothbrush, shoes arranged neat as a clock.
Her mother hangs wash in the side yard. Ella, above her,
cries at the pain she will add to that heavy load:
her sister's death, sure as the sun every morning,
knotted like washing, close as the houseboards' paint.
Still she shuts the grip and goes out to the bed of a sailor
whose question her father killed with a face of grief.
She leaves the zinnias, tongues of the late June morning,
loud in the jar mouth, hoping their words will heal.

Her Words

    You gotta strap it on
    she would say to me

there comes this hardship
and you gotta get on up the creek
— there's other's besides you —
so you strap it on
Oh, you give St. Jude what he'll take
hand it over like persimmons
with the frost on
it aint nothin
there's more stones in that river
than you've stepped on
or are about to
Once your hands
can get around sumac
once your feet
know the lash of a snake
you'll strap it on
that's what a good neck
and shoulders are for

In winter
at the settlement school
our wet hair would freeze
on the sleepin porch
and we'd wake up
vain younguns that we were
under blankets of real snow
Come Christmas
we'd walk sixteen miles
home to Red Bird Mission
only once gettin
lost in the woods
snowed over
down the wrong ridge

Nobody's askin
for what aint been done —
build against cold
and death scalds the dark —
you strap it on
there's strength in the bindin
I scrubbed on a board
I know what it's about

How the Letters Bloom Like a Catalpa Tree

in this poem, on a day when tulip bells
ring up from the ground, when the crab apple

swarms with blossoms. How I would like
the words to shine always like sword grass
and be stubborn as thistle and come to you
heady as lilac, as dandelion to the new bee.

But you have read this
so many times, the message
patched and worn like sleeves.
You've seen words die
down, thought ravel
as green comes on
and flowers are forced
to the ground. And you've
seen farther: green grown
ragged, the words old wood
storms break against the house.
What could I send you?

On Cowan Creek in Letcher County, Oaksie Caudill
is making a white oak basket. He cuts down a tree,
peels and splits it, pressing, whittling the ribs.
No waste and no hurry. He's got time as much as time's
got him. He makes the frame: two hoops, braces, and a binding
which at the handle looks like the old God's Eye.
Oaksie's not above impure improvements — tape and wire
to hold him as he goes. Still, it's slow, worrisome;
sometimes a splint turns brittle, sometimes a loop
whips back and stings the eye. Body gets cramped,
muscles like staves in the basket, all their tension bent
on springing free. Oaksie walks out, chews a twist
of Red Man, sees how burdock came on past the snow.
But soon he's back, bent to his wood-weaving,
the half-globe between his bony knees.

Oaksie's trade is this translating
of straight to curve, of fact to what we need,
tough as a poem for the burden that outlasts us,
for a heart leafed with words like a tree.

Looking at a Photograph of My Mother, Age 3

>Little one
>in the hand-worked dress
>let me lift you
>from the porch where you sit
>with two brothers and a hound
>while your father

the new baby in his arms
stands proud
at the gate.
Inside, your mother
beats biscuits, takes
a saucer edge to the meat.

Hard times
line your daddy's hands
with sawdust, hone
your mother's wits
and her tongue.
Seven children
quick as flesh can bear them.
Even deep sleep
cracks
with mouths.

Axe and saw
log hook and level
your daddy shaves hills
for your bread.
Your mother packs up
kettle and quilts
and piano when the sawmill
moves.

Crowded
at the foot
of some mountain
stashed at the head
of some creek
let me lift you.
You can look
like my son
over my shoulder.
I will hold you.
Tell me
what you see.

Jeff Daniel Marion

My sense of place is very limited—first, it is a rural one I'm speaking of. I grew up in Rogersville, Tennessee, and used to walk past David Crockett's grandparents' graves on my way home from school. In the evenings my father would take me with him to the "loafering place"—a combination store and filling station named "The 96"—where the locals gathered to talk, swap tales, and whittle, whiling away the hours. I spent hours and hours listening to those people (relatives, townspeople, farmers) and more hours listening to stories my grandmother told me. I spent time on her farm, watching, helping with the chores. Most of what I write either stems from a felt relationship to this rural society or in a more primal way to its natural topography—the rocks, wildflowers and weeds, sinkholes, trees, springs, whatever. So my knowledge of place is small and specific—a small town and a farm. But I carry a sense of it with me wherever I go—define myself and perceptions by that locus.

Yet I think that sense of place deepened within me only upon leaving the area. After spending a year in southern Mississippi, I returned to East Tennessee with a new awareness: the Southern Appalachian region was now mine by choice. So I returned to live within fifty miles of where I grew up and now try to maintain an on-going relationship with the area.

Farms have been at the center of my consciousness since early childhood, but one in particular stands out and has shaped my thinking more than any other. I am speaking of my Grandmother Gladson's farm in Mooresburg. While living and teaching in Mississippi, I made two discoveries about myself almost simultaneously: one, that I wanted to write, to be able to shape my experiences and memories into something durable and worthy; and second, that perhaps I wanted to write because I could not paint. As I began to write poems, I found myself compensating for my failure as a watercolorist by sketching details within the poem that would render sharp, sensory, and vividly realistic pictures.

But there was the small town, too, that shaped my consciousness: the experience of growing up there, of living in one place most of my life, and most significantly, later returning after being away some years and experiencing the effects of time, not only on the town itself and its buildings, but on the people, too, and perhaps most importantly on the person returning, the former member of the community, now returned as stranger, witness to change.

Sometimes the objects within the place of my childhood often seemed magical, mysterious. Within a moment, the commonplace suddenly became the extraordinary. As a child I always knew I was almost to Knoxville when just outside Blaine, grazing nonchalantly in the pasture, was this miraculous beast—a *spotted* mule. My father and I would eagerly watch for it—and it always became the highlight of the trip, usually occasioned by my father's words: "There he is." And, of course, the importance, the mystery of this creature's being was confirmed once and for all for me one Sunday when I read in the Comics section of the *Knoxville Journal* that this spotted mule was included in Ripley's Believe It Or Not.

But the common object can sometimes be just as mysterious, just as miraculous as the unusual. The worn, everyday object frequently has a curious attractiveness, as the poet Neruda reminds us: "The used surfaces of things, the wear the hands give / to things, / the air, tragic at times, pathetic at others, of such things — all / lend a curious attractiveness to the reality of the world."

Perhaps the most significant features of any region are the people within it. Certainly one of the major influences on my life was my Grandmother Gladson, a blind woman who taught me to see the world clearly and fully. Although I had few books as a child, she supplied a wealth of stories well-told, stories worth retelling and savoring. She taught me attentiveness to the world and to the word.

But not all was beautiful in that world, nor was all good there. I recall that as a child I witnessed many strange wanderers through that small town, a cata-

Jeff Daniel Marion (Doug Berryhill)

log, if you will, of human suffering, and sometimes the striking, the unusual, the so-called abnormal. The townspeople called her Rambling Rose, an albino woman married to a stooped, quiet man who always smelled of soured milk. I saw them often walking backroads and remember the image of her face against the red clay banks of the roadside. The story I heard as a child left a permanent impression: this couple sold their children shortly after birth, one at a time, and survived by this means of commerce. So I came to write about this memory, not as judgment or criticism, but out of a simple and profound need to understand, to cope with the darker ways of survival.

Thus my approach to writing is founded on the belief that there are forces, relationships, places, people, and things for which I try to find a voice — and it is through this voice that I am able to share and to shape imaginatively and creatively that which I love. Writing is for me more than finding a "subject matter" or "material," and it is certainly more than a matter of technique. It is a way of finding my life, imaginative and real, past and present, of finding the *ground* from which my experiences grow and from which my poems and stories can grow as experiences in themselves. Southern Appalachia has given me my life; these stories and poems are the seeds I sow back in the rich soil of this place.

The Last Man on Devil's Nose

The way up is always crooked.
Ruts of red clay in December
mire even the best efforts.
Sam McClain down at the store

leans against the Royal Crown
Cola sign & says, "You can't get there
from here." But 30 years ago
old Brummit did — cleared 2 acres by hand,
hewed the logs & set the frame.
One thing's for sure — his range
now is the summit view.
Got himself a mule,
two goats & an old Jersey cow.
Tends a scraggly garden
& has rabbit stew now & then.
By night a kerosene lamp & a keen ear
keep watch.
The seasons humor him.
Winter obliges & sews his pocket
shut. Nobody is going up there
in summer — not through the rattle
snake dens — sometimes as many
as 15 together, a knot
of diamond rope waiting.
But along about dusk
you might see him down near
Bledsoe's Spring. Comes to get
drinking water.
He'll have a cedar bucket hung on one arm
& a .22 slung on the other.
Probably checks his secret ginseng patch
on the way down.
Watch closely though —
he's like a whistle you thought
you heard — he cuts the air
& is gone.

A Mountain Fable of a Sort

Elwood Hurd remembers it well,
tells the boys down at the Silver Star
Garage about the day money
washed down out of the mountains
in mason jars, green rolled buds
of an April flood.
Brother Blazer slapped his leather
backed Bible across his knee &
shouted: "It's the Lord's manna
from above — we never had it so good.
Amen & keep it coming Lord."

And the whole town gathered —
lines, fishhooks, nets & long distance swimmers —
on the banks of the Little Pigeon.
So Sally Stipes bought a new
washing machine for her front porch
(the old one now rests less than
a fathom down on the bottom
of Sinking Creek)
and her boys went off to town
& got drunk,
the old man hasn't worked
a day since, but looks at the sky
every now & then
& says, "By God, I believe
Elwood's right
one of these days it's going to cloud up
and rain dollar bills."

Ebbing & Flowing Spring

Coming back you almost
expect to find the dipper
gourd hung there by the latch.
Matilda always kept it hidden
inside the white-washed shed,
now a springhouse of the cool
darkness & two rusting milk cans.
"Dip and drink," she'd say.
"It's best when the water is rising."
A coldness slowly cradled
in the mottled gourd.
Hourly some secret clock
spilled its time in water,
rising momentarily only
to ebb back into trickle.
You waited while
Matilda's stories flowed back,
seeds & seasons, names & signs,
almanac of all her days.
How her great-great grandfather
claimed this land, gift
of a Cherokee chief
who called it Spring of Many Risings.
Moons & years & generations
& now Matilda alone.
You listen.

It's a quiet beginning
but before you know it
the water's up & around you
flowing by.
You reach for the dipper
that's gone, then
remember to use your hands
as a cup for the cold
that aches & lingers.
This is what you have come for.
Drink.

Panther

For years they nursed the stories,
old men around a ring
of firelight, faces intent
for the flare of sound
now but memory:

shrill as a child's shriek,
yellow-eyed fear stalked
the darkness

only the old remember
remedy against that beast
who would steal a baby's
breath

only the old have seen

until yesterday

high on Devil's Knob
a lone trout fisherman
in that moment of backcast
turned

& glimpsed a sleek
shadow
slipping between rocks

his breath already stolen

Rambling Rose

I could give you a cameo:
finely etched lines that make

the face bold in relief
against its background.

But sometimes the gem that memory gives
won't cut to such a shape:
still it's the albino face
against red clay.

The fairest bride given to silence,
always trailing a stooped husband
whose milky-sour scent shadowed
the rooms where he went.

Almost yearly she nursed
a new child, seed to salve last year's
loss. Soon rumors swaddled the town
of sons sold in bondage:
survival is a dark background.

Down backroads
stories of her strange weathers
hover like icons in every home.
Pickups passing in swirls of dust
come to town with witness
of these wanderers:

from this heirloom
there is no relief.

Fall

Already sky is a scumble
of color where November
rain nails leaves
like shingles to the trail

alone on the crest
of Comby Ridge
a terrapin shell inverted,
bowl brimful
& bedded in moss:

slow pilgrim,
only wind whispers here
sipping at his bone cup,
the trickle of first chill
in his voice:

this moon will be sickle
honed on the whetrock of dark

& all will pare down,
pare down,
sliced to the bone

Hand-Me-Down Days

Girl in the backrow
   whose only gift for Christmas
     is a pencil box,

empty, its sole treasure
   your name crayoned in letters
     stark as winter trees:

you linger in the doorway —
   far away your father rocks
     in some dark corner of a tarpaper

shack, curses the wind whistling
   through cracks. Near the river
     your mother's new grave glistens.

Late afternoon light slants
   across our desks.
     We huddle by the stove

to read the lines of your hands
   hovering above the fire,
     scrubbed raw

on ridges of washboards.
   Wind skirls across rocky fields
     whipping you all the way home.

Winter Watch

So it comes to this, then:
backward toward a time when
memory is a scar cross-
stitching pain to joy, grief to loss
across a darkening valley where
already the horned owl waits,
perched in the larch for nightwatch,
his lantern eyes scanning the stillness
of abandoned home, woven tuft of weed
& matted hair nestling in the sycamore's crotch.
So begins the trilling of first cold,
crisp October whose blue clarity is

a lullaby to settle the cornshocked field
before winter locks in, setting its
teeth on edge & every eave:
wherever water seeks to run,
the hard cold fact glistens:
here winter nails us in
between hearth & dark
corners where already
our stories grow too dark to tell.

Michael McFee

I grew up in a log cabin in the mountains, ten miles from any real town.

— I'm tempted to let that stand as a single-sentence Autobiography of My Appalachian Years, from birth to departure for college. It sounds so "authentic," so "poetic," conjuring up images of the nascent writer reared in isolation, rooted in the remote hills, learning nature's text by heart.

But it's only superficially true. If it tells the truth, it tells it mighty slant.

For the log cabin where I grew up wasn't a pioneer family's cabin way out in the woods. It was a house in a new suburb halfway between Asheville and Hendersonville, a development called Royal Pines, "the Complete Suburban Home Community" according to its developers, the Mount Royal Company of Miami, Florida. My dad spent a quarter-century turning our raw little cabin into Everyhouse, putting in a ceiling, sheetrocking the paneled walls, and generally converting it into a comfortable, respectable place where kids could grow up. Which — I say this without irony and with gratitude — it was.

But it wasn't "Appalachian" in the stereotypical sense of that word; and that's my point. It could have been any suburb, Anywhere, U.S.A.; and I probably did the same things that any kid would do in such places. And I suspect that this is also true for others of my generation who grew up in the region called Appalachia but who were more influenced by the homogenizing effects of a nearby city than by any cultural tradition peculiar to the mountains.

But — again — that's only superficially true. Because being Appalachian is a deeper matter than that, something too stubborn to be obliterated by living in a suburb and watching dumb sitcoms on TV and listening to the Beatles on the stereo instead of indigenous folksongs. For me, there are two persistent aspects to being born and raised in Appalachia.

One is social, racial, familial, the inescapable blood ties, the troubled river of lineage whose headwaters lead back to an inaccessible cove, the mystery of origin. This fact of family grows more powerful as I grow older: it was there when I was a kid, but I took it for granted, all those aunts and cousins and curious grandmothers. But now that they're all gone, and my parents too, I'm obsessed with finding out the truth about these vanished people who made me what I am; and I'm convinced that my family's experience is typical of many Appalachian clans who began in such reduced provincial circumstances and struggled so hard to succeed. And did. But at an ironic cost.

The other is psychotopological, the imprinting that comes from growing up in the mountains, a blue indelible palpable longing for the literal hills. Once I finally escaped

Appalachia and got to college, I was surprised to discover how much I missed simply being in the mountains, their visual relief at the horizon, surrounding me in a comforting and yet sometimes chilling way. Whenever I drove back home on I-40 West, the first sight of the mountains suddenly rising up always produced an intense physical release, their relief my relief. *There they are, I'm home again.*

Though I've lived in nearby exile in Research Triangle cities for 18 years now, as long as I lived in the mountains, I still feel like an Appalachian writer, and am very pleased to be included in this anthology. Because the mountain material still stirs me like nothing else, whether it's looking at a family album or reading a history of Buncombe County or driving back homeward for the thousandth time, the foothills rippling in greeting. I feel an obligation to work out the curse, or blessing, or both, that the place laid into my family for generations before I descended to this Durham suburb and started fooling around with words. For it's through those foolish words, finally, that some measure of our Appalachian world will be preserved.

Michael McFee (Mary Moore McLean)

Reclamation

In a cornfield near Canton
by an easy bend of the lane-and-a-half blacktop
pebbled with the bed of the nearby Pigeon
leans an old drive-in movie screen.
Kudzu vines thread the braces
loose below and behind, buckling crazy
as the trellis some old lady
tacked on to the ticket booth seasons ago
when her boys took it for a tractor shed.
Panels warped and moonshot, like a drunk
checkerboard, the screen still

looks clear across the corrugated fence
into the next field, where cows cool
in the concession stand. In the shade
men sit on huge wooden spools
the phone company left behind, talking up
the loft, the other three walls
of the tallest barn in Madison County.

Family Reunion Near Grape Creek Church, Four Miles West of Murphy, N.C., 1880

Everybody moved. Only that background shed
is focused, its roof a black hat for the ladies
clustered toward the rear of this sober choir
behind the bearded blurs in Confederate dress,
the infants and the witch-like matriarch.

And nobody smiled, unwilling to suffer
minutes of breathless muscle before a camera
omniscient as the Lord or a ready predator,
forgetting that the involuntary subtle pulse
of simply being human and alive would erase

this effort at a record, sure as the weather
would wash its hands on their soapstone graves
until no text was left, sure as bitter years
would blight their genealogy with stillbirths,
death in the service, "bean lodged in throat."

Even the trees above moved. This might as well
be any family, Adam's fallen clan, regathered
outside Paradise for their farewell picnic.
What curse or promise do they bear, these men
with radiant chests and women brightly buttoned,

that tall unbiblical couple near the border,
her birdlike hands poised in some peculiar sign,
his right hand not sheathed over the starchy heart
but pressed to his temple, sharp index finger
cocked in some elaborate parody of suicide?

Vague old ghosts, "four miles west of Murphy"
might as well be four miles east of Manteo:
the dumbfounded verge of nowhere, a landscape
lost to heaven's shutter since the deluge
or buried for decades now under dammed water.

Cold Quilt

Our clear-eyed guide said it is the slick
cotton that makes quilts cold. I wonder
if it isn't the enduring dowry of bitterness
stitched into them that makes us shiver,
as in that quilt (unfit for hanging) handed
down to me from my father's mother, begun
the day her husband died, a lifelong lament
composed of old suits and shirts he'd worn,
threaded to her leftover dresses, its design —
each pane a basket of memorial flowers,
a dozen loud triangles tipped on their sides —
a stiff pastiche of grief and the solitary
nights spent trying to transform their bad luck
into something useful, used. No busy bee

touched that quilt. Her life became a patchwork
of quilted plenty, her backyard a dormitory
of vegetable beds, her table a dazzling pattern
of cakes and pies. But she stayed skinny
and wrapped herself in the plain handmade cocoon
of that death-quilt every night, even when
she began to fade in her children's spare beds.

At the funeral home, my uncle the soldier
draped her coffin with it, prayed, then handed
that life's flag to me, compactly folded, her
crooked stitches and nearly-rotten panes still
tenacious after half a century, the sheep
I count now in the inherited dark, her cold quilt
a poultice I spread on my chest before sleep.

Tinted Pictures

Someone has swabbed a rosy horizon,
a too-blue sky. There stand my sober
mother and her big sister, by the Pigeon
River, its skin a cheap hopeful mirror

of the sky. The backdrop trees, though
leafless, are a queasy rash of green,
like the grass underfoot in God's studio,
the deep fall mountains of nineteen,

what, twenty-seven? The girls pose
unretouched, awkward as brothers whose

mother has caught them in stolen clothes —
smocks, stockings, high-laced shoes,

worn britches hidden behind their backs.
The river drawls their secret to the bridge,
also untinted, its smooth concrete span
a perfect echo of the distant ridge,

and it sends the hint of its new highway
back through the young one's head, the idea
of riding all alone through a gap one day
to a world too quick for any camera.

But for now she has to wait, content
with this tousle of grass by the river,
with this stiff face, with the curious tint
that some stranger's hand may give her.

Plain Air

How hard to take the trail
as it comes, digressive,
narrow-minded with underbrush
or switchbacks, to expect
anything other than risers
of root and rock, brook and sky
retreating like careful animals.

How hard to settle for less
than luxurious prospect,
a log in a small clearing
quick with insects and curious
weeds, the song of descent
short, flat, blunt, never
hammered into a dulcimer form.

Shenandoah

Flurries of dogwood, fields clouded with cows,
Floridians climbing the slopes slower than spring:
time thins with air, whole hours suspended
perfect as birds gliding the wind's high ridge,
the blue earth's turning speed enough. Whole days

condense to a moment: the flame azaleas
and cardinals, the soft green curtain ridge
pleated between peaks, the vanishing points
soundless again under the sky's bright tiding
and remote as the blue relief of the heart.

Llewellyn McKernan

My poems about Appalachia come out of my deepest and oldest memories: those I have of growing up in the backwoods of rural Arkansas in the 1940s. (The closest town was Hampton, a tiny village with a population of 1,000.) Our way of life there was much like that in Appalachia at that time. And when I moved to Huntington, West Virginia, in 1967 — after receiving an M.A. degree in English from the University of Arkansas and later, one in Creative Writing from Brown University — I lived for almost twenty-two years in the heart of Appalachia, among people whose lives were still sustained by historical culture and traditions similar to those instilled in me in my childhood.

Llewellyn McKernan (Stephanie Matthews)

The Appalachia that infuses my poems is one that infuses my life — the happy continuity I found between the way I grew up, the way I chose to live the adult years of my life, and the things in that way of life that I must bear witness to in my work, whether I choose to do so consciously or not.

What are some of these things? A Protestant work ethic, with union and populist sympathies; close family ties that extend from parents to a vast and vigorous network of grandparents and aunts and uncles; a conviction that both religion and experiences in nature are redemptive.

I should add to all these ideals a last one of my own found in "At the Edge of Town": love is eternal. That belief lives, I suppose, in all cultures, or none. It is something only individuals, one by one, can accept or reject alone.

The narrow deep vein of life that runs through these rather old-fashioned values is female. These are primarily women's virtues, feminine characteristics, maternal qualities.

Is it any wonder — since my Appalachia is female spirit — that the two poetry books I've written about the region (*Short and Simple Annals: Poems About Appalachia,* published in 1979 by a grant from the American Association of University Women, and *Many Waters: Poems from West Virginia,* published in 1993 by Edwin Mellen Poetry Press) have in them many poems from the point of view of Appalachian girls or women?

Is it any wonder that the poems about Appalachia I've published in literary journals — like *Southern Poetry Review, The Kenyon Review, The Laurel Review, Appalachian Journal, Appalachian Heritage, The Agni Review, Kalliope, The Crescent Review,* and others — explore the two-edged sword of these old-fashioned values: the tragedy and triumph one finds in "The Strike" where the close-knit family and the union win, but the baby dies; in "The Shaker" where the woman's soul is purified at the expense of her body; and in "At The Edge of Town" where, though love may be eternal, kudzu threatens to squeeze the life out of everything else.

When I ponder all these poems and others I've written about the experiences of Appalachian women that parallel my own, each becomes part of a portrait I am painting of an ideal Appalachia. It still has many gaps and blanks in it, but it already looks like a woman who has the roughened hands of a servant who works daily with the abrasive materials of the real, who has grown calluses from deep cuts and burns, and who handles all she touches — roses, real estate, letters to the world, books, babies, household articles, and altar cloths — with gentleness, respect, and love.

> *So when the mines started at Black Mountain, they organized the union. I don't remember what year it was, but we had the awfullest strike you ever saw. There wasn't no big checks or nothing then. There wasn't no handouts. We was on our own.*
> — The Reverend Tag King, *We Be Here When the Morning Comes*

The Strike: A Bird's Eye View

I.

It is the dead of winter.
The school bus is stuck up to its axle
in mud. The bus driver is cursing.

I sit with my sister on a leather seat.
It's split badly. The cotton padding
bursts through, and the springs cut
our bottoms.

Up ahead is the bridge, crooked
like an elbow. Each day the weight
of the bus makes it sink a little bit lower.

No one sits with us because our daddy
is picketing, and we wear underpants
made from flour sack cotton.

I dream of being a great fiddler
and making it to the Grand Ole Opry.

II.

It's the first of March.
The icicles hanging from the eaves
have rainbows in them.

The kitchen is full
of the economics of coal dust
and sticking it out
for minimum wages.

Momma is cooking the last
of the fried ham and gravy.

She bends over the black wood stove
pumping heat into the room like
a weight lifter. Her belly bulges.

John L. Lewis, John L. Lewis:
Daddy repeats his name like
a powerful refrain in a song
about going to heaven.

The gourd hanging from the wall
glints like a penny.

Outside
the icicles come crashing down,
one after the other.

III.

There's a sudden freeze in April.
My sister's gray dress
is torn at the waist.
My toes are blue and swollen.

Scabs slice up my daddy's face.
All over his cheeks, little red lips
pucker, pus at the corners.

A gun thug bombs
the front porch of our cabin.
Momma's belly sags
like a sack of potatoes.

For lunch at school now
we have only one biscuit to eat.
Everyone laughs
when we walk and our soles
flap on our feet.

In the mornings I break the ice
around the pump and peer into
a world clear and fresh as a bell.

In the evenings Momma leaves us
and walks two miles
to visit our daddy in jail.

IV.

It is May Day, and Momma
in her new thin body
is doing the washing.

The scrub board bubbles
with blue, her fists make knots
of our clothing.

I can smell our family ties
on their hooks, the coat
of white paint on the table,

my own untidy hair,
newly washed, and the breath
of my sister as she bends

prayerfully over the pages
of her geometry. Outside
a cardinal sings the first
two notes of "Annie Laurie."

For the second day in a row
we've had nothing to eat.

No one
has anything to say.

On the hillside
where MawMaw and PawPaw sleep
Daddy's digging
another much smaller grave.

V.

Deep summer, smelling of roses:
I am cracking walnuts
and whistling through the gap
between my two front teeth.

The North Star trembles.
A pot of leather britches
boils on the stove.

We are all in the kitchen
with Daddy, who talks about
farming the coal. It's
a big black tree, secret
and deep inside the earth
falls the dark fruit
he brings home to us in white
flour, sugar, coffee, tobacco.

He says
sometimes in the light
of the carbide lamps
veins flash
like the constellation Orion.

The strike is over.
The gourd turns
the wind into music.

The Shaker

She programs her body
for the Whirling

She's an expert: her
gestures stately as

the revolutions of a
clock   Not too slow

Not too fast   Her feet
rise   shining like glass

Her gingham gown ripples
Her flesh turns fluid

as grass   She slides
out of its silver river

Her short blunt neck
glistening   Her ankles

bending   A breast hangs
in the air like a small

pink moon   One thigh's
still dark and moving

Then everywhere
the parts lie

Scattered   like
snow   Finer

At the Edge of Town

A house sits hump-backed
in the dark. A long hall where no clock chimes
runs mushroom soft
from the front door to the back, divides the house
in half. Something in the wall

throbs with a human pulse, and
the wind — clamorous as the mice who nest in
the chimney — opens and shuts doors
to rooms where no one is living, rolls empty beer
bottles clanking in circles, lifts
from a walnut dresser top old love letters faded to
a yellow stain, enveloped in dust.
They glide over an edge made raw by jackknife marks
and burns from cigarette stubs.
They flutter, the pages
coming apart, growing wings: pale moths flickering
in the monochrome
of the moon that shines its still water through
a window.
Drifting to the floor, they float on their shadows, each
one at sea among all the others,
though here and there words like the hieroglyphs
of some unknown tongue
swim up into the hallowed light:
love.. is... forever.

Meanwhile
a cracked pane endures the peepers' shrill cries.
The stars wrinkle
the thick scroll of the sky, and over the sill
the kudzu climbs steadily.

Irene McKinney

At the beginning of my conscious life I wanted to learn to pass in the mainstream culture. Some native Appalachians do that, but it's never quite right: the accent slips out at crucial moments; there's a tendency to guffaw when something ridiculous is said; there's a tendency to be blunt or joyous or anguished in polite company. I was born and grew up in West Virginia in a farmhouse built before the Civil War where no one but my family has always lived. We weren't genteel, and we were very poor. This made me associate everything about my culture with Doing Without and Being on the Bottom of the Heap. And so I tried to deny it, although to my credit that phase didn't last very long. When I write, the voice in my head has an accent and a distinctive vocabulary and diction. If I had truly learned to pass, I would be someone else. Maybe she would've been interesting in her own right. I don't know. Because I'm convinced that although the human mind is capable of ranging over an enormous amount of knowledge, there are only a few things we *really know,* and these things are basic human understandings indivisibly united with their origins in time and place and circumstance.

There were the objects I looked at and saw completely: shucking-pegs, horse-sweaty bridles and bits, potato graders, corn shellers, the stirring-trough for sugar cane, blue vitriol in the potato sprayer, piles of lime, big bins of wheat. These were objects of felt knowledge; they meant what they were, or their use was their meaning. All through my childhood I felt that my face was pressed up against the face of the natural world and the basic human world. Because we lived in an isolated place with no modern conveniences and very little money, it was as though I'd been born in the 19th century and thus came into the 20th with all the shock and fresh view of a time traveler. I was married when I was barely seventeen, had two children, and started to college at twenty-four after reading Betty Friedan's *The Feminine Mystique.* I'd learned to read before I started attending the one-room country school and had always read everything, literally, that I could get my hands on. And getting my hands on books was a central struggle in my early life. Whenever I chanced onto a box of old books at a neighbor's or a relative's house, I asked to have them, and people usually said, "Yes, get those dusty old things out of here."

In hindsight it seems odd to me now that *The Feminine Mystique* had such an effect on me. After all, what could have been further from my experience than the lives of a bunch of privileged Radcliffe and Smith graduates? But every education has a starting point, and that was mine. I was a raw but precocious country girl, and the world's rules and judgments and privileges had a hold on me even though I was only dimly aware there was a world out there, a culture with patterns filtering down into the most isolated regions of the country. I was able to begin to write seriously because I saw I had nothing to lose: I was a hillbilly, a woman, and a poet. I had no position to maintain, no vested interests to protect, no status to hang onto. So I might as well speak out of my deepest self and commit that self to print.

I eventually went on to earn two degrees, at West Virginia University and the University of Utah, traveled and taught for several years in California, Utah, New York, and most recently the Northwest. There is a politics of exile and a politics of coming home. When I was awarded a National Endowment Fellowship for poetry in 1986, I used most of it to have a small house built on the edge of the family farm in West Virginia. The familiar conflict is there, and the writing I do is irritated and powered by it. If I call myself an Appalachian, I do so knowing that Appalachia is a myth, but so are the other regions of the country. And myths must be revised, rewritten, to become real and humanized.

There's a myth of the South, and that's not mine. Mountain culture is more raw, less polite, less guilt-ridden, more isolated, less known by the rest of the country. West Virginia became a separate state because it wouldn't fight with the South in the Civil War. West Virginians weren't slaveholders, not necessarily because they were morally superior but because they were too poor to own slaves. So ours is another story entirely.

Irene McKinney

The pattern of exile and return, of alternately embracing and rejecting one's home, is enormously complicated, more full of the mystery of creation than we can hope to explain in terms of broad movements or groups or writers. I need the countryside and the people, but I need the larger world, too. I live on a margin, a narrow band between. I built my house on a margin, an edge between the deep woods and the cleared ground, just as close to the woods as I thought I could bear. I lived there alone for three years, revising the books I'd started elsewhere. When poverty, financial and intellectual, overtook me yet again, I went back out to elsewhere. And now, yet again, I'm about to come on back home.

The Anguish Lessons

Some of us will not learn our anguish lessons,
but plunge in again and again.
We dive into our names.

Under the dark porches of farmhouses,
in the gathering night light

on the white of the dogwood petals,
the oil pools.

With this our heads are anointed,
with this we wash the feet
of those who have come this long way.

For Women Who Have Been Patient All Their Lives

1.

There is anger in the stiff bedsprings
and under the house in the black powdered dirt,
ground into the blunt cracked hands of my father.

Something is coming, my mother says
There will be something for all of us

The strip-miners come, the loggers;
anger gathers at the lip of the cracked well,
in the bins of wheat in the shambled granary.

Someone will pay, it won't be us
We have learned to wait

in the cold morning with snow on the beds,
at night in the stale quilts
and worn grunts of our men.

2.

Mother, from the roots of your hair
from your heavy white body

from your great splayed feet
from the blue bowls of your breasts

from the steamy washtub
from the wet rags, sour milk

from the belly of the stove
from the lobs of dough, the biscuits

from the whine of the babies
I was one, dragging at you

from the dark burrow of your bed
where you wait in your sleep

What you have given cannot say its name

From blind love for your sisters
and the ease of women

from these, who you are
reach out to me

and I, your bony daughter
schooled in your kitchen

will reach back to give you
what I have, these words

the spilling of anger and love
saved like money for years.

Deep Mining

Think of this: that under the earth
there are black rooms your very body

can move through. Just as you always
dreamed, you enter the open mouth

and slide between the glistening walls,
the arteries of coal in the larger body.

I knock it loose with the heavy hammer.
I load it up and send it out

while you walk up there on the crust,
in the daylight, and listen to the coal-cars

bearing down with their burden.
You're going to burn this fuel

and when you come in from your chores,
rub your hands in the soft red glow

and stand in your steaming clothes
with your back to it, while it soaks

into frozen buttocks and thighs.
You're going to do that for me

while I slog in the icy water
behind the straining cars.

Until the swing-shift comes around.
Now, I am the one in front of the fire.

Someone has stoked the cooking stove
and set brown loaves on the warming pan.

Someone has laid out my softer clothes,
and turned back the quilt.

Listen: there is a vein that runs
through the earth from top to bottom

and both of us are in it.
One of us is always burning.

Visiting My Gravesite: Talbott Churchyard, West Virginia

Maybe because I was married and felt secure and dead
at once, I listened to my father's urgings about "the future"

and bought this double plot on the hillside with a view
of the bare white church, the old elms, and the creek below.

I plan now to use both plots, luxuriantly spreading out
in the middle of a big double bed. — But no,

finally, my burial has nothing to do with my marriage, this lying here
in these same bones will be as real as anything I can imagine

for who I'll be then, as real as anything undergone, going back
and forth to "the world" out there, and here to this one spot

on earth I really know. Once I came in fast and low
in a little plane and when I looked down at the church,

the trees I've felt with my hands, the neighbors' houses
and the family farm, and I saw how tiny what I loved or knew was,

it was like my children going on with their plans and griefs
at a distance and nothing I could do about it. But I wanted

to reach down and pat it, while letting it know
I wouldn't interfere for the world, the world being

everything this isn't, this unknown buried in the known.

Twilight in West Virginia: Six O'clock Mine Report

*Bergoo Mine No. 3 will work: Bergoo Mine
No. 3 will work tomorrow. Consol. No. 2
will not work: Consol. No. 2 will not
work tomorrow.*

Green soaks into the dark trees.
The hills go clumped and heavy
over the foxfire veins
at Clinchfield, One-Go, Greenbrier.

At Hardtack and Amity the grit
abrades the skin. The air is thick
above the black leaves, the open mouth
of the shaft. A man with a burning

carbide lamp on his forehead
swings a pick in a narrow corridor
beneath the earth. His eyes flare
white like a horse's, his teeth glint.

From his sleeves of coal, fingers
with black half-moons: he leans
into the tipple, over the coke oven
staining the air red, over the glow

from the rows of fiery eyes at Swago.
Above Slipjohn a six-ton lumbers down
the grade, its windows curtained with soot.
No one is driving.

The roads get lost in the clotted hills,
in the Blue Spruce maze, the red cough,
the Allegheny marl, the sulphur ooze.

The hill-cuts drain; the roads get lost
and drop at the edge of the strip job.
The fires in the mines do not stop burning.

Louise McNeill (1911–1993)

I was born in 1911 on a mountain farm in West Virginia. The farm lies on two small headsprings of Swago Creek which joins the Greenbrier River just below our small crossroads bridge. This section of West Virginia is bluegrass country, the "Greenbrier Lime," and is characterized by rich soil, limestone caverns, and the pink broken pieces of coral left stranded in the mountains when the last primordial ocean withdrew.

My family's original settler was Tom McNeel (later McNeill), a remote grandfather who, with his family, came across the top of Allegheny in 1769 and claimed the land by "tomahawk right"—not a strictly legal claim since by the Proclamation of 1763 all lands west of the Allegheny divide were forbidden to white settlers. Tom was a squatter, as were the two families he would find living nearby: John McNeel, in the "Levels" near present Hillsboro, and the Buckleys, nearer to Swago, just across the Greenbrier River from Swago mouth. Both of these families still hold their land today and will pass it on to male heirs.

Apparently the squatter claim was not so bad. When the claims were finally settled, Virginia had become a state in the Union. Tom's deed was signed by the governor of Virginia—three hundred acres, granted for service in the Revolutionary War since Tom was one of the many hard-grained settlers who had walked into the French and Indian War which then slid into the American Revolutionary War at Concord Bridge in 1775.

In the Virginia Archives there is also the war record of James Monroe McNeill, my father's father (Grandpa Jim), the rebel captain who went with the 22nd of Virginia, under the command of Colonel George Patton (grandfather of General George Patton of World War II). Colonel Patton was killed at Winchester, and Captain Jim was captured at Droop Mountain in November 1863, a battlefield which had been in the new "northern" state of West Virginia for four months. (The Trans-Allegheny section of Virginia plus a few unwilling counties east of the divide had been "war born or war torn" from the Old Dominion and on June 20, 1863, had become the thirty-fifth state of the American Union.)

Captain Jim lay in a Yankee prison at Fort Delaware from the winter of 1863 to June 1865. When he was released, he was taken to Staunton by box car and then walked through the mountains to Summersville where he owned two lots, purchased before the war. These he sold, and in late summer he came home to Swago, driving his oxen and ox wagon loaded with lumber, nails, and his carpenter tools.

In prison he had had plenty of time to think. He was past middle age, childless, and had been a widower for fifteen years. He started building his five-room Dutch cottage, backed up under the shadow of the mountains that reared darkly in the northwest. When it was finished, he took three or four trips into the "Levels" of Hillsboro, and one evening brought home dark-eyed hard-working Fannie Perkins, a Confederate war widow about twenty-eight years old.

When the Captain was fifty-four, Fannie bore him a big "brof" boy, my father, whom he named George (for Patton) Douglas, called "G.D."— born in the same cottage in 1877 in which I would be born in 1911 and also my youngest brother Jim in February 1918. When I was about fifty years old, my father gave me a little notebook of poems which Grandpa Jim had written while in Delaware in 1863–1865.

> "In the night there rose a star,
> Turnkey of my prison bar..."

I have spent my life as a teacher and poet, wife and mother: a second marriage to Roger W. Pease, a New England schoolmaster; a son, Douglass McNeill Pease, a physicist living in Storrs, Connecticut. I now live in Malden, West Virginia, retired, yet still writing poems and giving poetry readings. My education includes degrees from Concord College in West Virginia, Miami University in Ohio, and a Ph.D. in history from West Virginia University. Books of poetry include: *Mountain White* (1931); *Gauley Mountain* (1939); *Time Is Our House* (1942); *Paradox Hill* (1972); *Elderberry Flood* (1979); and *The Milkweed Ladies* (1988), a prose memoir. Poems have appeared in numerous anthologies and magazines. Among many awards and honors, I was appointed West Virginia Poet Laureate by Governor John D. Rockefeller IV in 1979 and serve as such to the present, have received both the Distinguished Alumni Award and an Honorary Doctorate in Human Letters from West Virginia University, and have been given the Governor's Award for the Arts.

Louise McNeill

Along the way there have been many failures, days of discouragement, massive work, and thousands of rejection slips. Among serious concerns about misuse of atomic power, pollution of the earth, and war, I have been involved with family, flower and herb gardens, baseball and football, Appalachian folk culture, and space flight. When my son grew up and went into solid state physics, he often sent me science paperbacks for the uninitiated. I read, began to believe the new science might be the metaphor of the next generation of poetry, and even wrote a few "science" poems. I always tell young poets to learn to make a living in some other field. I may also tell them there is so much joy *in the writing itself* that I would do it all over again.

Hill Daughter

Land of my fathers and blood, oh my fathers, whatever
Is left of your grudge in the rock, of your hate in the stone;
I have brought you at last what you sternly required that I bring you,
And have brought it alone.

I, who from the womb must be drawn, though the first born, a daughter,
And could never stand straight with the rifle, nor lean with the plow;
Here is ease for the curse, here is cause for the breaking of silence.
You can answer me now.

It has taken me long to return, and you died without knowing,
But down where the veins of the rock and the aspen tree run —
Land of my fathers and blood, oh my fathers, whatever
Is left of your hearts in the dust,
I have brought you a son.

Blizzard

In the blizzard night,
Bringing the cattle down from the hills,
We heard in our capped ears
The soundless screaming,
Sniffed in the ripped air the scent that has no smell,
Felt with our gloved fingers
The stiff bone formless and white,
Saw with our whipped eyes the shape unshadowed —

Only our blood recalled,
And the cattle calling
Answered the fear up there on the primal hilltops,
Where the frost grass whined,
And the naked thing crouched waiting

Mayapple Hill

Children warned against the Mandrake —
Apple of the twisted root,
On the hilltop every summer,
Suckle at the golden fruit;
Suck the pale exotic fragrance,
Revel in the mellow pome —
Children, drunken with the sunlight,
In the evening stagger home —
Nor at bedtime sense the fever,

Nor at morning any chill —
Taken from the tumored apple,
Golden on the August hill.

* * * * *

All the children of the summer
Sleeping drowsy in the sun
Of the upland, August meadow —
With their golden fevers done —
Children of the earth who reveled
In the sweetness of the fruit —
Lying with their limbs disheveled
In the Mandrake's twisted root —
Children of the twisted torsos,
Lying always, oh, so still —
Where the Mandrake's tumored apples
Ripen mellow on the hill.

Moonshiner

In a cave at the mouth of Dead Man's holler
Where the wild plums claw and the black haws twine
To cover the entrance, thorn and bramble,
I tend my kittles and still my shine.
Grain a-work in my barrels and noggins,
Corn and barley and rye and wheat.
A quart of ashes to make it sour....
A poke of sugar to keep it sweet....
A can of lye so the stuff will fizzle,
Fizzle, sizzle, and foam and swell....
Limestone water to make it clearer
Than rain on a huckleberry bell.

In a cave at the mouth of Dead Man's holler
Where the hills are close and the rocks are steep,
With my kittles red and the brass worm dripping
I work while the Revenooers sleep.
Bile and bubble and steam and trickle....
Jugs and bottles and jars to fill.
In a cave at the mouth of Dead Man's holler,
With my skunk gun handy, I run my still.

Timber Boom

The Gauley fox can scent the maddened rattler
And dodge the swift uncoiling of his sheath,

But now an unknown dread is whirring, whirring....
And green dust spurts before its jagged teeth.

The white pines quake against the Gauley sunrise
And shudder till they crash down Gauley hills,
The trout float belly-upward on the river
With sawdust raking blood around their gills.

Only the worthless clumps of laurel and scrub oak
Give hiding to the rabbit and the deer,
Pine thiskins flutter from the coneless branches
And groundhogs burrow downward from the Fear.

A Boom is rolling southward over Gauley
And in its wake the hills lie starkly skinned,
But it is not the pealing wrath of thunder....
And it is not the iron-fingered wind.

It rumbles from the hammers which are building
Slum shanties under fog,
(*Fifty a thousand and grub stake free at the cookshack
For a white pine log.*)

The Roads

(Appalachia)

Where do the roads go —
The ruined country roads flow,
Fern-clogged and weed-bogged, wandering the hills?
Nowhere that I know — by shad-blow and fence-row,
By woods where the lilacs grow,
By the rotted sills.

What can a road feel?
How can this sorrow heal?
Sole mark and wagon wheel passing through the day,
Grain load and apple load creaking down the hilly road —
All of the life that flowed —
Now gone away.

Where do the roads wind?
What do they go to find —
Crossing the mountain tops and meeting by the shores,
Swamp-locked and briar-blocked, searching for the rib-rocked
Men of the mountain stock,
By their empty doors —

Frost-pocked and burr-docked,
Winding through the passes

Where the dying chestnut trees reach their shriveled arms —
Thorn-crossed and time-lost, through the tangled grasses —
All the little country roads,
Searching for the farms...

Jim Wayne Miller (1936–1996)

I was born in western North Carolina (Buncombe County, Leicester community) in 1936. I am the oldest of six children (two sisters, three brothers) born to Edith Smith Miller and James Woodrow Miller. (I write in a partially autobiographical manner about Leicester, my parents, brothers and sisters, and grandparents in my novel, *Newfound*.) I attended Berea College and Vanderbilt University and since 1963 have taught German (language and literature) and Appalachian folklore and folk life in the Department of Modern Languages and Intercultural Studies at Western Kentucky University, Bowling Green, Kentucky. I met my wife, Mary Ellen Yates (from Carter County, Kentucky), at Berea College. We have been married since 1958 and have three children, James Yates, Fred Smith, and Ruth Ratcliff Miller.

A writer, Saul Bellow says, is a reader who has been moved to emulation. Or maybe also a listener who has been moved to emulation. My earliest memories are of my grandmother Miller reciting songs, poems, and stories she learned as a schoolgirl on Sandy Mush Creek in northwest Buncombe County. In the first or second grade I wrote a poem that tried to emulate something she had recited to me. Later I emulated things I read or heard on the radio. Once when I was eight or nine, I heard a radio drama that was so good (I thought) that I got out pencil and paper and wrote one (I thought) just like it.

I wrote throughout grade school, stopped during high school, and started writing again at Berea College where I learned that I was from Appalachia (Berea College draws about 85 percent of its student body from the Southern Appalachian region, its principal service area).

In the spring of 1963 after my grandfather Smith had died and while I was in the last year of a three-year residency at Vanderbilt University, I sent a sheaf of poems to Maxine Kumin who conducted the "Poetry Workshop," a bi-monthly column in *The Writer*. In the July issue she commented favorably on my poems and discussed them in terms of a sense of place, guessing that I came from "a backwoods section, the Ozarks, possibly."

That wasn't a bad guess. The scenes depicted in the submitted poems might well have come from the Ozarks, or from Kentucky or Tennessee, or from any number of American places. They happened to be drawn, in part, from my western North Carolina upbringing. But I think no one would ever have suspected that many of the details in the poems Kumin discussed came to me from New England—out of a passage from Nathaniel Hawthorne's *Mosses from an Old Manse*.

I mention this to make clear why I don't wish to impute a mystique to any particular place. And I hope no one finds any witless yodeling about mountains in my poems just because I come from the mountains of western North Carolina. For I am aware of a tradition, much in evidence since the 18th century, which romanticizes mountains and mountain people. Roland Barthes speaks of a bourgeois alpine myth — a mystique about mountains — which, he says, causes people to take leave of their senses "anytime the ground is uneven."

I do not wish to be associated with a romantic attachment to place. I have no literary enthusiasm for mountains and am not interested in them as mere landscape — or anywhere as mere topography or terrain. What interests me is people in their place — how they have coped, what they have come to be as a result of living in that place.

Jim Wayne Miller (courtesy of the Jim Wayne Miller Literary Estate)

William Butler Yeats said that when he was a young man, he had many ideas, but he had not discovered which ones belonged to him and to no one else. For Yeats, becoming a poet consisted in discovering which ideas belonged peculiarly to him. So it is with any poet, writer, or artist. There are things that belong to a person alone and to no one else which are tied up with a place — with a locale, a way of life, a collective experience in which the creative process and the person's capabilities as a writer meet.

My place is the Southern Appalachian region of America, a region which has, according to the historian Carl Degler, a complicated "triple history" — a history it shares with the rest of America; a history shared with the rest of the (lowland) South; and a third history, obscured by stereotypes, that is all its own. As a poet, I am interested in this triple history, in the individual and collective experience of the region's people and in the contemporary conditions and future possibilities that flow from this history.

I like to think that the figure of the Brier, who emerges in my collection *The Mountains Have Come Closer* and who appears again in *Brier, His Book,* is the embodiment of a theme in the place and people I write about. I like to think he is, as Wallace Stevens says, "...an invisible element of that place/Made visible." I didn't invent the Brier or the themes that concern him. But in thinking about place and one's relationship to it, I believe that with the Brier I have discovered something about Southern Appalachia, about America (this land which, according to Robert Frost, was "ours before we were the land's,") and about the American experience.

In the opening lines of *Look Homeward, Angel* Thomas Wolfe (a fellow Buncombe Countian) says, "Each of us is all the sums he has not counted." My poems, stories, essays, and my novel *Newfound* are ways of counting the sums.

Fencepost

Mending the fence we built one fall together,
I come to the spring below the mountain field.
This stake here by the spring drain needs no bracing;
it's sprouted now (you left the post unpeeled)
and feels so firm, so solid in the ground,
I'd say it's taken root.—Death's sickle-sweep
is wide:—bone-man on the branchbank,
in denims and an old black hat, still half-asleep
at foggy dawn, I've heard him giving his blade
a whetstone's lick and promise by the spill.
But death would have to be a newground
grubber, and dig out every root, and still
he'd not be sure roots wouldn't send down roots,
or sure that stubble wouldn't send up shoots.

How America Came to the Mountains

The way the Brier remembers it, folks weren't sure
at first what was coming. The air felt strange,
and smelled of blasting powder, carbide, diesel fumes.

A hen crowed and a witty prophesied
eight lanes of fogged-in asphalt filled with headlights.
Most people hadn't gone to bed that evening,
believing an awful storm was coming to the mountains.

And come it did. At first, the Brier remembers,
it sounded like a train whistle far off in the night.
They felt it shake the ground as it came roaring.
Then it was big trucks roaring down an interstate,
a singing like a circle saw in oak,
a roil of every kind of noise, factory
whistles, cows bellowing, a caravan
of camper trucks bearing down
blowing their horns and playing loud tape decks.

He recollects it followed creeks and roadbeds
and when it hit, it blew the tops off houses,
shook people out of bed, exposing them
to a sudden black sky wide as eight lanes of asphalt,
and dropped a hail of beer cans, buckets
and bottles clattering on their sleepy heads.
Children were sucked up and never seen again.

The Brier remembers the sky full of trucks
and flying radios, bicycles and tv sets, whirling

log chains, red wagons, new shoes and tangerines.
Others told him they saw it coming like a wave
of tumbling dirt and rocks and car bodies
rolling before the blade of a bulldozer,
saw it pass on by, leaving a wake
of singing commercials, leaving ditches
full of spray cans and junk cars, canned
biscuit containers, tinfoil pie plates.
Some told him it fell like a flooding creek
that leaves ribbons of polyethylene
hanging from willow trees along the bank
and rusty car doors half-silted over on sandbars.

It was that storm that dropped beat-up cars
all up and down the hollers, out in fields
just like a tornado that tears tin sheets
off tops of barns and drapes them like scarves
on trees in quiet fields two miles from any settlement.

And that's why now so many old barn doors
up and down the mountains hang by one hinge
and gravel in the creek is broken glass.

That's how the Brier remembers America coming
to the mountains. He was just a little feller
then but he recollects how his Mama got
all of the younguns out of bed, recalls
being scared of the dark and the coming roar
and trying to put both feet into one leg
of his overalls.   They left the mountains fast
and lived in Is, Illinois, for a while
but found it dull country and moved back.
The Brier has lived in As If, Kentucky, ever since.

The Brier Losing Touch with His Traditions

Once he was a chairmaker.
People up north discovered him.
They said he was "an authentic mountain craftsman."
People came and made pictures of him working,
wrote him up in the newspapers.

He got famous.
Got a lot of orders for his chairs.

When he moved up to Cincinnati
so he could be closer to his market

(besides, a lot of his people lived there now)
he found out he was a Brier.

And when his customers found out
he was using an electric lathe and power drill
just to keep up with all the orders,
they said he was losing touch with his traditions.
His orders fell off something awful.
He figured it had been a bad mistake
to let the magazine people take those pictures
of him with his power tools, clean-shaven,
wearing a flowered sport shirt and drip-dry pants.

So he moved back down to east Kentucky.
Had himself a brochure printed up
with a picture of him using his hand lathe,
bearded, barefoot, in faded overalls.
Then when folks would come from the magazines,
he'd get rid of them before suppertime
so he could put on his shoes, his flowered sport shirt
and double-knit pants, and open a can of beer
and watch the six-thirty news on tv
out of New York and Washington.

He had to have some time to be himself.

A Turning

Day-long drizzle out of a slate sky
low as the dripping roof of a mine shaft.
The Brier's thoughts work shifts, bent and cramped
in a day become a tunnel.

His mood damp and heavy as his old coat,
his spirit low as the shriveled arm of the lake
turning through stump-littered mudflats,
he walks up from the rain-black barn.
The drizzle hangs beaded on his hat brim.

He stands at the edge of the porch, looking
west: last light caught in the curve
of sky — rain in a mussel shell.
And then a bird calls — a thrush? The sound

springs up like a single blade of grass,
then cuts toward him through black limbs
like a smooth, silver plow point snapping tree roots
and turning up dark dirt in a newground.

Past midnight he comes suddenly awake,
lies in the dark, alert. One blade of birdsong
has turned the hollow of his mind a deep green
lapping bay where thoughts swarm like shoaling redhorse,
their speckled green and silver backs arching
out of shallows under willows by the shore.

On the Wings of a Dove

Once, after he'd come back from Ohio,
he worked at road construction for a summer
back up on the Laurel and Ivy Rivers
in Madison. After work, instead of going
all the way to Asheville, he'd stop by
a bootlegger's in Marshall, buy some white,
and drive to a place down on the French Broad River
below Redmon Dam. Pulling his car
down a sandy road, nosing it back
into the willows and sycamores so far
they closed around it, he'd sit there after sundown,
the smell of tar and sweat and asphalt in his clothes,
smoking and drinking white, listening to bluegrass
on the radio, watching the river, mountains, and sky
run together in the coming dark.

Catfishermen built fires along the bank,
and over on the island, and hung their lanterns
out over the water. His troubles sat
right under his breastbone, black
as a tree full of starlings, all talking at once.
But when Bill Monroe and the Bluegrass Boys
played *Wait a Little Longer, Jesus,* or *Blue Moon
of Kentucky,* and his mind throbbed and hummed
like pistons under the hood of a good truck
hauling his thoughts over a long open highway,
and the lights on the riverbank got in tune,
his mind turned into a whining sawblade
spinning so fast it grew invisible and quiet.

The starlings under his breastbone stopped talking.

Then white doves rose out of his rib cage
and flew out over the river toward the island.

The Brier Breathing

> In the evening
> when he walked

down
the steep slope
of his breath
into the hollow of sleep
he distinguished all
his different breathings —

breathing that fluttered
like swallows in a chimney

breathing that sang
easy rhythmical
a crosscut saw in timber

breathing short
shallow
strokes
chopping corn
hoe blade
clacking in rocks

breathing that never bottomed out
but kept on giving, going
down like plowed newground
still sinking underfoot
as he passed on
and came down soft again

breathing so deep
it went all
the way home
to a quiet cove
where peewees called

breathing that turned his body
leafy
turned it cold
and came up
out of a maze of passageways
a groundhog from its den

breathing from so far back
it trickled
transparent over rocks
and stood in sunlit pools
where ripples spread

wider and wider
where shadows of leaves grew gills
that slowly rose and fell.

Abandoned

Sometimes his mind flew black as a crow
over hundreds of coves and hollers
fallen silent since the people were swept
out like rafted logs on spring's high water.

Then his life would stand
empty as an abandoned house
in one of those forgotten places,
his days like blackened chimneys
standing in fields going back
to thickets of second growth —
untended tombstones in a cemetery
up some lost valley.

Sometimes he thought there was nothing left
but the life of a half-wild dog
and the shelter of a junked car
turned on its back in a ditch, half
grown over with honeysuckle.

Or else his life became the house
seen once in a coal camp in Tennessee:
the second story blown off in a storm
so stairs led up into the air
and stopped.

Robert Morgan

"Broomsedge" is a poem I have wanted to write for as long as I can remember. Every child imagines the grass is speaking. But broomsedge is so blond and bright, so whispery on a winter hill, it seems to have a special message. It grows most often in worn-out fields and pasture slopes, and the sigh of broomsedge seems to embody a wisdom that cannot be translated but echoes a voice in the pulse and in the earth. When I finally wrote the poem in the 1980s, it was as though I had at last spoken lines carried in the back of my mind for decades.

I was born October 3, 1944, in Hendersonville, North Carolina, and grew up on the family farm on Green River, near Zirconia in Henderson County, on land bought by my great-great grandfather, Daniel Pace, in 1838. All my great-great grandparents lived in the mountains of North Carolina or upper South Carolina, though my great-great grandmother Rebecca Ann Blocher Johnson was born in Walterboro, South Carolina, and married a mountain boy while she was visiting Flat Rock for her health in the 1850s. Both my father and grandfather worked occasionally in construction, as carpenters, masons, and housepainters, and we raised polebeans and other vegetables as money crops. But most of our farming was for subsistence: corn, garden, chickens, hogs, cow, a plow horse. Most of the bills were paid by my mother who worked in the cotton mill and later at the GE plant.

In 1971 I moved to Ithaca, New York, to teach at Cornell University. I had first left home in 1961 to attend Oxford College of Emory University, then transferred to North Carolina State University and the University of North Carolina at Chapel Hill and Greensboro. Between stints in school and coming to upstate New York, I taught at Salem College, worked as a salesman, freelance writer, housepainter, and farmer. I am now Professor of English at Cornell and live in Freeville. Tompkins County, New York, is also in the Appalachians, a landscape that is not much different from Western North Carolina.

Unlikely as it may seem to some, the mountains are a stimulating place and subject for poetry. Both the religious background of the people and the spirituality of the mountains themselves — their height, the covert hollows and misty remoteness — are essentially poetic. It only demands the vision to recognize and the rigorous accuracy of language to communicate that poetry. Also the terse mountain speech, an aversion to too much talk, and the pressure of inarticulateness, lend themselves to poetry and a love of music. Even the pain of isolation and poverty, the perspectives of difference and distance, and fear can spur the poetic and moral imagination. Southern literature has been most notable for its prose. Appalachian literature will be recognized for its uniquely intense poetry. The mountains are untapped and largely unmapped territory just beginning to be discovered by its poets. Poetry seems to thrive in periods of rapid and radical change such as we have seen in recent years.

My books of poems are *Zirconia Poems* (1969), *Red Owl* (1972), *Land Diving* (1976), *Trunk & Thicket* (1978), *Groundwork* (1979), *Bronze Age* (1981), *At the Edge of the Orchard Country* (1987), *Sigodlin* (1990), and *Green River: New and Selected Poems* (1991). I have also published a book of short stories, *The Blue Valleys* (1989), and a book of novellas and stories, *Watershed* (1991). I have been awarded fellowships by the National Endowment for the Arts, the Guggenheim Foundation, and the New York Foundation for the Arts, and have received the Eunice Tietjens Prize, the Jacaranda Review Fiction Prize, and the Amon Liner Poetry Prize. In 1976 the magazine *The Small Farm* published a special issue devoted to my work, and in 1990 *Iron Mountain Review* published a special issue containing the proceedings of the Robert Morgan festival at Emory and Henry College of April 1990, with essays, interview, checklist, and a new short story. I have given many readings at universities and colleges in the United States, including Duke, Stanford, Hawaii, Buffalo, Columbia, and in Europe at Oxford University, The American Academy in Rome, and the universities of Vienna and Bonn.

Robert Morgan (Dede Hatch)

Broomsedge

There is no whisper like the lisp
of broomsedge on the hill, the long
sigh of the afternoon feeling
around the pasture and combing
out the blondest grass, the wheaty
stalks with thistle in their ears
that lean and straighten away from
the prevailing voice. On the poor
land, the grave land, the oldest fields,
the broomsedge whisks and strokes bright
rumor from the air, a vowel,
a long slow ease of song below
the threshold of song, an ancient
lull almost unheard but coming
along the world's edge over
clay and subsoil, like the faint
music of ancestors in our
bloodsleep who tell with bending blade
and downy seed everything we

know and nothing we remember
at this poorest elevation.

The Hollow

First travelers to the coves of the Blue Ridge
up near the headsprings,
found no trails between
the cabin clearings. Each bit
of acreage along its branch
opened like an island inside the wilderness,
with paths to water and to the turnip patch
always stopping at the margin where
a groundhog sunned its gob of fur.
The children chewed tobacco or drank corn,
when someone picked his way
out through the thickets to obtain some.
Their best diversion of all, their most
accomplished: watching the mountain haze, the blue
haunt overhead that cooled
and lulled even the August sun
and lay out along the slopes like
a smoke of silence, an incense of their
lifelong vigil between the unstoned graves
and the wormy appletree, a screen
sent up from the oaks and hickories
to keep them hidden from disease
and god and government, and even time.

Nail Bag

When a cleared farm wore out or washed
in three to seven years, the soil
bleached and threadbare, they just burned the barn
down for the nails and moved on,
wagon banging buckets, babies
howling, oxen straining at fords
and ridges. To the next claim. And
once the trees on that acreage were
girdled and felled, they burned the logs
and plowed the ashes around stumps,
bringing in enormous yields from
the singed ground. Then took out the sack
of nails like slivers of crystal
that hammered right would summon

wilderness into new structure.
As though all husbandry and home
were carried in that charred handful
of iron stitches, blacksmithed chromosomes
that link distant generations.

Lost Flower

Old Asa Gray from Harvard looked high
in the mountains for the shortia
that Michaux had discovered and plucked
on the Blue Ridge and dried for his collection
back in France almost a century before.
No botanist had seen its bloom, nor
knew where to climb for the dazzling beds
the Frenchman had extolled in his journal.
Professor Gray named it *shortia galacifolia* for
a friend and sent assistants every summer
to the highlands to explore the summits
for the herb that had no relative except
one cherished breed in China,
a sacred mountain flower.
But when they found the shortia abloom
in oriental profusion all over the south
flank of Transylvania County late in the last
century, it gloried slopes lower
than expected, haunting just above the coves
at the edge of South Carolina and in the shade
of heavy woods, curd-white and shy in the
trash of forest floor, smaller than its
Chinese twin, and called by neighbors
the Oconee Bell for where it rang quiet
on the lower elevations, no higher
than the best-fed springs.

Death Crown

In the old days back when
one especially worthy lay dying
for months, they
say the feathers in the pillow would
knit themselves into a crown
that those attending felt in perfect
fit around the honored head.
The feather band they took to be

certain sign of another crown,
the saints and elders of the church,
the Deep Water Baptists said.
I've seen one unwrapped from its
cloth in the attic, the down
woven perfect and tight for
over a century, shiny but
soft and light almost as light.

The Body of Elisha Mitchell

The body of Elisha Mitchell
when it lay in the clear pool
beneath a waterfall below
his named and measured peak, white as
marble in the laurel gloom, was
stirred by shock ripples from the falls
and turned by eddies like a compass
needle pointing to the summit.
The icy spring water had kept
the body perfect for two weeks
as the searchers crisscrossed the Blacks,
Big Tom Wilson the bear hunter
and the Reverend Mitchell Junior
hacking into thickets to look
at every twig for sign of tracks.
They came to a cliff edge and saw
the body fifty feet below
staring past them at the peak
he'd measured highest in the east,
his eyes wide and blue and clear
as the eye of his barometer
used to get elevation. The
snowy body was unbruised by
rock or tree in the plunge, untouched
by fish or animal, though prick
marks would hint a rattler strike
may have sent him reeling down
the slope and over, falling numb,
the venom perfect for embalming,
the body white as a breathless statue.

Whiskey Tree

Tree on the mountainside, hickory
or ash, the bottle bush, oak

sapling stronger than a man and
high above the valley road, back
above the branchhead at the end
of the haul road where the boys
come to loaf on Fridays after
quitting time, away from children,
disapproving wives. They sit on
the high ground under the protecting
limbs and watch the stars appear through
the washy lens of liquor, yell
and laugh and sing to the radio
in someone's truck, or look into
the dark and end up weeping.
But always tying, fixing with
a string or wire, lace or bandaid
their empties to the limbs above,
climbing into the forks to stick
a pint or jug on the end of
a twig, until the sapling seems
some Christmas tree in sunlight,
or starlight, bearing its yield of
bulbs that pull like enormous tears
as the tree is stunted, bent and
burdened under its cold harvest,
a tree of the knowledge of
forgetfulness, radiant with
memory on a winter morning,
as crows avoid the shining bush.

New Organ

Without a dollar in the house
he offered the peddler sixty
bushels of his finest sweet
potatoes, then seventy, eighty,
and the deal was inked. A season
he'd given to the yield of those
great milky nuggets in the red
clay, crisp and delicate as glands,
fat twists of gold below the white
convolvulus vines shawling on
the hillside. He picked each swollen
root from the soil like a note
and filled the basket eighty times,
and then his wagon, thinking
one hamper for each key, the milk

becoming the strains of music
from the bellows inside the chest,
as Wessie pulled the stops and pedaled,
walking as she played, stepping
on the red carpet treadles to
the edge of another weather
to look over. The lungs inside
seemed a big harmonica,
a louder accordion. He frowned
and never spoke approval as
the family sang and the young
gathered to the heat of his labor
transmuted into a movement
of the air, a stir of air in
the shudder and breath of the pedals
and a dance of color in sadness
of the hymn's expectations, in
the gathering of voices and
the light and shade of the fireplace,
now the hillside was frozen over
and snow shawling over the clay,
the rows hard as a file's ridges,
each line become a phrase inside while
the carpet wore out on the pedals
as from a long pilgrimage.

The Flying Snake

The giant rattler that lived in
the rocks above the Gap Road
watched teams and passing
riders from its summer ledge,
almost invisible in moss.
If bothered it could drain
its black feet into a crevice
or, provoked, spring on a horse or driver,
raking the neck with its
loaded fangs and flopping off
into the brush below the trace
before one had mastered
panic enough to
shoot the leg-sized whip of lightning.
Four settlers had died, and many
mules and oxen.
Even the old Cherokee formula
of singing the snake its own song
was useless if it struck before seen.

Once a posse climbed up in the cliffs
and shot a dozen small ones but
the old killer sank back
into the mountain, and seemed
to know just like a crow if one
was coming armed.
It was Great-grandpa as a youth
who thought of tying his seine net
around the yoke and under the chests
of his steers, and drove standing
in the wagon with a shotgun in the hay.
That cool August noon the jarflies
sang like rattlers in the trees
and ripe huckleberries
sweetened the air.
Flying squirrels swept
in the high branches of the oaks, and
way down the valley he could hear
Aunt Tildy's chickens
routed by a hawk.
Coming near the rocks he crouched
to cock the gun and let the team
nose slowly into the shivering
spots of sunlight.
He heard the cold thunder necklace fling
off the shelf above and as it caught
in the webbing by its barbs he
just had time, before it
thrashed free, to raise the
barrel and cut the jeweled blur in two.
The head piece bit a rock
and soaked the ground with venom.
The tail twitched on for hours
like something dreaming.
The two halves filled a half bushel
and he sewed the sixteen rattles to his hat.
Years later he'd imagine spiders
falling from the sky like snowflakes,
and mad dogs and angels in storms,
and once in a nighmare he shot
by mistake Jesus as he came
through the east in Rapture light.

The Gift of Tongues

The whole church got hot and vivid
with the rush of unhuman chatter

above the congregation,
and I saw my father looking at
the altar as though electrocuted.
It was a voice I'd never heard
but knew as from other centuries.
It was the voice of awful fire.
"What's he saying?" Ronald hissed
and jabbed my arm. "Probably Hebrew."
The preacher called out another
hymn, and the glissade came again,
high syllables not from my father's
lips but elsewhere, the flare of
higher language, sentences of light.
And we sang and sang again, but
no one rose as if from sleep to
be interpreter, explain the writing
on the air that still shone there like
blindness. None volunteered a gloss
or translation or receiver
of the message. My hands hurt
when pulled from the pew's varnish
they'd gripped and sweated so. Later,
standing under the high and plain-
sung pines on the mountain I clenched
my jaws like pliers, holding in
and savoring the gift of silence.

Valerie Nieman

I grew up in Appalachia without recognizing it as such and live today in an Appalachia which seldom matches that metaphor worn thin by the popular consciousness.

I was born and reared in western New York State, in the soft undulations of farm and forest land which birth the Allegheny River. In hindsight, it was a natural progression from headwater to headwater, from the streams that fed the Allegheny to those that swell the Monongahela.

Transferring from Jamestown Community College in New York to West Virginia University, I chose journalism for my major and West Virginia as my home. I graduated in 1978, married a fellow ex–New Yorker, and began work.

By 1981, my husband John and I had purchased a bit of pasture field near Fairmont, West Virginia. We later bought more acreage and built our home with our own hands — and the help of family and friends.

The ability to "do for yourself" is a truly Appalachian trait, I believe, mothered by the isolated family's need to be its own builder and butcher and baker, plumber and veterinarian, roadbuilder, lumberjack, horticulturist. My family on both sides counts small farmers in the majority, though by my parents' generation, many had gone to work in factories while continuing to farm or at least garden.

True to that heritage, I combine careers today. I have worked as a reporter and editor since my college years. With my husband, I manage an organic garden and small orchard. We occasionally keep beef cattle. And, of course, I write.

I work in several genre and forms — that same blessed small-farmer tenacity to do the best with what you have! My first novel, *Neena Gathering,* a science fiction tale set in West Virginia, was published in 1988 by Pageant/Crown. I've recently completed a mainstream novel set in the early 1970s in a West Virginia town. One of my short fiction pieces

Valerie Nieman (Jack Hobbs)

received a PEN Syndicated Fiction Award in 1988. And I have been awarded a National Endowment for the Arts Fellowship in Poetry as well as a Kentucky Foundation for Women grant in fiction for 1991. My poetry has appeared in a number of literary magazines, including *Poetry, The George Washington Review,* and *Kentucky Poetry Review,* and in 1988 a chapbook of my work was selected in a national competition sponsored by *Sing Heavenly Muse!* magazine. That collection, *Slipping Out of Old Eve,* had twin themes of feminism and the land.

The land — and our attachment to it — is what defines Appalachia for me. The region is too various to be bound by images of coal fields or hill farms or rugged mountains. Appalachia exists in the land-consciousness of its people, whether in West Virginia or Georgia.

There is an inner awareness of time and season, of the relationship among people and animals and plants, and of the soil that nourishes them all. This land-consciousness may or may not have an element of preservation. In wild lands — and much of Appalachia remains wild — the Biblical imperative to subdue the earth retains some meaning. That pacification has had a terrible cost, both for the land and its people.

Appalachia's people share another awareness, becoming equally rare in a world devoted to maintaining the appearance of youth. It is an acknowledgement of mutability, change, and loss. A nodding acquaintance, if you will, with Death itself. Religion plays a role, of course, and the ethnic strains which have blended here. Some say this is only fatalism, but it is more than that. It is especially pronounced in these coal mining regions of the mountains where we admit that the layers of stone underfoot are tunneled and undermined and may falter beneath us. We live with a certainty that the earth is hollow.

At the Union Picnic

He sits, for a time,
in the shadow of a home built
on the rock of his wife's worry.
They talk, he and the others,
of shifts, sections,
and the numbers of men who went down
and were found later
by the gleam of a watch crystal
in a sullen fall of slate.

Then he rises, deliberately,
as though there were a weight on his neck,
a memory of a collar, more recent
memory of a load. Muscles flex
in his back, along the sure seam
of his body. He bends
to pick up a tennis ball, yellow,
piercingly yellow on the grass,
yellow like the sun.

He pitches it in a low arc
to the boy who stands

against the sun, his eyes
sunken in darkness. The ball
strikes the boy on the thigh.
His face wrinkles.
"Come here, come here," the miner
calls, and his voice echoes strangely
on the open day and is lost.

The boy watches the ball
roll away, like the sun
in its circle. He doesn't cry.
And the miner gathers up his
child in his arms and holds him,
                        holds him.

Reclamation: Washing Machine

A pickup truck sidles along a back road, stops;
a man muscles off its bed a broken washing machine
and heaves it down the loamy gap that spreads its legs upon
the stream. The machine bumps and tumbles,
agitator spinning out the dark rinse of the night.

    This is the hatred that men have for the hollow:
    the unfilled clefts of the land which are dark and wet,
    riotous with gathered April waters
    where trillium bloom, virginally white,
    and their broken stems stink like a shallow grave.

In the cab of the truck a woman sits, staring
into the thick of trees consorting into darkness,
her face following the coal of a lighted cigarette,
thinking: the last spring flood had clensed each cleft
of this accumulated domestic wrack.

Expedition

She walked until the river split into streams,
streams to creeks, creeks to runs
and the last run like a dark thread
drawing her into the land itself,
into a closed wound.

She had lenses for looking up and counting
the stars and lenses for looking down
and counting springtails in the blackened leaves
and some that were only mirrors.

She penciled entries on the pale
machine-drawn lines of her journal —
the first morning bird (indigo bunting),
the way the alder leaves were chewed and tattered.
At first she ignored broken beer bottles,
plastic jugs impaled on branches —
until they disappeared.
"One tire in the water," she wrote,
then left the rest of the page blank.
"A girl's hair ribbon, brown with algae,"
and she walked upstream, the ribbon
waving behind her, a single meager thread
useless in the great maze of the land.

Once people came past her camp,
sang hymns
washed in the blood of
the sweet by and
nearer My God
and she thought they were angels
until a voice broke and she cursed
them and their victim.

The moon came night after night,
round then horned.
When there were clouds then the sky
was a perfect swollen gray,
like the inside of a ball of wool.

A hunter stood at twilight on a ridge,
listening to distant hounds.
He tended a fire, stirring it with a stripped
and broken limb. Sparks whirled up.
He might have worn a red plaid coat,
a letterman's jacket with demons
or dragons, something extinct,
might have worn leaves for leggings
and braided vines.
She watched his movements
until he became a figure
marked with a burnt stick
on the wall of the sky,
jumped into life by a fire's emaciating light.
She turned to her own small flame.
Her arousal spiraled into the night air
and extinguishment.

The land shut around her.
She tried to climb the bluffs

but found the way too vertical,
treacherous with abrupt springs,
spalled stone and clay.
The water no longer seemed to flow past
but knot and tangle, a black net
heaving in the rapids, at the narrows.

She fished with a line twisted
from her hair and knotted
to a hawthorn hook, caught minnows
and ate them quivering whole, their silver eyes
seeing the way down her throat,
scales clinging to her fingers
like the light of the absent moon.

In the fall came a flood. Her books,
pages long sealed with mold and fungus,
went like unearthed coffins
on the brown tide.

She ate lethargic ants
and grubs with useless fat-man's legs,
peeled the bark from cherry trees
and chewed the green lining, like the frayed
lining of her coat.
She killed a belling hound lost to the hunter,
and fallen as she had
to the bent snare of the land.
She seared its flesh over a fire lit
with alder leaves and berry canes
and fed with the litter that accumulates
on the upstream side of a leaning snag.

The trickle of water was a gash in the frozen land.
She wore the dog's hide on her blackened feet
and the dog's head on her own,
fangs permanently bared.
She watched ice creep out from the banks,
knit itself together the way
bones heal, swords cross,
random marks of the unlettered
are sent tongueless to the future.

Lee Pennington

I was born May 1, 1939, in a place called White Oak, one of Kentucky's many hollows, located in the western end of Greenup County. My parents were Andrew Virgil Pennington and Mary Ellen Lawson. I was eighth in a family of eleven children.

We lived in Baltimore during the early part of World War II where Dad could work in the shipyards, then returned to Kentucky in 1942 and bought a $265 farm—a log house, a good well, and 32 acres of steep hillside which the whole family worked. I attended the same one-room school of my parents, carved my initials near theirs on weather-beaten boards, and taught my first class, a first grade class, when I was in the fourth grade (the teacher spent most of her time making "hook" rugs and had older students teach the classes). After the seventh grade I knew I would go to college. I didn't know how, since we were poor hillside farmers grossing about $2,000 only in a good year ($1,000 below the poverty-stricken level by national standards). But some way, somehow, I knew I was going to college.

While attending McKell High School in South Shore, Kentucky, both Jesse Stuart, my principal, and Lena Nevison, my English teacher, encouraged me to write. In fact, one theme I wrote for English class, "Toadfrog Tears," became my first published short story, appearing while I was in college in *Mountain Life and Work*. I also wrote up all the high school sports and school news for local newspapers for which I was paid $3.00 an article.

On the basis of a newspaper article about Jesse Stuart and the influence of Robert Burns on his life I was offered a scholarship and workshop to Baldwin-Wallace College in Ohio. There has never been a happier young man. My mother and father had not gone even to high school, and no one in my family line (which can be traced back to 1132 in England) had ever graduated from college. Near the end of the first semester, however, I was notified that I would owe almost $400 at the end of the term. I telephoned Mr. Stuart who advised me to transfer to Berea College where I could work my way through school. At mid-year, January, 1959, I was one of eleven students accepted at Berea. I thought to myself, "You, farmboy, are the luckiest man alive."

Among a variety of literary activities at Berea I worked one year as head news bureau writer for the college, one year as publicity writer for the Council of Southern Mountains, and wrote and directed *The Porch,* a one-act mountain tragedy presented at the college during my senior year. I also met my greatest critic and editor, Joy Stout, who became my wife during my last semester there.

After graduation Joy and I went to New York to teach English at Newburgh Free Academy. Then we earned our M.A. degrees in English from the University of Iowa. In 1965 we began teaching at Southeast Community College in Cumberland, Kentucky. Coming back to the mountains was like coming home. It was our heritage.

It was also a challenge. These Appalachian students, the sons and daughters of Bloody Harlan County, regarded by the rest of the country as having the worst of everything, had lived life more deeply than other students in America. True, they had mechanical problems, but they became interested quickly and worked harder than any place I've been, publishing in two years more than 1,000 pieces of writing in over 30 magazines and anthologies. However, their book of poetry, *Tomorrow's People,* in which they looked closely at themselves and their land and spoke honestly of what they saw, resulted in our being run out of Harlan County. For what I call the "Power Structure," it was too much. There were threats, contracts, shots fired, dynamite put in our stoker. Our boss, the president of the University of Kentucky, concerned for our safety, demanded we leave. With an armed car in front and one in back, with ourselves armed, we left in the middle of the night, traveling 4,000 miles during the next two weeks although we never got outside of Kentucky.

Lee Pennington

In the autumn of 1967, Joy and I came to Jefferson Community College in Louisville. We have been here ever since, and I continue to encourage my students to write, publish, perform, and perfect their vision and voice.

My first book was also published in 1967, *The Dark Hills of Jesse Stuart.* Sixteen others have followed, and I have ready for publication twelve more books. My poems, short stories, and articles have appeared in hundreds of magazines, anthologies, and textbooks in America and abroad. Among many awards the most significant perhaps were the Pulitzer Prize nomination for my book of poetry, *I Knew a Woman,* in 1977, and my being named Poet Laureate of Kentucky by the House of Representatives of the General Assembly, a lifetime appointment, in 1984. In 1983 Joy and I established the International Order of E.A.R.S., Inc., a group which promotes the ancient art of storytelling and produces the annual Corn Island Storytelling Festival, the largest of its kind in the world.

Sometimes I'm asked, "If you had to decide, which one thing would you choose from the things you do? Teach? Write? Tell stories? Sing?" The answer is simple. Whatever it takes, one or all, I would search life, discover life, and live. And everything I do, without question, is connected to my Appalachian past, my roots, where both ideas and ideals were firmly established. Every river, no matter how large its flowing, has a million smaller feeder streams giving it volume and force on its way to the sea. My own, of course, is Appalachia — its land, its people. My stream cannot help but know with a deep sense of reverence the rush of all those smaller streams.

Return

I return again; but it is not much, not here
where earth once more is green and fields
are gone, where all is scars of sunlight,
a purple stone face some night artist builds
of the last long streaks falling west.
It is not much for now sprouts are timber
and the tall rows of corn in a plowed
newground earth are about all I can remember
of the time you stood by the spider roots,
spoke of the land and sky, spoke of needs
for one schooled in fighting a stone-loved hill,
yet never a single victory with the weeds.
But know this, my father, with the world in stress,
I battle now not against but with the wilderness.

The Hounds Are Restless

The hounds are restless, their minds
clouded moons where dark wild
runs in blood, moves in veins
cool as wind.

The muddy red river rips
their brains. They stare and bark
in a mountain wilderness—
noses lifted in the dark.

Something out there, where trees
close the fields in.
They can't see it, but they know.

Inside their eyes dark rivers splashing.
Inside their minds a wild afterglow.

Dark Smell

This night smells of Appalachia,
Dark Eden earth spilled in a coal dust sun
seeping like the milk of your face into rains,
counted tracks cracking from coal dust wheels,
from coal truck wheels and two-eyed dragon
food rolling on the line, child of blackness
whimpering at each curve, whispering sudden
echoes on otherwise forboding silence,
white silence of a baby's hand,

green silence of a mother's eye,
black silence of a father's misery,
and the dark bird, blackbird, red-
winged blackbird silence inside
a coal miner's mind watching rats
scampering on grey feet pulling long
grey hairless tails, silent rats dancing
from the pits
before the final slatefall.

Lady Sewing Songs

Lady, your fingers talk blackbirds,
clip violets from the dark stillness,
stitch love-bright willing patterns,
sunrise eyes above yes whispering willows.

You slip through, songs breaking memory
to crying, laughter to greening
and wildflower purple dance among May
as lying deep in lilacs
dreams wake the mind's river.

Flinging songs bloom flower-wise
and thread-sure, you touch bee wings
to sing a sweet working,
a poetry, an art,
a moon-honey heart.

Billy Edd Wheeler

When most men go to fight a war, they take a gun,
But you do battle with a big guitar and the type of run
That carves out notes with a calloused finger strum.

Going down a coal town road or up some hollow
Your songs and strums form attacks that follow
Flame thrower coalbins full of red-hot guitar.

And songs that rise like approaching bomber rains,
Like handgrenades in dancing dust of hurricanes—
Exploding in the ears: shrapnel thoughts and ideas.

Vibrating strings, lonesome twangs, and silver lips
Shape up this dust, rip off its crust like burning nips
Of the last laid frost biting through and hanging on.

Kentucky Lucky

You go ahead and talk about Kentucky,
about black winter buzzards flying in your eyes,
and I'll tell you, you don't have kin
left around anymore to hear you speak.
I helped bury Clyde Dillow last week.
His sons are Dayton men, now just Dayton men,
and don't you stand there acting like it's a surprise.
If sons can't claim their dad, he ain't lucky.

You just tell me how roots go down deep
in this gully-forsaken earth, this coal-sucked land,
and how Lexington highbrows love niggers in the street,
and I'll say, by God, ain't that sweet.
Makes me want to lick the ground
and kiss a race horse's feet.
Maybe you don't like the sound?
Maybe you'll tell me go dig a hole in the sand,
crawl inside for a long night's sleep?

Listen, I've heard talk since I could hear.
I hoed a steep hill against the July sun.
I guess I know pains in the ribs and on shins
a broken arm couldn't bring. I know roots
and every fog horn talker who toots
and every coward who drops his pants to run
and every farmer picking nubbins to fill corn bins.
But I'm not afraid. Not now. Anymore I can't fear.
It's like my wife said, what's to fear now?
We've fed our lives to the lions more than twice.
We've had dynamite at our backs for years.
We've watched bullets crack the bark of trees.
We've seen mules die at the plow.
We've seen enough broken women pay the price.
You just let the yellow clay soak up your fears;
not me. They can scare me cold, but I'll not freeze.

So you go ahead and talk and have your say.
You tell 'em about horses and highbred grass.
You tell 'em Abe Lincoln walks here on Sunday
and good folks get out to hear him pass.
And I'll show you barefoot blood prints in the snow.
I'll show you some people dying to feed the gutter.
I'll show you a thousand faces wanting love
while you turn your head away and point above.
Don't give me that God will help; it's sour butter.

To Be

He wanted to be a carpenter,
the finish kind driving nails home
against the grain, locking but not
splitting wood.

But his worth, or bent as the family
would say, left him only enough
to guide a hoe against the weeds,
not drive a nail blind

as he wanted half as much again
as anything. Still, with no hope left
to think strings of steel into wood
and structured finish smooth as glass,

he became the best with hoe he could
learning each new day to make a cleaner, wider slash
until every swing down the hoe to hammer understood
building newground dreams from brushpile ash.

We Came

We came, you and I, feeling old
Leaves sink down under nervous feet,
Our own, searching footing on ancient
Hills where river sounds trace our steps.

We came, you and I, suddenly on a tree,
White birch, I believe, where woodpeckers
Were strange sculptors on stranger wood —
Carving out distant sounds of hammers.

We came, you and I, and felt this common art,
Born of us and birds, half the earth,
Half a tree gone dead of worms and poetry
Red-headed wings pound into a still world.

We came, you and I, mysteriously by the water,
Climbed and stood and tore, from this tree, a face,
Already made, already rotting of wetness,
Already eyes dark set in gentleness of our mirrors.

Poet of the Soil

You stood there against the Kentucky sky
And watched the wind settle the dust

Following your plow like birds, and I
Under your shadow, proud, with a gooseneck hoe
Leaned to watch the soil where you'd been.
It must have been your hand, loose from plowlines,
Around my shoulder and then your mountain voice
Pointing like echoes across the ridges,
For I remember coming back from where romping
Thoughts had played in the growing corn
And standing there by your side and hearing
You say it takes a million tumbling stones
To make soil worthy of the earth.

Ron Rash

Shortly after my grandmother's death in 1979, I found the following comment about her marriage in a diary: "I guess it worked out pretty well. We had eight kids and too much to do to even think whether we were happy or how the marriage was working out." This quote exemplifies the experience of my people in the Appalachian mountains — my mother's family in Watauga County, North Carolina, and my father's family in Buncombe County, North Carolina. And though much of my life has been spent in the Appalachian foothills, growing up in Catawba and Cleveland counties in North Carolina, and now living in Pendleton, South Carolina, it is the experience of my family in Appalachia that has shaped my sense of the world. Their *Weltanschauung* has instilled in me a fierce belief in individual responsibility; a distrust of human nature, government, and progress; a perception of nature as being terrifying as well as beautiful; and most of all, that though a better life may await us beyond the grave, the present one is more often to be endured than to be celebrated.

Nevertheless, though my Appalachian heritage has bequeathed to me an essentially tragic view of life, my kin have taught me through example how to live with courage and dignity in a fallen world. My grandmother, for instance, wrote the earlier quoted entry without a hint of self-pity; she was merely stating a reality. Although I was only five, I still vividly remember my dying grandfather's refusal to allow his cancer-ridden body or his doctor's orders to stop him from planting crops he knew he would never see harvested. I remember my aunt taking me aside the day after her first-born son had died in a car wreck, softly but without tears asking if it would be too much of a burden for my brother and me to be pallbearers.

Ron Rash

Much of what I write is an act of homage, a way of remembering my Appalachian kin, but writing about these people and their world is finally more: it is a way to discover who I am.

My Grandmother Speaks of the Early Years

He gave up whiskey and I gave up
believing marriage was anything more
than two people trying to survive.
After one summer's hoeing
my hands were rough as his,
my face burned and cracked.
I quit looking in the mirror.
The bulbs I planted that first fall
never blossomed. Nothing tender grew
on that rocky mountainside.

When our first child died
my heart withered
like a drought-scorched stalk of corn.
I didn't cry the next year
as a hard rain washed
a season's sweat down the valley.
Tears were for folks expecting life to get better.
We did what we could. We got by.

In a Chilren's Graveyard North of Newry

There was no order to their grief.
Like wind-blown seeds these marked stones
bloom in disarray across the field.
Faces forgotten in the great forgetting,
only fading names and dates
remain for strangers to read like braille
in this nursery where
the children are always sleeping.

As I wade through knee-high weeds, my child
wakes. I listen to her short, sharp breaths
and wonder that fierce salt tears
could leave this earth unseared
where fathers come, awake or in dreams,
carrying children in firm, frail arms.

July, 1947

This is what I cannot remember —
a young woman stooped in a field,

the hoe callousing her hands,
the rows stretching out like hours.
And this woman, my mother, rising
to dust rising half a mile
up the road, the car
she has waited days for
realized in the trembling heat.

It will rust until spring, the hoe
dropped at the field's edge.
She is running toward the car,
the sandlapper relatives who spill out
coughing mountain air with lint-filled lungs,
running toward the half-filled grip
she will learn to call a suitcase.

She is dreaming another life,
young enough to believe
it can only be better —
indoor plumbing, eight hour shifts, a man
who waits unknowing for her, a man
who cannot hear through the weave room's
roar the world's soft click,
fate's tumblers falling into place,
soft as the sound of my mother's
bare feet as she runs,
runs toward him, toward me.

A Preacher Who Takes Up Serpents Laments the Presence of Skeptics in His Church

Every Sabbath they come,
gawk like I'm something
in a tent at a county fair.
In the vanity of their unbelief
they will cover an eye with a camera
and believe it will make them see.
They see nothing. I show them Mark: 16
but they believe in the word of man.
They believe death is an end.

And would live like manure maggots,
wallow in the filth of man's creation.
Less than a mile from here
the stench of sulphur rises
like fog off the Pigeon River.
They do not believe it is a sign

of their own wickedness.
They cannot see a river
is a vein in God's arm.

When I open the wire cages
they back away like crayfish
and tell each other I am insane —
terrified I may not be.
Others, my own people, whisper
"He tempts God," and will not join me.
They cannot understand surrender
is humility, not arrogance,
that a man afraid to die cannot live.

Only the serpents sense the truth.
The diamondback's blunted tail is silent,
the moccasin's pearl-white mouth closed.
The coral snake coils around
my wrist, a harmless bright bracelet,
in the presence of the Lord.

Sunday Evening at Middlefork Creek Pentacostal Church

Like poets, they know a fallen world's
words fail a pure vision,
so would wrench from the heart
a new language, and feel
sound pour from their mouths
like a hemorrhage, and fall
white-eyed to the concrete floor,
epileptic in the ecstasy
of the word made flesh.

Having Foreseen the Deaths of Others, the Old Mountain Woman Awaits Her Own

I've felt the bone beneath the flesh,
smelled death's stench on a young man's breath.
Neighbors said it was God's gift
yet shunned my eyes when I walked near.

What power did they think I had?
That I could choose is a lie
my cancered body proves.
What do they know of suffering —

I died with every one of them.
Tonight I die alone.

Six months I've closed my eyes and seen
a black tree branching in my chest.
Limbs sprout through limbs, straighten
my arms. Roots pierce my feet.
I rise outstretched against the sky.

Having Recovered His Sight After Being Struck by Lightning, the Old Farmer Quiets Those Who Would Question Him

Let words die unheard on your tensed tongues.
Drive nails into my ears if you must speak.
A bloody, sighted silence I'd prefer.
I've had enough of words, they always seek
to be more, more than what they are — a heap
of pits and peels. Stir them all you want and find
a man cannot live by words alone.
The blind pass their lives gnawing a bitter rind.

When lightning slapped me hard against the ground
and I smelled my shoe soles burning yards away,
I woke from that darkened other life.
No words came. There was nothing I could say.
I lay hours wide-eyed in a damp, bright field,
knowing what I felt words could only kill.

Raising the Dead

The quick left weeks ago, most voluntarily.
Those who remain are brought up, row by row,
into the fading light
of this November afternoon.
An eviction notice served on the dead
days before the Horsepasture River
is dammed, drowns in itself,
and this valley becomes a lake.

Believers among them knew the time would come
but no trumpets herald this resurrection,
only the curses of weary laborers,
recruits from another county
who take plundered bone and dust
to higher ground.

Nor will souls stay behind
to tangle every fisherman's line
that drifts across this consecrated earth,
to trip skiers who glide over
what was once a sky,
to rise like mist off the lake at midnight,
seep into the suburban sleep
of powerful men
and make them dream of drowning.

But some future fall may find
a man alone on this lake,
no rods or skis, his boat just drifting,
the silence of this place
moving like river current through his heart.

Good Friday, 1995, Driving Westward

This day I feel I live among strangers.
The old blood ties beckon and I drive west
to Buncombe County, a weedy graveyard
where my rare last name crumbles on stone.

All were hardshell Baptists, farmers
who believed the soul is another seed
that endures when flesh and blood are shed,
that all things planted rise toward the sun.

I dream them shaking dirt off strange new forms.
Gathered for the last harvest, they hold hands,
take their first dazed steps toward heaven.

George Scarbrough

I was born in the extreme southwest of Tennessee's extreme southeast county, the mercifully undeveloped backcountry of Polk, and grew up in what I came to term my personal Mesopotamia: a stretch of country lying between the Hiwassee and Ocoee Rivers and west of the mountain range that splits the county in two, from which both rivers flow out onto the lowlands among small hills. I knew the Hiwassee first, as a young child holding my mother's hand and walking weeping across the loose planking of the tall, black iron bridge that spanned the river at Patty, a small whistle-stop on the L & N not far from the newspaper-imprinted walls of the cabin from whose near-windowless, dark interior I first saw the light of day. Walking the groaning timbers, I could see the blue-green water far below and sensed something in the strange shifting element that has always touched my life immensely and intensely, from the cold, clear-running spring at the foot of the great oak to the nights spent on a troopship floundering about in a mid–winter storm in the middle of the North Atlantic.

Water, then, more than mountains, more than the worn-out farms in the county which my family share-cropped for parsimonious landlords, more, even, than books has influenced and shaped my thinking. For I am volatile, too, and always running away. When I sang the hymn in church whose central trope was the river — or water — of life, my mind was not on celestial watersheds but on those rearing ridges to the east from which the bright streams of the county came, well-supplied.

As for being a part of Appalachia, I am, though more ancestrally than personally. My mother, Louise Anabel McDowell, was born in the mountains of western North Carolina and was brought at age two by her parents across the outermost western range into Polk County where my father's family, millwrights, lived along the shores of Chestua Creek. Sixteen years later she would marry William Oscar Scarbrough whose own ancestors had come into what is now Anderson County in 1790 to begin building a line of mills. (The Scarbroughs came from London to Bucks County, Pennsylvania, in 1640, then followed the mountains south as they migrated through West Virginia into the valley where Oak Ridge stands, where I now live.)

So I've had an Appalachian ancestry but have not associated myself especially with a mountain background. The mountains were there, at a distance, lovely in their purple casts but not intriguing: to be entered and come away from on a chestnut-hunt; to be crossed eventually, passed over in two senses; to be viewed from peripheries as essential but unintimate facets of my landscape.

Books, taking me immediately away from locale, influenced me more than terrain, reading having been available to me as long as I can remember. I was born into the alphabet, as it were: though its primary function on those cabin walls was to keep out the wind, I became warm in other ways from headlines that loomed large and gothic black above my bed. My mother's love of reading and her habit of reading aloud engrossed me in the shapes and meanings of words, a temple she lived in which became my one and only house of worship.

Rather than Appalachian, I've always considered myself Southern. From the beginning, my daily intake was Southern history from my history-loving mother whose name was famous not only for its Civil War generals — one on each side — but also for McDowell County, North Carolina, whence came the aggravating McDowell Gang, guerillas who helped themselves to whatever was available from the stores of both parties in the conflict. As a Southerner — and as a "hillbilly," I suppose — I've always heartily despised those who held us in contempt down here, south of the Mason-Dixon. Certainly we were isolated, land-locked, language-locked — and willingly left so by outsiders for a good while. But some of us were learning to read, to find in words the key that enabled us to go beyond pre-set limitations.

As a sharecropper's son, I had a chip on my shoulder which grew to chop block size under the scorn of many men on the Sewanee campus in the early forties. I was a fellowship student at the University of the South and referred to then as a covite. But they did not, to paraphrase William Gass, cut my tongue out, as he says America has done to most of its poor. I won't be allowed, again in Gass' words, a language as "lousy as their lives," meaning the isolated and deprived. From infancy I wanted more than that. The sunflower told me a story about that as did the wandering cosmos, that startling starry flower which strewed its pink and white flowers over an ancient earthen dairy on one of the many farms we were always in transit to or from.

As far as being recognized by outsiders, I've been published in such magazines as *The Atlantic, Harper's, The New Republic, Saturday Review of Literature, The Sewanee Review, Poetry,* and nearly a hundred others. I've published three volumes of poetry by E.P. Dutton, one by Iris Press (Binghamton, New York), and the latest, *Invitation to Kim,* by Iris Press of Memphis which, I hear from the publisher, has been nominated for a Pulitzer Prize. My novel, *A Summer Ago,* was published in 1986 by St. Luke's Press, Memphis. Several grants from the Carnegie Fund, the Authors' League, and P.E.N. American and a few poetry prizes, notably from *The Sewanee Review,* complete the account — for all that any part of it may be worth.

George Scarbrough

Tenantry

Always in transit
we were always temporarily
in exile,
each new place seeming
after awhile
and for awhile
our home.

Because no matter
how far we traveled
on the edge of strangeness
in a small county,
the earth ran before us
down red clay roads
blurred with summer dust,
banked with winter mud.
It was the measurable
pleasurable earth
that was home.
Nobody who loved it
could ever be really alien.
Its tough clay, deep loam,
hill rocks, small flowers
were always the signs
of a home-coming.

We wound down through them
to them,
and the house we came to,
whispering with dead hollyhocks
or once in spring
sill-high in daisies,
was unimportant.
Wherever it stood,
it stood in earth,
and the earth welcomed us,
open, gateless,
one place as another.

And each place seemed
after awhile
and for awhile
our home:
because the county
was only a mansion
kind of dwelling
in which there were many

rooms.
We only moved from one
room to another,
getting acquainted
with the whole house.

And always the earth
was the new floor under us,
the blue pinewoods the walls
rising around us,
the windows the openings
in the blue trees
through which we glimpsed,
always farther on,
sometimes beyond the river,
the real wall of the mountain,

in whose shadow
for a little while
we assumed ourselves safe,
secure and comfortable
as happy animals
in an unvisited lair:

which is why perhaps
no house we ever lived in
stood behind a fence,
no door we ever opened
had a key.

It was beautiful like that.
For a little while.

Winter Bread

In my mother's kitchen
The meal bin
Was a fine oak barrel
With stout staves and
Scrubbed brass bindings,

By all odds the best
Furniture in the house
In its corner
At the head
Of the long table.

My mother dipped
Her head in, dipping,
Straightening
With a scoop
Flaked and spilling

Back rough bran
That smelled of old
Whiskey and popped corn.
Fruit-jar bouquet.
I begged permission

To dip my head in,
And she allowing,
Came up ineluctably
Drunk with
The yeasty atmosphere.

How bright the hoops,
Evenly stacked on darkness,
Shone in the half-
Light from the stove.
I could hear,

Outside,
The wolf-wind
In the valley.
It was December.
It is again December.

The wolf-wind howls
In the valley. This
Is a comfortable house,
With certain not-
Plain appointments,

(Among the best
Of furniture there is
No best furniture),
But there is nothing
I would not forego

To lift again
The lid of the meal
Barrel in my mother's
Kitchen for one deep
Unreconstructable

Breath
Of winter bread.

Hiwassee River

    Down there is the river
fresh from the mountain notch,
touched with sulphates from
    the copper veins

    in the higher peaks:
shallow, it runs clear: deep
a blue tinge assesses the truth
    of its origin:

    let us go down to
the blue river where it enters
the savannah and green corn grows
    for miles along

    flat river bottoms
kept from the river by a hem
of bright green willows:
    let us go down:

    the afternoon's gold
light enters the green, is yellow
above the river's bright blue:
    it is time to go:

    later, we'll seek
the shallows where spun water
runs and trout swim upstream
    in the cold rushes,

    pausing along in the sunshot
eddies over the polished stones, their
stipples red and gold under
    rockbrown shoulders:

    we'll take the cow-
path down to the water, follow
the wide laterals cut to fit
    the winding sidehill:

    we'll move slowly
like the gold Jerseys: there is
no hurry there in the water
    where it idles before

    plunging to deep blue
and the cows drink amiably
at the clean rock edges:
    their stances are calm:

let us go now:
while the vessel of willows
holds the young water contained
 as in a worked wicker:

nothing can change:
the afternoon lingers like a warm
hand in the grasp of the current:
 the corn will not

be drowned, the cornland
will run down to the sunset hill
in slow, drilled hours: *next year*
 the dam will be built.

Bettie Sellers

Although I have always claimed Georgia as my home state, I was born in Tampa, Florida, where my young father had gone to make his fortune. The combination of the Great Depression and a hurricane persuaded him and my mother to come home to Georgia when I was but a few months old. Four siblings and I, then, grew up on a 58-acre farm outside Griffin, a small town about forty miles south of Atlanta.

My father's people had come over from England in 1640 and over the years had migrated from Virginia to North Carolina, my great-grandfather having arrived in Oxford, Georgia, in 1837. He was a builder and furniture maker there. His children spread across the state, and my father was raised in the rural community of Rico, west of Atlanta. All of these forbears were some wonderful combination of farmers, teachers, and preachers—a situation which continues into my generation since my sister and I teach, Brother Bill farms, and Brother Ed preaches (the only one who has migrated to the North, near Chicago).

When I came to live at Young Harris, in the mountains of northern Georgia, I felt as though I were coming home to a place I had never been. My maternal great-grandparents brought this about. Great-grandfather Seale was a circuit-riding Methodist preacher in these hills and had some connection with establishing the mountain mission school that has since become Young Harris College where I now teach English. When I was a little girl, my grandmother used to tell me wonderful stories of when she was one of the first students to come to Young Harris in 1889, of the adventures they had at the little mountain school. In those days, I had no reason to know that one day, I would be led here by a husband who had come to love the school from his own student days. Twenty-five years later I feel as though I have never lived anywhere else.

That same story-telling grandmother may have been responsible for my being a writer. When she died, I wanted to write her stories down so they wouldn't be lost to my children and their children. It was a small step then to deciding to write my own stories, to find my own voice.

I based my poetic theory on a line I found somewhere in Faulkner's memoirs: "Beginning with *Sartoris*," he wrote, "I recognized that my own little postage stamp of earth was worth writing about." There was my license to write! And over the years, I have told my stories, from the Shoal Creek farm where I grew up through the Depression as well as from the mountain top where I have watched the seasons turn for twenty-five years. I am at home here as nowhere else.

I am a fortunate woman to have found a vocation that is such a joy to me as teaching is and more than blessed that my writing fits into my working life as hand does in soft glove.

I'm as proud of both careers as I am of my three children and five lively grandchildren. Over the years there have been prizes both for poems and books of poems (*Spring Onions and Cornbread, Morning of the Red-Tailed Hawk, Liza's Monday and Other Poems*); a Georgia Emmy and other awards for a documentary film on the life and works of North Georgia poet/novelist Byron Herbert Reece (1917–1958); and the 1987 Govenor's Medal for the Humanities for my work in the preservation of Georgia's unique cultural heritage. This award reflects my interest in and concern for the career of Byron Herbert Reece over a period of almost twenty years.

My chief concern for the Appalachian landscape is that the largely unspoiled beauty of the mountains appears to be disappearing rapidly. The intrusion of many roads and houses is both thoughtless and destructive. Attempts to pass a ridge law have thus far failed in the Georgia state legislature. I keep hoping this will change in order to protect what is left. My people have lived on and loved this Georgia land, and I would protect it for my grandchildren if I could. They are the thirteenth generation to live in this great country of ours. I would hope there would be many more.

Bettie Sellers (Heirloom Images)

And All the Princes Are Gone

She sits beside the oak fire, Lilah, pale,
intent on nothing here where mountains circle
Brasstown tight as walls around a medieval
castle formed. She holds the book, its cover
gone, its pages tissue thin with fingering.
She peers through smoke to where the men,
their coats brocaded, satin tight around
their thighs, bow to ladies in a banquet
hall. Soft music sounds around the spitting
of the logs that Samuel dragged from Double
Knob behind his lumbering ox, a mild and
placid beast who chews his hay as though
in contemplation of the history of his kind.
She sees the ox, a Yule log chained behind,
crossing the drawbridge to a castle court,
and servants hanging holly boughs to grace
stone walls, and torches shadowing a feast.

Her cabin is not here, nor Samuel's supper
simmering on the hook above the fire. Dark
comes, and Lilah watches dancing figures spin,
a pleasant dream to warm this wilderness where
life is hard, and all the princes are gone.

Naomi's Nerve

Naomi Davis died this morning, did ya hear?
Now, there was a woman with nerve! Some past
ninety she was, and it forty years since she fought
the wolves all night. I remember hearing how she
throwed rocks to keep 'em off her calves over
by Lick Log Creek. Ain't been no wolves around
here in many a year, but I heard tell of times
when they run in packs all through these hills —
stole stock and younguns too, if'n they was left
alone too long. Usta be powerful bad over to
Lick Log, drawed by all that Davis stock, I
rightly suspicion. And no man on the place the night
Naomi fought! Them Davis men was bad to wander —
allus flitting off over the Gap for some cause
or nother, they was. Naomi never said a word,
though; all them Davises has some pride to burn,
would of let them wolves tear their throat afore
they'd speak any word to let the family down.
I don't doubt none they'll bury Naomi proud.

Pink

Her Mama called her "Pink" when she was born,
to match a tiny flower pressed in Exodus —
from Charlestown gardens, its like not found
among the blossoms wild in Brasstown soil.

She called the two boys "Flotsam" and "Jetsam,"
having heard such words ring somewhere
with all the strength of heroes: Samson, Saul —
though never could she find them in The Book

no matter if she searched to Revelation's end.
The last child Mama named "Rebecca" to be sure,
make up for giving wrong names to the boys —
and those now stuck too tight to budge.

Then Mama died, not knowing just how right
she'd called her boys, hell-bent to leave the plow

and hoe for parts out West where gold grew common
as the stones they cursed in winding valley rows.

In time, their faces faded as Pink brushed
Rebecca's long red hair, the color of her own.
She washed and cooked, up on a wooden stool
that Papa made so she could reach the tubs and stove.

She stitched the gown for Rebecca's wedding day,
embroidered it with pinks and ragged robins
around the neck and sleeves. In other springs,
she knitted caps for babies never hers.

She did for Papa till his days were through
and kept the cabin neat as Mama ever could.
Alone, she withered slowly, frail and dry
as petals caught and pressed by Exodus.

Miracle at Raven Gap

"If I could have a mess of greens
just once before I die."
Old Mary Dean lies pale and thin,
her kinfolk standing by.

"I've got a patch of turnips, Min,
don't guess they'll hurt her none.
I'll fry a pone of cornbread too,
be back here when the sun

sets down in Raven Gap." So Nell
went home and fixed a plate
for Mary Dean's last dying wish —
and with a will she ate.

Next morning, Nell thought ghosts could walk.
She started, gave her head a scratch
when out her window saw at dawn
Old Mary digging in her turnip patch.

Liza's Monday

She has left her tubs and boiling sheets, fled
north across the woodlot, heard no grumble
from the pigs as she passed, the chicken shed
where eggs wait to be gathered, felt

no pain as December's harsh wind dried
lye soap on her arms, reddened hands held

stiff by her sides, palms forward as to catch
the gusts that sweep the slopes of Double Knob.

Inside the cabin: Ethan's shirt to patch,
the fire to mend, small Issac sleeping
in his crib, soon to wake for nursing.
These and other chores are in her keeping,

but she hurries up the mountainside
as on an April day to search for mint
and cress, to find first violets that hide
in white and purple patches by Corn Creek.

The ridge is steep and rocky, sharp with briars.
Raked inside by gales howling bleak
as northern winds around the cabin whine,
she does not feel the laurel tug her dress,

the briars pricking dark red beads that shine
on bare arms. All winter afternoon she climbs
until she gains the highest rocks, the knobs
where one can look out, trace the spines

of distant mountains, scan the valley floor —
black dots for shed and cabin, smoke only wisps
blown by the wind. Liza sees no more:
not broken stones underfoot, not heavy sky

holding snow. She sits on Double Knob, back
against the ledge, and watches night come by
to close the valley, wipe her clearing out
as though it has never been. Snow clouds

roil around Liza's head, wrap cold arms about
bent shoulders, fill her aproned lap, open hands.
Below, the wash-fire has burned down to embers;
Ethan long begun the search across his lands.

Vivian Shipley

I was born in Chicago, Illinois, in 1943 but returned within a year to Kentucky with my parents where both my mother's and father's families have lived on farms for several generations. I was raised and went to high school in a small town. During the summers I stayed with my grandparents on their farms. The Todds on my mother's side had a small farm where there was very little to do. There was no indoor plumbing, so pulling up water from the well was one of my major chores. There was electricity, but the stove for cooking and the stove for heating were fueled by wood. When I was there, I was responsible for carrying wood, work which truly gave me a direct relationship to eating and keeping warm. Preparation of food was very time-consuming because everything was made from scratch. Also Grandma Todd canned all of her food, including pork.

In the summer we fished, killed chickens, and caught frogs to eat. Gigging frogs at the pond was a major attraction for me. Going to the little store down the road, swinging on the front porch while watching cars pass by, and going to church were my only diversions from work here. My greatest anxiety was provided by trips to the outhouse which was at some distance from the house. Snakes were always a threat, and once in an inopportune moment a chicken bit me. I always checked for chickens in the outhouse from then on.

After Grandma Todd died in her sleep at eighty-five, Grandpa Todd sold the farm. The day after the papers were signed, a tornado ripped down the house, barn, and shed. Now a modern ranch sits on the place where I rocked, and I can't recognize anything. A big old cherry chest survived the tornado, and it is the only thing I own that is left of their lives.

Visiting the Shipley farm at some distance outside of Cecelia was an easier and more exciting experience. There was indoor plumbing, an electric stove, and coal-burning stoves for heat. My only real responsibilities here were bringing up food from the cellar house and weeding the garden. At times, Grandpa Shipley would make me help sucker tobacco. Since I was afraid of worms and snakes, all of these jobs held considerable fear for me. However, going down into the cellar house was the worst because the stairs were falling apart.

My Grandma Shipley, Minnie Tabor, had a reputation for miles around for her cooking, in particular her jam cake. Grandpa Shipley was also known for his ability to cure ham. The first thing I always wanted when I visited was fried country ham and jam cake. Grandma Shipley also had a reputation for fried chicken. The ritual of chopping off the chicken's head and watching it run around the yard until it dropped has never left me. An unconscious relationship between eating meat and killing was a daily part of living on the farm — the ham from hogs Grandpa Shipley raised to be killed and the chicken from pets I made when I gathered eggs.

Vivian Shipley

Socially, life was more exciting on the Shipley farm with trips into Elizabethtown every Saturday and several little stores near the farm where the men always gathered to tell stories. Since both families lived near each other, there were always gatherings of cousins, aunts, and uncles. It seemed as though I was related in one way or another to just about everybody I met. Church, although a weekly ritual, did not dominate the Shipley's social life, but there was always a big outdoor picnic in the front yard on Sunday afternoon with each relative bringing the food for which he or she was most famous. This farm, the location of many family memories, has since been sold. The picture on my most recent book, *Poems Out of Harlan County*, was taken of the back door of my great-grandparents' house which is still standing. Change, however, is apparent because in front there is a house trailer and a high chain link fence.

After graduation from high school, I went to the University of Kentucky in Lexington. My most notable achievement there was being the only homecoming queen who was never crowned. I was elected and stood in the middle of the football stadium in front of thousands of people while the runner-up was given the roses, crown, and trophy. The mistake was corrected on the sidelines as other mistakes made later in life could not be. After graduating in 1964, I married and came to New Haven, Connecticut, where my husband was enrolled in medical school and where I taught seventh- and eighth-grade English for three years. When my husband decided to go to Vanderbilt University for his internship, I applied to and was accepted into the Ph.D. program in English. When my husband came back to Yale in New Haven, I came too, and got a job at Southern Connecticut State University in 1969 where I have been teaching ever since. During that time I have had three sons, divorced their father, and married Ed Harris. Ed, our three sons, and various animals live in North Haven, Connecticut, where the only farming I do now is to grow perennial flowers.

When not teaching, mothering, or gardening, I write poetry, something I started to do in 1974 after having a large brain tumor removed. The tumor was discovered in conjunction with the birth of my second son, Todd, which required an operation the doctors thought I could not live through. I suppose I started writing poetry because the near-death experience taught me there were words I wanted to say, a heritage I wanted to celebrate, and names, places, and activities which were part of the everyday life on farms in Kentucky that I wanted to preserve. Voices, unless they are written down or recorded, are lost.

Worms

Hands dried to apple skin
twitch as horse tails

do at flies. Plucking
at covers, you
remind me of Daddy
picking worms off tobacco
already suckered. Always
I was scared
to curl them in my palm.
Even tomato worms
smaller and greener
made me shrink back.
You laughed at me,
old woman. Now
you know fear of worms.

Horse Breath Winter

I won't look like you, old
black walnut. Thick
shelled, shrunken meat, you
will be too small under ground.
Cake flour clung to your face
like snow shrouding chopped
wood as you leaned on the door
frame holding the brown
sugar frosting while we danced
the parlor where you laid grandpa.

You're not even a ghost
now, just a victim
of decrease unable to swing
my grief like a child
between us. I rub
lotion to soften your skin,
transparent waxed paper
pressing a veined leaf but
white will not sink, films
knotted hands. Pulling away,
I remember rocks rising to surface
in the bed of a drying creek.

White Chickens

The idea of a strait jacket
has come into my head. Flat,
folded together, sleeves open
to reach like white chicken

wings flapping the backyard
my father fenced. He remembered
farm chickens that ran, roosted
in a barn and laid eggs in hay.
Bred for slaughter, crowded together
after hatching, those fryers
never walked but each morning
before his coffee, my father
positioned them, statues on
our grass. Cooped too long, muscle
would never again be regained.

Tethered to those chickens
even as their meat withered,
it could have been so easy
to wring their necks.
Was it boyhood need for chase
that left him unable to kill?
Or perhaps my father imagined, even
expected, the chickens to rise
resurrected, to rush the yard,
plastering grass with their blood.

Outside Cecelia, Kentucky

Born at the head of Rough Creek,
in half-dovetailed logs daubed with mud,
she claimed the one window
to watch two woodpeckers clash
for a nesting cavity in dead oak,
one golden shafted flicker,
the other she couldn't name, blue-black
and white with a ruby velvet head.
Mother chased out dirt in that house.
The odds were against her.
I counted white-eyed vireo,
grosbeak colored the lapis lazuli
I dreamed while reading
Browning's bishop order his tomb.
I would not marry back to naked barnyard.

Building castles in damp yellow sand,
my foot shaped a shed that did not fall.
Ocean was in early morning fog
resting heavy on ridges in Harlan County
and the frost, ribbed
on the leaf of blackberry bush.

Ignoring the log, hanging to rope
over holes, I ran right across
missing boards in the swinging bridge,
fearing the fall in the creek
full of crawdads,
hornyheads and jackfish.

I cannot string boards together,
bruise myself a crossing
for the quiet smell of ashes
or a drink, my hands cupped,
from the clear cold spring
where water began
its long journey. No escape
from its banks when traps
closed, many a muskrat had
gnawn away a leg
for the creek to swallow.

Nancy Simpson

I believe the mountains are my natural home on Earth although I was born in Miami, Florida. My parents, both sets of grandparents, and literally all my kin were born and raised in Atlanta, Georgia. I lived in Atlanta most of the first five years of my life, but more than once my parents felt the tug of the great Atlantic Ocean and moved back and forth from Atlanta to Miami during the time Miami was a boom town. Finally, as the story goes, my mother got sand in her shoes and did not want to live in Georgia any longer. I began first grade and stayed in Miami during my school years, graduating from Miami Jackson Senior High in 1956. Miami was a beautiful, sophisticated, and exotic city. I am certain now that I am wiser for the experience of growing up there, but at the time I felt I was living in exile and brooded continually for my "lost home" and my Georgia cousins.

I came to Western North Carolina with my husband and sons in 1960, part of the "back to the land movement." It was the happiest time of my life. I felt I had found my home. We bought wilderness land on Cherry Mountain near Hayesville and by the spring of 1969 were living year round on the mountain in a small cabin we built. In time they all left, and only I stayed. I learned abruptly why "life begins at forty"—because it ends at thirty-nine. Life ended for me at thirty-nine. At the very least, nothing familiar remained. I was no longer a wife, no longer a mother. I had to start over, and it seemed all I had to help me start my new life was an undeveloped mountain.

I earned a B.S. in Education at Western Carolina University and began pouring out my grief in poems. Writing saved me. I became a teacher at the local mountain school, and I kept writing. I studied poetry in writing workshops at Callanwolde Fine Arts Center in Atlanta with any master poet who would give me time—Richard Hugo, James Seay, Philip Levine, and Donald Justice. Twice I was awarded the Callanwolde Poetry Award, and that early recognition kept me on task. I wrote daily. For a period of two years, I met one evening a week with a small group of professional writers affiliated with Young Harris College in a small mountain town just across the state line in Georgia. Steve Harvey, the workshop leader, was my first formal poetry instructor and my true mentor. Others in the group who encouraged me were Janice Moore, Bettie Sellers, and Blanche Farley. Across the mountains in the other direction was Kathryn Stripling Byer, a fellow poet who was most generous and supportive. She invited me to read at Western Carolina University Mountain Heritage Day and even wrote critical essays about my poems.

For a couple of years I worked in solitude and brought my first collection of poems near completion. My poems were being published in such magazines as *The Georgia Review, Southern Poetry Review, Indiana Review, Florida Review,* and other literary magazines. Some were

Nancy Simpson

printed in *The Anthology of Magazine Verse & Yearbook of American Poetry*, and I was awarded the Florida Fine Arts Festival Poetry Award judged by William Stafford.

But I was not satisfied. I wanted to know about the writing process. At that exact time the then famous Goddard Writing Program folded its operation in Vermont, and the original founders came south searching for a new home for their unique program. It is still a miracle to me that they decided to reopen their program at Warren Wilson College in the Southern Appalachian Mountains, a short drive from my home. I entered their first class in the summer of 1981, and in 1983, shortly after my chapbook *Across Water* was published by State Street Press, I earned my MFA in Writing. *Night Student*, a full-length collection, was published in 1985.

Presently I continue to teach English and Language Arts to normal, exceptional, and gifted students. I also teach creative writing workshops occasionally and English Composition at least one evening a week at the local community college. Writing is a daily part of my life. Recently some of my poems were included in a special southern edition of *New Virginia Review* edited by Dave Smith, and others were included in a special southern issue of *Confrontation* (Long Island University) edited by Martin Tucker. New poems are forthcoming in *Georgia Journal, Lullwater Review* (Emory University), and *The State Street Reader.*

I have come to believe that poetry is a way of thinking—a way of knowing how to live and how to die. Nature informs me whether I am at the ocean or on a mountain. At times my poems superimpose topography of ocean and mountain simultaneously. "The Girl with the Black Innertube," an early poem, surprised me for it revealed to me this mixed, inner landscape. It shocked me into knowing I can defy the dimensions of time and space and at the same time remain sane and sure-footed in the physical world. In time I came to understand the phrase "there is no home" to mean that one carries around an inner haven of sorts that consists of all the places he or she has ever been. This means I have dinosaur bones in me that I found once on a mountain in Utah. I have a Georgia cornfield, a hurricane, Ten-Thousand-Islands, and a Winter Park. But the imagery of the southern mountains seems to be the most prominent in my poems. Clearly, I am captivated; in fact, I did not write before I came to live in the mountains.

Night Student

It is the first shooting star my eyes have seen
breaking blackness above the university parking lot.
I am impressed with Jones,
the spectacular mark he made on my paper.
I have it beside me two hours from home.

Truth is up there over the steering wheel,
keeping up, 60 mph on Franklin-By-Pass.
Socrates said so. I would like to ask
the Know-It-All what makes stars break.

I drive slow on Standing Indian Mountain
and count the times Jones asked in class,
Is it logically consistent? Ten.
On the radio, static reception,
Linda Ronstadt is singing about a broken lady
waiting to be mended.

I see my face in the rear view mirror,
not a wife anymore, not a mother,
a thirty-eight-year-old freshman
chewing left over cheese crackers
that crumble on my fingers, star showers
into the floorboard.

What was it I saw up there, white against black,
like white hairs in brunette,
like the white line on pavement?

What is it as two minutes past twelve,
this funnel cloud in me, this song of Forsythia
makes me stop my car at Shooting Creek
to search in space above trees
where headlights do not reach?

Star, one cut with your sword,
you have sliced the night open for me.

Crowded House

The young in me are leaving,
a whimper, a tear drifting off
so I assume they take their wounds.
God knows I have taught them and taught them.
I put down my switch to count
which ones are left. Thank goodness.

The busy girl is gone, tied up in traction,
a bad back and a hateful disposition.

She never minded a word. Stand, I said
but she slumped.

The believer is here part time, a student
inquiring into books stacked to high-heaven,
The Apology, Crito, Phaedo. She thinks
truth was written long ago.

The one who loves men left and came home
married and pregnant. Now I am mother-in-law,
and grandmother to her noisy daughter.

As for the peacemaker, she is going off to war
and has forgotten how our feet pounded the pavement,
how many marches it took to end just one war.

The intuitive one walks on the mountain.
I know how she dreams to get free.
She brings phosphorous and a creekstone,
a salamander crawling in the palm of her hand.
She wants me to like her, and I like her, that one,
keeper of the crowded house.

White Lie

End of May, and we have nothing
better to do than walk on the mountain,
our cardigans closed against the cold.
You cannot take back one lie,
not even white ones, subtle

as berry blossoms beside this path.
I kick a stone and tell you I believe
we will pull free from the brambles.
Old timers call this Blackberry Winter,
a temporary cold spell, quick to pass.

Lives in One Lifetime

Sometimes you get what you asked for,
to be left alone. All day
not once the sound of a motor,
one sailboat only with a yellow flag waving.

From this shore I see where sky begins,
blue between oaks on top of the ridge.
Across Chatuge, the lake made by man,
a whole mountain rises out of the water.

I have no boat and no way to cross over
this flooded valley except to walk.
Where the road was, my feet can touch asphalt
if I let myself sink.
                              Here the house stood.
There is the roof of the barn, buried forty years.
Yes, I am sinking in doubt.
Rubble from lives in one lifetime passes before me.
This is the end, the new start,

rock I remember, and clay soft beneath my feet.
An old logging road leads me up the mountain
where trees stand apart,
where sky begins.

The Wreck

Witnesses saw it all, heard the crash
the speeding blue Camaro stopped dead
at Pinelog Bridge. Sam Beck insists
he saw a man fly through the windshield,
careening through air, velocity 100 mph,
maybe more. Searchers dragged the river,
trudged bottomland three days, hunting.
We all stop sooner or later
but something in me wants to know
why they never found him, where he went.
Something in me moving fast
wants to fly out through my eyes
like the body thrown free of the wreck.

Leaving in the Dead of Winter

Ghosts push up through soil, pale mushrooms
and Indian Pipe clusters, the little saints.
Let the land moulder, October, November.
Oaks look finished but they will come back.

Some pretend to be dead and lie morbid
on the ground. Saplings rise from the rot.
At night phosphorus glows
in the heart of the oldest stump.

It is natural to live with decay,
to notice the life of a tree and say we die
many times, mutable, all of us.
Still, one must learn how to act,

when to come, when to go.
Here is a scene. In wintertime
a woman packs to go someplace.
Torn photographs fall to the floor. She sees

herself, and the one man she loved, young.
He looks dependable. Now she smashes a red
crystal bowl, and wants to cut everything.
Wait. This is not the end.

The woman drives away fast.
Or take it from this point of view —
leaving Cherry Mountain in the dead of winter,
you look up and see a backbone sticking out,

huge curve of the ridgeline
shaped like a great whale beached and dying.
The ground has already stiffened.
No one can live this close to death.

Bridge on the River Kwai

All those times, all those bridges,
Georgia to Forida, sand
in his shoes, red clay in his pocket,
I wonder what passed through my father's mind.

He never said much about hurricanes
or corn, except that you pull it not pick it.
One summer in Georgia I promised to pull
all the corn in ten acres he planted.

Indolent girl, red clay in my pocket,
I remember a movie in East Atlanta.
Prisoners built a bridge across water,
building, building, the whole movie.

I was too young to know why
they blew it all to pieces in the end.
This morning a half drowned woman wakes me.
I open the window. She has come many miles

across water. Her memories are mine.
She gives me one starfish, one mango
and reminds me how I climbed the tree
when the flood came, after the hurricane.

I give her anemone for starfish.
I give her a mountain, the safest place to be.

R.T. Smith

If demography is one of the unholy arts, it is still perhaps a necessary one, so I'm willing to submit myself to it. In fact, I rankle less under the auspices of "Appalachian poet" than under "Southern poet," probably because most people already have some limiting idea of what the latter might be. But about the only thing that can be said of the former is that it applies to people who have some strong connection to that dragon-tail-shaped earthmass that passes for mountains east of the Mississippi. Although I often assail my writing students at Auburn University with questions about when the tobacco is cut, how indigo is grown, what "Seminole" means, and what is it we call a red-crested finch (all relevant to their South), I'm of half a mind that writers don't come from anywhere in the same sense that other people do, that they create themselves as they make their artistic choices and strive to build the poems they most need to read, bridges to the places where they want to go.

In this light, I should say that I was born in the District of Columbia, that I have a mother and a father and a sister, and that I'm less likely to write about literal memories of them than to splice them with anyone else unlucky enough to cross the path of my imagination, all to the end of discovering what I don't already know. I was raised in North Carolina and rural Georgia and seem to have hung around the summits of the Blue Ridge since I was old enough to hear about them. The literal truth is that I first became a writer while in graduate school at Appalachian State University. I lived in Boone for three years and in Spruce Pine for the richer part of two, and what I learned there travels well: a bit of clogging goes a long way in a Galway pub; slope terracing for corn works in Mexico; herb cures are not far from Jamaican bush medicine; and an attention to words as spiritual entities will float on any water.

When I look at my poems chosen for this anthology, I see that my Native American roots and interests are obvious, as are my rural ones and my obsession with the mysteries of trees and birds. Different kinds of making also riddle these pieces, and I guess that suits, as I'm always aware of my surname's origin and meaning. I've never been bothered by the knowledge that a smith's making involves extreme heat and force and that it happens in a place called a forge.

On a first visit to my home, a friend once said it appeared to be the nest of some sort of archaeologist. She was right. The physical objects — Civil War Springfield, Lakota hatchet pipe, Acoma Pueblo vase, Andean pan pipes, a Celtic bodhrán, slat pew from the old Bandana Baptist Church — all preserve the stories of people who are not quite my people. They provide access to someone else's bloodroot, but they are also reminders of my own search, a sifting through of memories and dreams for artifacts that will help me understand the experience of the quite small tribe that I represent. The same friend also noted the sparse population of my poems and, I suspect, wondered if my habits of mind don't incline to solipsism. I hope that's less true, for I always feel the presence of others in the shadows of the ridges and the echoes of the crows and in the silences behind words. I like to think my explorations are kin to those of any pilgrim.

Joan Didion once wrote that a place belongs to whoever loves it most strongly and possesses it most fiercely. I think the Appalachians are mine for reasons stronger than geography and topography, stronger than citizenship or habit, for they possess me. I hear the sound of the rivers and see the twilight mists rising in my dreams, and I never wake from them without wondering how I can maneuver myself back there. I don't think I could stop returning in body or thought if I wished to, and when consideration of this mountain obsession comes over me, I agree with W.S. Merwin that "...it seems probably/Sometimes that the slope, to be so elusive/And yet so inescapable, must be nothing/But ourselves." It would be lovely to think so, even if only as metaphor, even if in the service of some unholy art, which by now begins to sound like a contradiction anyway, if it comes round in the end to the mountains.

R.T. Smith

The Call

Calling the distant owl
who is greedy with the season,
I recall grandfather's voice
becoming the voice of the owl
to mate with some wild thing
cautious on the edge of the forest.
In this time of brown red leaves,
blood turning silently in my heart,
I crouch in the fog's blue shroud,
try to find the screech owl's tones
deep in my throat and legacy
where they have slept unfed
for more than a dozen years.
Through the cave of my hands,
the thicket of fingers meshing,
I hoot twice the old way and wait.

An answer forms on air, westward;
a time-streaked face rises,
resembles me, smiles wide and flies.
Strong wings beat the night.
It takes my breath away.

The Bird Carver

All winter I perch on my bench
and draw the Buck knife blade
through pine, ironwood and birch.

My steel is the shape of a feather,
and from it fly merganser, heron,
mallard and gallinule, sliver by sliver.

An ash slab's texture counterfeits thermals,
a solstice wind swirling as primaries
emerge, and a beak of heartwood and knurl

extends to test weather. My fingers
trace the deft scapular lines,
sleek edges, articulation of crest, spur

and eye. I work while the cold light
nurtures my craft or until dulled
steel needs the grindstone's bite.

In the hearth, flame's bright plumage
rises, a thicket of frail reeds,
a nest. My eyes linger there, and forage.

Out the window, then, I watch the thin
gray woodgrain of sky, the late sun
a knot from which all sap unfurls. Again

I rub my fingers, touch healed cuts,
the fresh nicks on my skin's whorls.
As the metal's temper whets on grit,

I listen; it whispers of wings, a throng
of nomad harlequins returning. My blade's
rasp, inspired, imitates their song:

simplicity, the grace of handmade things,
things that last and belong.

After an Image in Faulkner

The rusted chain once wrapped
about the limb of a catalpa tree,

now ingrown as fate,
has held the heels
of a hundred hogs,
throats slit in first frost,
blood spilling in a tin bucket.
I can see granddad
aproned, wearing a felt hat,
the knife red
and silver in his hand,
just past dawn when
the chosen shoat hung
perpendicular, as if running
after his last blood toward
the earth's secret center,
slightly spinning,
the tallow-colored carcass,
clapper of an unseen,
unforgettable bell.

Yonosa House

She stroked molten tones
from the heart-carved maple dulcimer.
My grandma did.
She sat like a noble sack of bones
withered within coarse skin,
rocking to snake or corn tunes,
music of passing seasons.
She sang the old songs.

Her old woman's Tuscarora uncut hair
hung like waxed flax ready to spin
till she wove it to night braids,
and two tight-knotted ropes
lay like lanyards on her shoulders.
On my young mind she wove
the myths of the race
in fevered patterns, feathery colors:
Sound of snow, kiss of rock,
the feel of bruised birch bark,
the call of the circling hawk.

Her knotted hands showing slow blue rivers
jerked nervously through cornbread frying,
pressed fern patterns on butter pats,
brewed sassafras tea on the hearth.
She wore her lore and old age home.

They buried Yonosa in a doeskin skirt,
beads and braids, but featherless,
like a small bird with clipped wings.
I cut hearts on her coffin lid,
wind-slain maple like the dulcimer.
The mountain was holy enough for Yonosa.
We kept our promise and raised no stone.
She sank like a root to be red Georgia clay.
No Baptist churchyard caught her bones.

I thank her hands when the maple leaves turn,
hear her chants in the thrush's song.

Weave

Indian women once believed
that to appease the evil spirits
they should burn the first piece
woven on a new frame loom.
Tonight's moon washing through
your bedroom window falls
across the handmade floor loom
you have spent a year constructing.
The white warp strands tremble
to feel such pure light's touch.
The dark weft dovetails
across the idle web as I move
my hand along your ribs
and feel the pale pine of heddles,
breast bar, knee bar, treadle.
You dream of magical fabrics:
the winter hunt, a burning river,
red berries spilled on snowdrifts.
In your breathing I feel patterns
your heart creates from the cloth
of sleep. Indian women dance
intricate patterns for a burning.
Your breath entwines with miles
of taut and legendary thread.
The moon's lost fibers knot.
Your touch becomes the tribe.

Beneath the Mound

Deer, lightning, bluebird, toad —
someone has drawn figures

on the small walls of my chamber,
this hollow under a hill.
I can hear the thirsty roots stretching.
I can feel the damp soil settling.
I sleep uneasily and long to be whole.

Most of my weapons, masks and tools
are dust. Most of my vessels
are broken, returned to their source.
The cloth that once wrapped me
has lost all holding power.
My bones are strewn out
and cannot be healed.
Dark stones in a pattern
are the only stars I behold.

Who remembers that night,
that fire, the weeping women
and a procession, slaves hauling
earth to build this mound?
Who recalls the sacred chants?
Who can dance the steps of death?
Who knows the dialect
and stories that named my tribe?

If I could weave my spirit to memory,
my memory to ligament and muscle,
I could gather these fragments,
scattered and anxious to be found.
If I could recover the taste
of the black yaupon drink or skills
that kept my hunting silent,
I could refledge this dusty flesh.
I could quench this urge to move.

But history holds me in its grip,
an owl with his captive rat
moving deeper into night,
a rock preventing the spring's water
from surfacing under the moon.
If I could get this cracked jaw to move,
I could rise to summon the rain.
If I could see the sky at all,
I would catch the bluebird by his wing.
If I could speak,
I could sing.

Hill Woman

(for Hilda)

There are always women and women, but they can't
all bury you. Only one.

I see you as a quiet child picking
red wildflowers on the banks of Roses Branch,
or older lying in a field near Bandana,
deep in Queen Anne's lace at night
and counting constellations. Then you might have
walked Roan Mountain's crest through rhododendrons
budding into life. You might have seen blue ridges
like the silhouettes of sleeping women
fading into distance and know already "only one."
Then did you drive breathing holes like stars
into the tin lid of a Mason jar and dance
at twilight, hand-catching fireflies to swarm
in glass and light the twisted path home?
Perhaps you cupped your hands and dipped
deep into the stream to drink from your image,
already knowing the way your breasts would swell,
the blood that would come from the moon,
this man then a hundred miles away,
who was looking over his shoulder,
into a mirror where already your face
was forming a smile, your green eyes blazing.
And perhaps he already foresaw you alone
and dressed in mourning under stars,
wildflowers again in your hands, fresh
dirt caked on your walking shoes. And who
could blame him for being thrilled and afraid,
feeling a shiver down his spine to recognize
what you saw long ago in your body and in the stars?

Bob Snyder (1937–1995)

I was born in St. Marys, West Virginia, a town founded (according to legend) by the Virgin Mary, for reasons best known to herself. I've never figured out why divine intervention was required. Maybe she was fed up with Eliot and Stevens, not to mention Jesse Stuart.

My father was a still operator — at an oil refinery, let it be known — and my mother, secretary at the county health department. My dad's people came from around St. Marys and from Helvetia, West Virginia; my mother's, from the Ireland-Frametown area of the state and, on her father's side, from Germany by way of Cumberland, Maryland. My maternal grandfather spoke German and was a glassworker and a follower of Eugene V. Debs. He died when I was 13, and my self-education began with my going through his books. "Ode to a Grecian Urn," which I found in an anthology, put me in a spell and sent me down the rocky road of poetry.

I have been lucky in my teachers. In grade school and high school I had Audrey and Joe Samuels, both inspirations. At West Virginia University I fell in with an interesting New York crowd. In the 1960s Joe got me a job at the University of Cincinnati. I got in trouble with anti-war activity and drifted into Over-the-Rhine, where I could lean back in an old German saloon and listen to a hillbilly band.

Bob Snyder

I worked there in various Poverty War jobs. That's how I met Ernie Mynatt who introduced me to black lightning and who could walk into a sad situation and light everybody up in a way that was just amazing. I was first president of United Appalachian Cincinnati. I also met Hank "Boatwhistle" McIntyre, a bass player and comic who put me on the good road of bluegrass. I had a lot of black friends, too, and was fascinated by the people and politics of Avondale and the West End, especially musicians like Don Thomas, Billy Brown, Charlie Wilson, Fruitbowl Reeves, and Bobby

Crowder. I was moved by the devotion of musicians to their art, and I still remember Earl Taylor with his head bent over a speaker and tears in his eyes, making me play Bill Monroe's "Rosa Lee McFall" over and over.

My black colleagues helped me get a job at Antioch which developed into Antioch College/Appalachia in Beckley, West Virginia. There some of us formed the Soupbean Poets. We put out the magazine *What's a Nice Hillbilly Like You...*, and I worked up my collection *We'll See Who's a Peasant* (1977) under the pen name of Billy Greenhorn. When Antioch backed off its minority centers, I worked in Charleston, West Virginia, for a black CAP agency. Now I'm finishing a doctorate at Harvard University with a dissertation on Susanne Langer.

I write mostly about lost love and Buddhism. Meter interests me a lot, and I have a nine-syllable line which I've progressed up from Villon. I think Hölderlin covered the whole scene of "modernism." I like collaborative writing and have created along with Pete Laska and Joe Barrett the book *Old Martins, New Strings* by the Mason-Dixon Trio. Every year I read at Baber Mountain in Richwood, West Virginia, and at Dick's Den in Columbus, Ohio, where I'm backed by altoist Joe Diamond and his group. I try not to forget what Boatwhistle once told me: "When you tell a story, you got to live it for the truth."

Comfort Me with Hyssop

in soft pencil my great grandmother Caroline
underlined all the most pessimistic parts
of her cheap littleprint 1880s Bible —
how like a flower we spring up in the morning
are cut down by evening: no wonder

what with Lloyd's lifelong whiskey habits
Eva her youngest dreadfully burned to death
while stirring the kettle of family clothes
not to mention the vast screendoor boredom
of dingly back country cattle farming.

Wonder at her finding the inside outside
in the giant void growing on Mill Creek.
Wonder her way into the quiet mineral grass,
how many keys there are to heaven's rooms
but a broken heart's the axe to every door.

Pilgrim Number One

on those raw foggy restless schoolmorns
the rheebodendrons folded or invisible
sky heavy-shrouded whose darkness
reaches into all rooms, all hearts
the body itself sick of life
in the hazy orange light and gloom
of the painful gradeschool corridors —

the one thing definite and clear
was your long and level grin
even with your lip bit white below —
and not till later did we fathom
the secret of your eagerness
how your mother's female fears
your father's chasing you with a butcherknife
put you up in the foreground of yourself
with pure politeness of your mouth and eyes
laughing, saying, "NO MORE TROUBLE PLEASE!"

The Shoenatural Prophet

I smooth the page and touch all time
like a cold girl friend face
far far a-walking and anxious of report
though as poor old Aunt Becky said
it is no wonder there is a great
running to and froe in the earth
the devil in sutch rath and furiey
racing up and down the roads of mountains
for reality   the athlete of detail
knows that his reign is short
and love the angel of freedom
is nearing the last and final battle

Merle

the whole outfit under grass:
            I can't believe it! why
they were the whole slow life of me
and I was the kid at every funeral
Guy's with the four old farmers singing
their billygoat song up in the hills
Hughie's when I saw with a chill
that just like Uncle I too must die
Neilly's the baby of the family
that one really tore up her sisters

but I knew the hour had come
when at Lena's service up in Akron
my father stood blankly in front of Hughie's widow
"why my Lord Merle I didn't recognize you..."
Merle unrecognized by the eye of man!
Merle the prize by marriage
Merle Cotton and Buddy's mother
the family beauty a big sound forceful blonde

whose name people liked to say Merle Merle Merle
who always stood intent arms folded leant forwards
as if she were patiently enduring the cold
and you sort of want to offer to
run and get the poor woman a sweater
but no no Merle says
           and its your move pilgrim
Merle looking you dead square in the eye
and you can't tell if Merle'll speak or laugh
both start the exact same frank way

Hiding

the rain picked up at Milroy Grose Road
the fog intensified at Possum Creek turn-off
tingling silver overtones were growing everywhere
brightness from some hidden source
everything hidden save me
my brown Valiant and my little hyphen of road

I know there's a bright sun in here somewheres
as the morning rain rages
           the morning fog obscures
my mind blocked free of created things
high over the New River Gorge

out there is the cave we like to sit in and watch
  the river
drinking Gallo and smoking reefer
                          but now
coming back from the party on Fenwick Mountain
over the Rainhenge Foggyhenge Funkyhenge Bridge
  of Enlightenment
hide shivering at the nearness of uncreation
I'm a skeleton smoking a seegar
amid the tough adult Buddhist stardust
KEEP ON BOY JUST KEEP ON
               YOU'RE NEVER SATISFIED

Guard Duty

I wake up at night in the hills of West Virginia
in the house of my eighty-four-year old cousin
a single star lights his bathroom window
and an old white doorcurtain window with tree in fog behind
takes me back to you
           love old snake
here comes the aw shucks love feelin

I run my hand over the tufted bedquilt
trying to recall my dream of raccoon-faced leaves
     dawn's arriving
I will fill one of your old stockings
with Blue Dragon Sevin Dust
and sprinkle for the bugs
I will pick the wax beans
thinking of the old folks fingers
I touched in their coffins

Dogwood Farmstead

Daughter feels always silhouetted by it
feels so followed by the sky space around
feels she belongs to the place so
much more than it belongs to her
and that — just that right there —
is what the thing of it is
the site so off to itself feeling
stuck up on a hill full of fears
where the clouds strip you naked
and everyone stands to the wind
dark-socketed under the porchroof

pine shadders tighten and loosen
their star claws on the swing
according as the clouds recess
the house has too much personality
has an anxious inner sashaying
that needs to be put to laughter
has planks that open the nose
with a hundred year skunky gossip
WHY WOULD ANYONE BUILD A BIG HOME
OUT HERE WHERE NO ONE CAN SEE IT

Daughter makes up hymns of her own
spends all day practicing whistling
"the rock is embarrassment
   the hard place joy"
softening the light she lets in
hardening the light she lets out
Daughter walks the Devil by the deep blue sea
Daughter waits for the earnest unknown
trombones in the graveyard perhaps
forever humming high board well set
the happy home the seek-no-further

Katherine Soniat

When I was four years old, I moved south with my mother from Washington, D.C., to New Orleans where I was to live for most of the next three decades. My first impressions of that city were of flying cockroaches gusting out of the live-oaks, the rainy heat of summer afternoons which seemed to extend well into December, and the sweet-olive laden darknesses of November when the weather might, just might, turn cool. This was indeed an alien and visceral landscape in which I found myself immersed.

I note this "change of life" when I was four for when it occurred again some thirty years later, I had almost the same hypersensitive reactions to my new environment. I had spent a long time in the midst of New Orleans flora and strangely wingéd fauna; I had spent an equally long time imagining mountains and dry air. This wintry imagery had even started to appear with frequency in my poems. Once a student from Hamilton College in New York called long distance saying she was writing a paper on my work and wondered what my "mountain experiences" had been. None, I said, with great disappointment. Then, a few years later, my life took me to southwest Virginia, and there were my mountains of wandering cows and valleys of blowing corn. This was like exiting my "house on marshland" (I take this from Louise Glück) and landing in a preconceived heaven.

Katherine Soniat

I would hope that the freshness of the Appalachian region comes across in my poetry as well as it did to my southern senses in those first months here. Whether my poems concern the "deep" south or my present home in Catawba, Virginia, I think they begin with an almost photographic impression and then start translating into metaphor. Let me comment on the inception of two of the poems included in this anthology.

As I drove the windy mountain roads, I

was struck by a repetitive presence — that of the abandoned farm-truck in a field. There was a paradox in that its emptiness was so unsettling it came almost to contain a life of its own — the life it once contained. Thus, "Truck at the Top of the Field" was written. The poem "A Shared Life" is a narrative which originated from the finally disastrous confrontations between dogs, cows, farmers, and pheasants. After these episodes ended in the shootings of two dogs, I thought what if there were a world which could exist without fences, a world such as the one the birds fly through. Thus, the opening lines of that poem. The form was experimental for me, one in which I allowed the poem's content to shape the form. It was an exciting approach that I have since found fits itself to the uniqueness of each poem's initial impulse.

I often find a voice inside saying watch your material, your content, write about the urban landscape, but more and more I know that we cannot tell ourselves to write a conscious agenda. Poems flash out of a dark root and come to a life of their own; they must "need" that life. I will always recall those heavy scents and twilight visions of a childhood in New Orleans. I only hope I will bring that same well-trained nose and eye with me into all my journeys, be where they may, rural or urban.

My most recent collection of poems is *Cracking Eggs*, published by The University Presses of Florida. My work has recently been in such journals as *Poetry, The Kenyon Review, The North American Review, The Ohio Review*, and *NER/BLQ*. Presently I am working on a collection which combines my beginnings in New Orleans with that city's own historical origins.

Truck at the Top of the Field

It does not move,
but waits like a relic
pawnshops grow quiet with —

pocket watch run out of time,
gold rings finished with names.

Not one cow peers through its slats
into summer
            where once this truck
headed out, headlights flickering
the road, cows moaning, almost dawn
and somewhere to go.

Summer Tea

At first, the shape was a thing —
a blowing bag? hat in the field?
Then she saw the whining coon,
her dogs tossing him like an old
summer doll. Once she had pictured

fear like this — it gloomed windows,
hung in the imaginary trees

making cat-whines as she sat
arranging her dollhouse, its tiny
folk for August tea.

Now that cry was coming clear,
swift as the knowledge of waking
alone and knowing *alone* is the first
and final private thing. The coon's
whine came clear and she came

with a leash, thrashing two dogs
and a coon, not knowing
just what was being saved, the four
of them swirling before something
brisk and unquestioning on the other side.

Later, she returned to that coon,
dog-crippled, now undergoing men
with their shovel as he hunched
to the ground as if to pull it
up for privacy, one of them

mumbling *rabies* and *go on, hit him.
You afraid?* The man beat slowly.
And the coon's whine slowed
to that windy sound outside
a dollhouse.

A Shared Life

The horses nuzzle,
and bluebirds scatter from the fence post
like Sunday's children at a picnic.
But who promised all would be this idyllic
                                      with the fences up
or down — the black dog shot today, bleeding
among the farmer's dead pheasants, the brown dog
uncontrollable in his pursuit of cows,
the cows bemoaning the fenced life
the dog charges through.

Even the dozing cattle settle
under a tree house
                    not made by children.
Platform nailed high in a field oak,
where at night deer will arrive with eyes
                                    like porch lamps snapped on
                                    in the mist

as flashlight and double-barreled shotgun
                              plug each in turn,
                              mindless
of the limits.

And there is no end to limits: no end
                    to how the guinea hens can't
                    fly high enough, to how the pheasants
                    can't run far enough, to how the black
                    dog ran straight for the pheasants
                    and now is laid out in a patch
                    of bronze feathers, while the cows
                    flee the brown dog, flee
                    in four directions like the simpleminded
                    or an early fall wind, the animal warden
                    speeding across the beeline of 311 North
                    to say he don't want to cause nobody
                    no heartbreak, but those two dogs
                    broke the law; and behind him, by noon
                    comes the woman in the gray sedan,
                    taking a skiddy turn up to the dead
                    dog's porch to yell that the radio's so loud
                    it's spooking her cows. Oh, woe

unto all these dismal marriages in the fields,
woe to those with the vacant
                         or intelligent brown eyes,
to those with talons, canines, or cuds.

Even on calm days, cows press their hides
to the barbed wire
                  like noses to the window —
                  a wish, perhaps, to be one of the lost,
to be one of those with secret paths in sunlight,
hidden compasses for midnight.
A wish not to be
              one of these cows who rush
              each dawn ahead of this dervish of a dog,
              every breath a puffed remnant

of those lost to the fog a year at a time —
our animal universe tail to mouth,
tumbling into a rosy, beastly oblivion.

James Still (1906–2001)

The following excerpts were taken from *Foxfire,* fall 1988, an issue devoted to James Still.

My forebears from both sides first settled in Virginia during pioneer days. The Lindseys set down near Berryville and the Stills in what is now Lee County near Jonesville ... up the road from Cumberland Gap where I came to attend college in 1924. I didn't know then I was completing a genealogical circle. We've figured that my ancestors fought in the American Revolution and frontier land was allotted them as reward for their services. The Lindseys in Georgia, the Stills in Alabama. And not many miles apart....

I was born in 1906 on Double Branch farm just outside LaFayette [Alabama]. Sometimes I tell people I was born in a cotton patch. Anyhow, I came to consciousness there. One of my first memories is of running about with a small sack on my back Mama had sewed up for me. I'd pick a boll here and yonder and everywhere.... Aside from the Holy Bible, in our house there were three books: *The Anatomy of the Horse, The Palaces of Sin, or the Devil in Society,* and a heavy volume with a missing back, *Cyclopedia of Universal Knowledge.*

The *Cyclopedia* opened my eyes to the world. Many a subject was covered such as you'll find in a modern reference work. And more still. How to prune a fruit tree. The language of flowers.... Twenty-five sample words in several languages. A collection of classic poems. I got the poems by heart.

I wrote my first story when I was eight or nine. I still have it. I titled it "The Golden Nugget," and it was written with a lead pencil on a school tablet. Hard to read now, after seventy years. I found it recently, and I'll declare that I saw my future in the piece. A foreshadowing, you might say, of all the scribbling to come....

I never got to read the great books until I attended Lincoln Memorial University which was over the ridge from Cumberland Gap, Tennessee. I arrived with sixty dollars in my pocket and was starved for reading material. Every student earned his keep at LMU, and after morning classes I worked afternoons in the rock quarry feeding a rock crusher and was the library janitor. When the library closed at night, I swept the floors and emptied the wastebaskets and rubbed up the tables, and then with the door locked, the several thousand books and collection of magazines were mine until daylight. Many times I stayed the night, too drowsy to make it to the dormitory, and slept on newspapers in the storage room. I was like a child in a candy store. I hardly knew where to start. Somehow I found Thomas Hardy and Joseph Conrad and Hawthorne and Walt Whitman. The library was what Lincoln Memorial meant to me. I was saved by it....

At Lincoln I was holding a work scholarship provided by a benefactor. As did most of

James Still (Brunner Studio)

the others. When I was to graduate, I found out his name and address and invited him to the ceremony.... He was driven down from New York in his chauffered Cadillac. His name was Guy Loomis, heir to a sash and blind fortune.... Afterwards Mr. Loomis offered to pay my way to a graduate school of my choice in the south. He also said, "I'll make it possible, not easy." That proved to be the case. I chose Vanderbilt University.... On graduating in June my benefactor offered one more term of schooling.... A year later I was back home with three diplomas, no job, and no prospects....

I came to Knott County, Kentucky, to help Don West and his wife, Connie, with a summer recreational program.... I stayed a week at the Hindman Settlement School, and when I returned home, they sent a letter offering a job as a volunteer worker. They would shelter and feed me but couldn't pay me. I was willing, having no other prospects.... My assignment was the library.... I worked three years without pay. With the times improving, the fourth year I was awarded fifteen dollars a month. Slightly more the fifth year, and the sixth.... The publication of a few poems and short stories had kept me in razorblades and socks. And I'd published my first book, a collection of poems reviewers were uncommonly kind to. As I tell it, I was so rich I retired. On a day in June, 1939, I moved to an old log house between Dead Mare Branch and Wolfpen Creek, facing little Carr Creek.... The log house I moved into was built in 1827, or as the state historical association claims, 1840. I went there to finish writing the novel, *River of Earth,* for which the Viking Press had offered a contract. I had found a home....

People here are more likely to express themselves in an original manner than any place I know. I think it is something to celebrate. I don't want or expect Appalachian speech to be like any other. It has its own individuality, its own syntax. To be unlettered is not necessarily to be unintelligent.... What my part of Appalachia had in common with other parts for a long time was isolation from the main stream of American life and neglect by both our state and national governments. The neglect has only partly been addressed. Yet things are changing. Almost from day to day....

I don't know where Appalachia begins, or where it ends. It's like a fellow once told me: When I was in the eighth grade, my geography teacher kept mentioning Appalachia, and I couldn't find it in the textbook anywhere. I asked my Pap, "Pap, where is Appalachia?" And he said, "Son, you're sitting square in the middle of it." That's where I have a feeling I am and have been all these years.

Spring

Not all of us were warm, not all of us.
We are winter–lean, our faces are sharp with cold

And there is a smell of wood smoke in our clothes;
Not all of us were warm, though we hugged the fire
Through the long chilled nights.

                          We have come out
Into the sun again, we have untied our knot
Of flesh: We are no thinner than a hound or mare,
Or an unleaved poplar. We have come through
To the grass, to the cows calving in the lot.

Drought

Troublesome Creek is a highway wandering more than natural
For a passage going somewhere and arriving at certainty;
A road aims at straight lines, though accepts a curve or two
And a rise and fall to make a scheme and nature agree;
A creek pays less mind to man than to geography.

It would take a lot of rain to span the banks of Troublesome
And fill them up and start a respectable flowing,
And waken the rushes and dampen the hair of the mosses,
Liven the spring and start the draws a-roaring;
It would take a master rain to set the creek road going.

Pattern for Death

The spider puzzles his legs and rests his web
On aftergrass. No winds stir here to break
The quiet design, nothing protests the weaving
Of taut threads in a ladder of silk:
He is clever, he is fastidious, and intricate;
He is skilled with his cords of hate.

Who can escape through the grass? The crane-fly
Quivers its body in paralytic sleep;
The giant moths shed their golden dust
From fettered wings, and the spider speeds his lust.

Who reads the language of direction? Where may we pass
Through the immense pattern sheer as glass?

Passenger Pigeons

Here was a symphony of wings,
An aerial river of birds across the sky in thunderous floods
Of slate-blue feathers, a host of violet throats
Splitting the sky with one unerring thrust.

Here were red feet of pigeons spilling
Like blood through the trees, breaking the forest down
In their dense roosting wild with guttural cooing.
Here in this weight of wings were folded death and dust.

Dulcimer

The dulcimer sings from fretted maple throat
Of the doe's swift poise, the fox's fleeting step
And music of hounds upon the outward slope
Stirring the night, drumming the ridge-strewn way,
The anvil's strength...
                        and the silence after
That aches and cries unhushed into the day.

From the dulcimer's breast sound hunting horns
Strong as clenched hands upon the edge of death,
The creak of saddle-bags, of oxen yoke and thongs,
Wild turkey's treble, dark sudden flight of crows,
Of unshod hoofs...
                        and the stillness after,
Bitter as salt drenching the tongue of pain:

And of the lambs crying, breath of the lark,
Long drinks from piggins hard against the lips;
And with hoarse singing, raw as hickory shagbark,
The foal's anxiety is woven with the straining wedge
And the wasp's anger...
                         and the quiet after
For the carver of maple on a keen blade's edge.

Banjo Bill Cornett

Singing he goes, wrapped in a garment of ballads,
And his songs are his own, and his banjo shaped
By his own skilled hands. This is his own true love
He grieves, these his winding lonesome valleys
Blowing with perished leaves and winds that starve
In the chestnut oaks, and these the deaths he dies.
His voice is a whispering water, the speech of a dove.

The banjo is a part of him, his waking and his sleeping;
It is his bread and meat. Here his heart's peace lies.
It is his tongue for joy, it is his eyes for weeping.

Night in the Coal Camps

Cold yellow windows to the night, the trees
Frozen with dark, and eyes sleepless
Along rutted streets. Clear the sparrow words
Pierce thumb-latched doors; blowing they pass
Like field larks dustily through seeding grass.

Drawn faces on pillows, mouths hollowed in breathing
The unquiet air; and the million-tongued night tremulous
With crickets' rasping thighs, with sharp cluckings
Of fowls under drafty floors. In the caverns deep
The picks strike into coal and slate. They do not sleep.

Earth-Bread

Under stars cool as the copperhead's eyes,
Under hill-horizons cut clean and deft with wind,
Beneath this surface night, below earth and rock,
The picks strike into veins of coal, oily and rich
And centuries-damp.

They dig with short heavy strokes, straining shoulders
Practiced and bulging with labor,
Crumbling the marrow between the shelving slate,
Breaking the hard, slow-yielding seams.
Bent into flesh-knots the miners dig this earth-bread,
This stone-meat, these fruited bones.

This is the eight-hour death, the daily burial
In a dark harvest lost as any dead.

White Highways

I have gone out to the roads that go up and down
In smooth white lines, stoneless and hard;
I have seen distances shortened between two points,
The hills pushed back and bridges thrust across
The shallow river's span.

To the broad highways, and back again I have come
To the creek-bed roads and narrow winding trails
Worn into ruts by hoofs and steady feet;
I have come back to the long way around,
The far between, the slow arrival.
Here is my pleasure most where I have lived
And called my home.

O do not wander far
From the rooftree and the hill-gathered earth;
Go not upon these wayfares measured with a line
Drawn hard and white from birth to death.
O quiet and slow is peace, and curved with space
Brought back again to this warm homing place.

A Man Singing to Himself

They were a man's words, a ballad of an old time
Sung among green blades, whistled atop a hill.
They were words lost to any page, tender and fierce,
And quiet and final, and quartered in a rhyme.

This was a man's song, a ballad of ridge and hound,
Of love and loss. The words blossomed in the throat.
This was a man's singing alone behind his plow
With a bird's excellence, a man's shagbark sound.

Wolfpen Creek

How it was in that place, how light hung in a bright pool
Of air like water, in an eddy of cloud and sky,
I will long remember. I will long recall
The maples blossoming wings, the oaks proud with rule,
The spiders deep in silk, the squirrels fat on mast,
The fields and draws and coves where quail and peewees call.
Earth loved more than any earth, stand firm, hold fast;
Trees burdened with leaf and bird, root deep, grow tall.

John Foster West

My branch of the West family has lived in the Appalachians since 1772 when Alexander West I removed from Orange County, North Carolina, to Wilkes County on the Yadkin River. My great-great grandfather Alexander West II fought in the Revolutionary War, against the Cherokee Indians and at the battle of Camden, South Carolina. My great grandfather Baylus West one of the first settlers on the Lewis Fork Creek at the foot of the Blue Ridge, owned a large area of land which was divided among nine children, leaving little for my grandfather John Witherspoon West and none for my father, John Wilson West, who was born in 1867.

After the death of his first wife (and siring five children), my father married my mother, Elvira Foster, when she was 17 and he was 42. Of their eight children, I was the fifth. My first novel, *Time Was* (published by Random House, 1965), is based on my parents' lives from 1906 to 1918.

My father worked twelve and fourteen hours a day until his mid–60s to pay for 120 acres of sorry upland, then sold it and became a tenant farmer, moving from farm to farm, from shack to shack. During these itinerant years, I attended eight different schools, two of them one-room affairs, and studied at home by kerosene lamps. When I was a child, it required a whole day for my father to haul a load of mule-drawn lumber or tanbark from our home to Wilkesboro. Not long ago, I drove the distance on Highway 421 in thirteen minutes.

My family were devoted readers, and we would walk for miles to borrow books and magazines. I started writing poetry around the age of seven or eight. In the fourth grade, I won a classroom poetry contest. The first short story I sold (for $50) was written when I was a high school senior.

After graduating from Morgantown High School in 1938, I worked at an expensive psychiatric hospital for two years, saving $200, and entered Mars Hill Junior College where I worked my way through, writing both sports and general news. When I graduated in 1942, I owed only $125 which I paid at the end of two weeks of working in the Navy Yard in Charleston, South Carolina. That fall, I entered the University of North Carolina as a junior but was called into active service as an aviation cadet. During these years, I continued to write stories and poetry. Returning to the University of North Carolina in 1946, I received my A.B. in journalism in 1947 and my M.A. in English Literature in 1949. While there, I was co-founder of *The Carolina Quarterly* and runner-up in a Dodd, Mead national novel contest.

My career as a professor began at Elon College in 1949 where I taught for nine years. During that time my first collection of poetry, *up ago!*, was published, and I also studied eight weeks at a summer creative writing workshop at the State University of Iowa.

In 1958 I began teaching at what is now Old Dominion University, Norfolk, Virginia. While there, I published my first novel. After ten years, I moved to Appalachian State University to begin a creative writing program. After twenty-one and a half years at ASU, I retired on January 1, 1990, as emeritus professor of English.

Over the years my poetry has appeared in anthologies, quarterlies, and such magazines as *The Atlantic*, *Southern Review*, *The Southwest Review*, *Southern Poetry Review*, *The Appalachian Journal*, and the *North Carolina Folklore Journal*.

In recent years my second novel, *Appalachian Dawn*, a sequel to *Time Was*, was published along with *The Ballad of Tom Dula*, a researched study of the Tom Dula-Laura Foster murder case (which inspired the old ballad "Hang Down Your Head, Tom Dooley"). Also published in collaboration with Pulitzer Prize–Winning photographer Bruce Roberts was a book of poetry and photography, *This Proud Land*, in praise of the Blue Ridge country. My second volume of poetry, *Wry Wine*, followed.

John Foster West

In 1987 my novel *The Summer People* won the first Appalachian Consortium Press's Appalachian Fiction Award (published in 1989). One of the themes of this book is a protest against ecological destruction in the Appalachian region, focusing on the summer people who destroy forests and dig holes in the mountains to build chalets which are then occupied only three or four months in the year. I continue to protest this destruction of the Appalachians in my fiction, poetry, and my letters. Much of my best poetry in recent years has dealt with the region, but it is not propaganda poetry. Instead, I try to capture the spirit of the Appalachians through writing about my feeling and love for the region.

In progress are two novels based on my marriage to Nan Love West, who was killed in an automobile accident after twenty-two years and three months of marriage, and on our three children, Betsy, Leah, and John Kimrey. However, my continuing concern will be the preservation of the Appalachian mountain region.

Appalachian Nativity

As new wine bloats an old skin,
her girlhood gorged his gaunt shack;
where six were, another mate had been;
and never looking back,
she heaved aloft the yoke of each dour day

beneath the shadow of an austere man
double her years. Without stay,
new offspring followed seasons in the land.
Thus, in a winter of chill and plague
she waded alone through hot flame
of fever, down to the feverish vague
door of death, then turning, came
back, back, a new son in her arms —
a son unfed, cold, coldly assailed
by harsh life; though imperiled,
she rose up and, shivering, sloughed off death
and fed him and warmed up all December.
She gave life to go with meager breath,
in that chill time to remember.

Dark Lake

Once a valley lay here, where cows cropped
tilted pastures and the creek cut in two
his world. Smoke stood straight up
above black shingles once sliced like mica
by the iron froe of a grandsire lost in the past,
and the house by the stream was a safe place
where parents, all patience, awaited his coming.

Now a lake, valley-deep, covers
old hunting grounds where rocks were tools
and grassy slopes slanted up toward tomorrow.
He misses that old world with a dull ache
akin to dread. Sometimes trapped in sleep,
he dives down through watery gloom
searching, finding a chimney stump and stone steps
leading nowhere. In sudden panic
he flashes upward like a fleeing fish
all silver in moonlight, eluding the maws
of something huger than fear.
He wakes in sweat, weeping for anyone
who might have survived that place Atlantis,
to tread alone alien shores.

Aunt Orlena

Folks always called me Aunt Orlena.
Face wasn't much to look at, cross-eyes and all,
but I rid muleback and shanks' mare

through thunderstorm and blizzard fetching bairns
into a cold, cold world.
When my mount couldn't foot the ice,
I driv nails through my shoes, inside out'ards,
so's to stand up on icy slopes.
Birthin don't wait for no fair weather much.
Started young and fetched a thousand into life,
my last'un the year I died at a hundred and two.
I held up now and then jest long enough to get
twenty-four of my own and, don't you know, not one
lived past babyhood. But a thousand
is a fair crop, I'd say, in one-o-two years.
Not many men folk ever growd crops that long.

Pink Washborn

Me? I'm called Pink Washborn.
Never struck a day's work in my life,
unless you could call walkin and banjer pickin work.
Walked from here to yonder, slow as molasses,
seein what folks was doin, saying howdy
to stranger and kinfolks, jest anyone,
pickin and singin for bread and bedtick.
When I went, they found me settin agin a tree
my banjer on my lap, a grin on my face,
it snowin like hell, and me barefooted.

Winterfolk

Winter is a rebel way up here
on the west incline of this blue divide,
a reluctant refugee from his own occupied land:
in April you pass puddles of jonquils
sunning like blonde girls in yellow shorts
on a south exposure,
followed by a rocky mouth baring icicle fangs
facing north, standing off spring a day longer,
with here and there a swatch of snow
like feed-sack patches on worn green sleeves.
When spring does come, it's not with a charge
but stealthily, like an Indian stalking
the sleeping occupants of an isolated cabin.
One day you look up and behold! it's spring—
until you step into shade and inhale winter air.

The older folks have been up here so long
they half believe they beat Boone and the Alamance men.
When they ride out, it's on old buffalo trails.
On summer nights they carry winter in worn pockets
and snow beneath battered hats.
Let low-country intruder approach a cove,
and eyes as gray as icicle fangs measure stranger
for size, honesty, and intent.
If he smuggles in warmer times and brighter blossoms,
he can plant them the hell on some other farm
and leave this one to the familiar winter
of hard, honest labor,
the way God Almighty meant it to be.

MacKenzie Gap's Namesake

Had me one wife and three other women,
each livin in her own house, her own boss.
Got forty-seven younguns, thirty of them
boys, all big and stout as mules.
Told the folks hereabouts, in my religion
a man could have one wife and three
concubines; told them the name of my religion
was You Tend to Your Business, I'll Tend to Mine.
I was six foot, eight; weighed
two eighty, and had fourteen boys
my size. When my families went to church,
folks moved over for us.
The preacher kept preachin about
them giants in the earth,
but never said nothin to me face to face.
He knowd, and I knowd, size is
nine-tenths of the gospel,
whether you're a mule or a man.

Bull's Branch Revisited

The red clay hills have disappeared.
The rock-ribbed ridges, slashed slopes,
dirt that "would not sprout a pea,"
(but for two hundred years grew shaggy corn)
are covered over now, a mantle of green
with fieldpines having been lapped
across the land's scarred face.
The gaunt old shack still squats

black as weathered cowdung in the step
notched in the steep slope.
Creature of an austere past, it clings
to two electric wires, its only link
with a time just down the road.
Bull's Branch is hidden in a sleeve of green.
On the mountainside beyond,
the pasture is a forest; timber-tall
tulip poplar, oak, and pine vie for room.
The spring is lost beneath a slide
where Daniel Boone and I both knelt
to satisfy our upland thirst.
If, at this moment, he should come along,
striding up the branch in battered hat
(his coonskin cap relegated to myth),
I would meet him on familiar ground.
He would need to know what happened here
between his day and mine. "Not much,"
I'd say. "Six generations come and gone,
a good many crops of corn, no spring now."
The comfortable green forest all around
would put him at his ease, and he could choose
to disbelieve that time had passed at all;
for even time stumbles and stays its pace
passing among tall trees.

Charles Wright

The following excerpts were taken from *Contemporary Authors Autobiograpy Series,* Volume 7, Gale Research Inc., Detroit, Michigan.

I was born by the water and grew up on lakes and rivers. The first of these places was Pickwick Dam, Tennessee, where I was born 25 August 1935 (my father's thirty-first birthday) at 6:45 on a Sunday morning in the TVA hospital. My fame spread quickly throughout Hardin and adjoining counties as the first baby to be born in the new government hospital.... About a mile from Pickwick Dam is Shiloh National Park, scene of the Civil War battle of Shiloh and Pittsburg Landing. Family history has it that my great grandfather Charles F. Penzel, for whom both my father and I are named, was wounded out of the war during this battle.... He had arrived in this country in 1857 as a young man of sixteen from Asch, Bohemia, a second-son victim of primogeniture and anxious to escape the fighting in the Austro-Hungarian Empire at the time....

My mother (raised in the Mississippi Delta country) came from generations of farmers, ministers and itinerant preachers, tavern keepers, and Shenandoah ferrymen who had been in northern Virginia for over two hundred years.... My parents were married on 5 June 1934, the depths of the Depression ... not a good time for a banker's son. Not a good time for a cotton broker's daughter. My father (a civil engineer) signed on with the government, the Tennessee Valley Authority, and proceeded for the next eight or nine years to bring electricity to parts of the rural South, first by damming the Tennessee River, and later the Powell, the Clinch, and the Hiwassee, among others, first in Tennessee and then in North Carolina....

I remember a lot about Hiwassee.... In the lower southwest squeeze of the state, between the Cherokee National Forest and the Nantahala National Forest, between Ducktown, Tenneseee, and Murphy, North Carolina, the village had been hacked out of the wilderness, and the wilderness was not much bothered by it, or changed.... But my memories of it are golden. No matter how difficult it might have been physically for my mother, we must have been a very happy family there as that's how we all remembered it, the family albums replete with young boys holding up stringers of fish, lake views and mountain views, tiny houses and tiny yards, pine trees and undergrowth....

The summer I was thirteen, I went to a place that made an indelible marking on my life at the time and has continued, in imperceptible ways, to ink in the outlines of how I look at things, and how I go about things. The place was called Sky Valley and was a summer camp ... on two thousand acres of land outside Hendersonville, North Carolina. I spent three summers here and one entire year, in the tenth grade....

The overall override of Sky Valley was self-help: in the summer the campers helped build the physical plant, from the central eating pavilion to the barn to the individual cabins ... it was not a baby sitting organization, and the boys were inordinately proud of their summer accomplishments. The school worked less well, perhaps, but it was a noble experiment and gave me a lifelong weakness for solitude and contemplation....

I matriculated at Davidson College in the fall of 1953 ... by the time the four years were over, I had a diploma and a commission in the U.S. Army Intelligence Corps, which was, it turned out, to be my passport to the world.... I was in the Army for almost four years, three of them in Italy, in an apartment in Verona.... It gave me a whole new life ... the Army got my body, but Italy got what passed for my soul in those days....

I was more than fortunate to get a job in 1966, as I did, with my background — about seventeen poems published in magazines, a handful of translations published, and an MFA degree (from the Iowa Writing Program).... Offered a half-time, visiting, nine-month lectureship (at the University of California in Irvine) ... I stayed for seventeen years.... I spent my first two years in California in pursuit — of my first book and my first (and only) wife.... During this two-year stay I went to Montana, a place that has played, to this day, an important part in my work, both exteriorly and interiorly.

Charles Wright (Nancy Crampton)

My in-laws-to-be, John McIntire and his wife, had had a small ranch in the mountains of northwestern Montana since the late 1930s, a half-section of one of the last homesteaded areas in the continental forty-eight states. Surrounded by wilderness, twelve miles from the nearest neighbor, thirty miles from the nearest town, it was one of the truly unspoiled natural areas in the country.... Over the past twenty years, as a place and landscape and source of energy, it has joined east Tennessee/western North Carolina and Italy as one of the areas so much of my work has drawn sustenance from....

In the spring of 1986, forty-five years after I had first been there, I went back to Hiwassee for a few hours' visit ... Cherokee County was still an isolation of deep remove, and the village really had not changed much. The government sick-yellow siding on all the houses had been covered over by a stained upscale, dark green siding, the village complex was now called Bear Paw and was a "private community," but nothing was very different.... It was still sacred soil and still looked like a wonderful place for someone to have a childhood in.

Blackwater Mountain

That time of evening, weightless and disparate,
When the loon cries, when the small bass
Jostle the lake's reflections, when
The green of the oak begins
To open its robes to the dark, the green
Of water to offer itself to the flames,
When lily and lily pad
Husband the last light

Which flares like a white disease, then disappears:
This is what I remember. And this:

The slap of the jacklight on the cove;
The freeze-frame of ducks
Below us; your shots; the wounded flop
And skid of one bird to the thick brush;
The moon of your face in the fire's glow;
The cold; the darkness. Young,
Wanting approval, what else could I do?
And did, for two hours, waist-deep in the lake,
The thicket as black as death,
Without success or reprieve, try.

The stars over Blackwater Mountain
Still dangle and flash like hooks, and ducks
Coast on the evening water;
The foliage is like applause.
I stand where we stood before and aim
My flashlight down to the lake. A black duck
Explodes to my right, hangs, and is gone.
He shows me the way to you;
He shows me the way to a different fire
Where you, black moon, warm your hands.

Dog Creek Mainline

Dog Creek: cat track and bird splay,
Spindrift and windfall; woodrot;
Odor of muscadine, the blue creep
Of kingsnake and copperhead;
Nightweed; frog spit and floating heart,
Backwash and snag pool: Dog Creek

Starts in the leaf reach and shoal run of the blood;
Starts in the falling light just back
Of the fingertips; starts
Forever in the black throat
You ask redemption of, in wants
You waken to, the odd door:

Its sky, old empty valise,
Stands open, departure in mind; its three streets,
Y-shaped and brown,
Go up the hills like a fever;
Its houses link and deploy
—This ointment, false flesh in another color.

*

Five cutouts, five silhouettes
Against the American twilight; the year
Is 1941; remembered names
— Rosendale, Perry and Smith —
Rise like dust in the deaf air;
The tops spin, the poison swells in the arm:

The trees in their jade death-suits,
The birds with their opal feet,
Shimmer and weave on the shoreline;
The moths, like forget-me-nots, blow
Up from the earth, their wet teeth
Breaking the dark, the raw grain;

The lake in its cradle hums
The old songs: out of its ooze, their heads
Like tomahawks, the turtles ascend
And settle back, leaving their chill breath
In blisters along the bank;
Locked in their wide drawer, the pike lie still as knives.

*

Hard freight. It's hard freight
From Ducktown to Copper Hill, from Six
To Piled High: Dog Creek is on this line,
Indigent spur; cross-tie by cross-tie it takes
You back, the red wind
Caught at your neck like a prize:

(The heart is a hieroglyph;
The fingers, like praying mantises, poise
Over what they have once loved;
The ear, cold cave, is an absence,
Tapping its own thin wires;
The eye turns in on itself.

The tongue is a white water.
In its slick ceremonies the light
Gathers, and is refracted, and moves
Outward, over the lips,
Over the dry skin of the world.
The tongue is a white water.)

Firstborn

— Omnia quae sunt, lumina sunt —

1.

The sugar dripping into your vein;
The jaundice rising upon your face like a blush;
The glass box they keep you in —

The bandage over your eyes;
The curdled milk on your lips;
The plastic tube in your throat —

The unseen hands that linger against your skin;
The name, like a new scar, at your wrist;
The glass box they keep you in —

We bring what we have to bring;
We give what we have to give;
Welcome, sweet Luke, to your life.

2.

The bougainvillaea's redress
Pulses throughout the hillside, its slow
Network of vines

Holding the earth together, giving it breath;
Outside your window, hibiscus and columbine
Tend to their various needs;

The summer enlarges.
                     You, too, enlarge,
Becoming accessible,
Your liquid reshufflings

Protracted and ill defined,
Yet absolute after all, the new skin
Blossoming pink and clear.

3.

You lie here beside me now,
Ineffable, elsewhere still.
What should one say to a son?

Emotions and points of view, the large
Abstractions we like to think
We live by — or would live by if things

Were other than what they are;
Or we were; or others were;
If all were altered and more distinct?

Or something immediate,
Descriptive, the virtuous use of words?
What can one say to a son?

4.

If it were possible, if
A way had been overlooked
To pull that rib of pure light

Out of its cage, those few felicitous vowels
Which expiate everything ...
But nothing has been left out,

Nothing been overlooked.
The words remain in the dark, and will
Continue to glitter there;

No tricks we try to invent,
No strategies, can now extract them
And dust is dust for a long time.

5.

What I am trying to say
Is this — I tell you, only, the thing
That I have come to believe:

Indenture yourself to the land;
Imagine you touch its raw edges
In all weather, time and again;

Imagine its colors; try
To imitate, day by day,
The morning's growth and the dusk,

The movement of all their creatures;
Surrender yourself and be glad;
This is the law that endures.

6.

The foothills of Tennessee,
The mountains of North Carolina,
Their rivers and villages

— Hiwassee and Cherokee,
The Cumberland, Pisgah and Nantahala,
Unaka and Unicoi —

Brindle and sing in your blood;
Their sounds are the sounds you hear,
Their shapes are the shapes you see

Regardless, whenever you concentrate
Upon the remembered earth
— All things that are are lights.

Homecoming

(M.W.W., 1910–1964)

I sit on my father's porch.
It is late. The evening, like

An old dog, circles the hills,
Anxious to settle. Across
Our road the fields and fruit trees,
Hedgerows and, out beyond, in
Another state, the misty
Approaches to the mountains,
Go quietly dark. In the
Close corners of the yard white
Cape jasmine blossoms begin
To radiate light, become
Cold eyes. Into the sky the
Soft, loose Milky Way returns,
Gathering stars as it swarms
Deeper into the west. Now
Fireflies, like drops of blood, squirt
Onto the stiff leaves of the
Ivy vines, onto the bell
Lilies. Now I remember
Why I am here, and the sound
Of a breathing no longer
My own cuts through as I wait
For what must happen, for the
Flurry of wings, your dark claw.

Isabel Zuber

1912. A mountain man moves his growing family out of the North Carolina hills, away from the steep and stony farms his people have tended for five generations, and settles on broader, richer lands near the Holston River Valley in Tennessee. The covered wagon takes three days to go less than fifty miles, a journey made possible by hard work, thrift, a good price for the home place, and inspired by his wife's passionate desire to see her children better educated and off the land.

The education is a success, comes to include masters degrees, a doctorate. The adjustment to the flatlands is not. After the young mother sickens and dies, her husband sells out, moves halfway back. Over time, all but two of the children resettle in the upcountry, two sons returning to Watauga, the county of their birth. Eventually, even the dead are brought home to lie on a gentle slope not far from where they first set out.

A familiar enough story in Appalachia. In this particular version the couple are my grandparents, John and Anna Maud Eggers. They were brought back and reburied above Union Church in the community of Mabel about the time I was born to their eldest son, Herman (one of the returnees) and his wife, Elizabeth, in the small college town of Boone, North Carolina, some ten miles away.

I lived in Boone until I was married. At length, I found myself transplanted to Winston-Salem, but the hills are home to me still, as they were to those before me. The dream is always of going back, if only as dust that belongs there.

So I'm from Appalachia, am of the mountains, qualify as an Appalachian writer. But what does that mean? I confess I don't know. The argument seems endless as to whether Appalachia has a distinct and isolated culture or is really like all the rest of the country, at least like the South, with a few, not too significant, colorful characteristics exaggerated in print and other media.

I'm not trying here to settle this issue or to give evidence for either side. Personally, I would like to believe that we are, or at least have been, different and therefore special, though it may be only the wish that makes us so. For my part I have kept up the old connections to a large, extended, and clannish family. I have grown up hearing the grim stories of illness, accident, and crime without remedy or recourse, know that life is somber, to be taken as it comes, without sentimentality. And I know that a couple of generations ago the land was near unbearably lovely, that bees could be followed into the woods to their wild tree nests, and arrowheads of the Others were plowed up in the fields. Their mother's horn sounding from the back doorstep called my father and his brothers home to supper, and one day two of them

Isabel Zuber (Elizabeth Zuber)

sat on a sunny bank by a small stream with onions and some of her cornbread and told each other that no one in the world could be happier than they.

But where is this in the poetry I write? Not obvious, perhaps, but somewhere there, surely, underneath in what has been called the "compost." I may not be thinking of the mountains when I write, but perhaps they are always there anyway, with the wild strain coming through. I hope so.

My writing also owes a great deal to the help of supportive friends and encouraging teachers. I am grateful for publication in *The Arts Journal, The Laurel Review, The Small Farm, Poetry, Whetstone, Wind,* and others, and for recognition in awards for the Irene Leach Literary Contest, the North Carolina Writers' Network, Weymouth, and the Appalachian Writers Association.

I would especially like to thank Kay Byer, my most supportive friend; Jonathan Zuber, my most careful critic; and A.R. Ammons, who has been an encouraging teacher for me, as well as many others.

Your Old Ways

How would I know
if your old ways
work? Is there more
promise, less risk, the right
amount of danger?

What are you waiting
to tell me? I raise
beds in the garden, graft
a bud, root my cuttings uneasily.

What is it I don't know
that might save us all?

Our Lands and Fields, Mother

What shall a daughter
know of inheritance?
Morning and evening
milk will come down

through her fingers.
She'll stand in the furrow,
tend, care and none
of it be hers.

Father — leave your son
his birthright. Mother — give
your daughter lentils, secret
of bread, a worn spindle.

Didn't I work?
Didn't I die here? Isn't
this my dust? Sing what we were —
a hard narrow song.

The Decrease of the Tribe

They sold an L of acreage for
a new plant that makes a part
of something that is a part of
something that controls emissions.
Boards are falling off the barn.
Burdock grows in the lane.
No garden this year.

She rests her swollen leg on
a folding canvas chair as she
quilts. He spits tobacco juice
in a paper cup and watches the
screen. The table is set with
a white cloth, good food and
it is very quiet.

From the hill where the peacocks
scream for the peahens stolen
last fall you can see the new
highway in the valley, always
with trucks. The fat pony
grazing has not been bridled
in four years.

Since I was here last they've
sold all the pigs, are down
to five cows. The gamecocks
fight and kill each other off.
One wet and dead I found under
the boxwood. You will find us
much changed she said.

Before the Preacher Went Blind

Before the preacher went blind (and
could only hear his congregation
listening) he had visions. Eight
moons hung in the sky — eight suns
by day if he'd been able to look.
In his study at night a single
candle whirled big as
a spinning wheel, other lights
scattered, broken, over the rim.
Camp fires of the protracted meeting
doubled, redoubled, till from the pulpit
all souls seemed to move, sway
in circles touching a circle of flame.

At last the ground itself — as a wall
without gates — stood on end before him
and every worldly thing pushed up
into his very face.

After that he said
it was better not to see.

Made

    Creating the viper
    the great hand
    sketched; swerve,
    curve, flash, slash.
    When all was done
    even the Hand
    drew back.

What the Hunter Brings Home

But very little of the wild
and recently dead will fill a room.
It's the smell goes everywhere.
I spread papers for the blood,
fur, guts, head and feet, work
on my knees, my knife heavy,
sharp. Under membrane
the liver's free of spot,
eyes unclouded. I pull the skin
up over them quickly. Wholesome

meat, plentiful little rodents.
I clean the floor, won't think
of what I've done, what he's done.
We'll eat.

Thriving to Fail

I

One generation out
and already we don't
remember how the pick
slashed again and again
and ice chipped
like radiance
into the enameled bowl.

II

Before our eyes
our country vanished.
A faint scent
of the spicewood
hung in the air a moment,
was gone. Images
thus became more
necessary.

III

They drank from clay
they formed themselves
and so were more
fortunate than we.
Neither our cup
nor our water
is our own.

Another Misty Morning

Fog comes.
We bend to it, yearning
in gray. Oh, we long
for the leather clad
men promised of old.
We wait in the wet
and rain, drops

running off our hems,
down our heels,
for them to step —
aged, blithe and jaunty —
out of their cloud,
swinging their satchels
full of centuries of
compliments. We
stand, our noses growing
colder, stiff fingers
extended, smiles
freezing on our faces.
We wait, sir, by chance,
by chance, only for chance.

Offerings of Light

What is the cost
of all this yearning?
And what could be done
profitably in the time
spent at the window
watching the gray
stones, green iris sword,
imagining trout somewhere
in streams beyond, with
more than echoes of story?

Prophet, hold out your hands.
Refuse regret, for
offerings of light
are being given
in a cobweb and dew.

Solstice

Longest night
the sacred sweep
from light to dark,
dark to light.
We draw the rhythm
of our breath
rise, fall, ease, flow.

In the kitchen
a woman sings

hymns of another
time, an easier
faith, and a winter
rose blooms on
the window sill.

Glossary

Brier: a term used to refer to migrants from the Southern Appalachians who went to work in the steel mills and auto assembly plants north of the Ohio River. It came into use in Ohio in the early 1900s (Jim Wayne Miller's poems from *The Brier Poems*).

hoop: in West Virginia, a country person (Mark DeFoe—"Emergency Re-pairs").

leather britches: a colloquial name for a variety of half-runner green beans preserved by drying, a process that originated with the pioneers and persisted in the Appalachian mountains well into the 20th century. The entire bean pods (after the strings were removed) were strung on a strong thread and hung in a warm place to dry. For cooking, they would be soaked in water overnight or longer to soften (Llewellyn McKernan—"The Strike: A Bird's Eye View").

man trip: a low, flat, box-like metal cage with a roof to protect against cave-ins that runs on tracks to carry miners from the mine entrance down to where they are working. Described as being cramped and uncomfortable, the ride is all the more unpleasant when it takes an hour or longer to reach deep, underground work sites (Mark DeFoe—"The Former Miner Returns from His First Day as a Service Worker").

Melungeons: a race of tall, bronze-skinned, black-haired people, often with dark blue eyes, located in isolated communities in the mountainous regions of Tennessee, Kentucky, Virginia, and North Carolina, first encountered by expeditions to these areas as early as 1774. Their origin is unknown. Theories range from their forebears having been Portuguese sailors shipwrecked along the Carolina coast in the mid–1500s, members of Sir Walter Raleigh's Lost Colony, deserters from Spanish expeditions to the area in the mid- to late 1500s, to their belonging to a band of "white" Indians from pre–Columbian times, first noted by De Soto in 154 (Don Johnson—"Sailin' On to Hawaii").

Mstistry: a dream word invented by P.J. Laska. Freely-associated, it evokes words and concepts such as *mystery, missed history, history* shrouded in *mist,* etc. Consonant clusters *ms* and *mst* are impossible in English but are common in Slavic languages like Russian and Polish which were spoken by immigrants in the coal mining regions of West Virginia (P.J. Laska—"Mstistry").

Omnia quae sunt, lumina sunt: Latin for "All things that are, are lights," a quotation from Ezra Pound (Charles Wright—"Firstborn").

Shaker: 'In the Shakers' religious services at Pleasant Hill, Kentucky, a believer would come to the front of the meetinghouse and begin to whirl, an ecstatic exercise in which he would shake off the old body (Adam and the sins of the flesh) in order to make room for Christ" (Llewellyn McKernan—"The Shaker," quoted from Notes in her book *Short and Simple Annals: Poems About Appalachia*).

Teays: refers to the Teays River of prehistoric times which emptied into a great inland sea covering the interior of the North American continent. Existing until the Ice Age, it is the ancestor of what is now known as the New River, making this "new" river one of the oldest rivers in the world and the only river system to bisect the Appalachian plateau from east to west (Stephen Knauth — "From the Cherokee").

Vandalia: almost became the state name for West Virginia. It originated as the name chosen for a proposed 14th colony after the French and Indian War in an attempt to win favor with the king who would have to approve its charter (English royalty had a distant connection with the French Vandals by way of a former queen). Not until 1861 did statehood become a possibility for the frontier of Virginia at which time "West Virginia" won out over "Vandalia" as the state's name (Bob Henry Baber — "Vandalia").

witty: a retarded or mentally deficient person believed to have the gift of prophecy. It originally comes from the Old English word *wittig,* meaning "wise." A variation of this meaning is one who is a trickster and whose behavior may be outrageous or wily (Jim Wayne Miller — "How America Came to the Mountains"; Richard Hague — "Greenbrier Portraits").

Notes on the Poets

Since these poems were collected, many of the authors have received honors, awards, and publishing credits not covered in their autobiographical essays. Some of that information is listed below. Also included is a brief summary of the literary careers of those poets who are deceased — their legacy to the literature of the Southern Appalachians.

Bob Henry Baber has published a chapbook, *Assorted Lifesavers from the Mountains,* and a children's ditty, *Ice Sicle Soup,* and edited *Old Wounds, New Words: Poems from the Appalachian Poetry Project* with George Ella Lyon and Gurney Norman (Jesse Stuart Foundation, 1994). He received two Andrew W. Mellon Appalachian Studies Fellowships from Berea College. His journal "My Exhilerating, Self-Destructive, and Near-Criminal Candidacy for the Governorship of West Virginia" was published in *The Appalachian Journal,* 1997. In 2004 he was elected mayor of Richwood, West Virginia.

Joseph Barrett (1950–1990) published two books of poems, *Roots Deep in Sand* and *Periods of Lucidity,* and had completed a third, *Blue Planet Memoirs,* at the time of his death. He studied in Oxford as an exchange student and also in the Middle East. Many of his poems were published in literary journals in Japan, France, Canada, and Australia as well as in anthologies and literary periodicals in the United States. He studied Chinese and Japanese poets and experimented extensively with new forms and styles including haiku and senyru. He was one of the original Soupbean Poets, a group that emerged in the 1970s during the poetry renaissance in the Appalachian South, a reawakening of the area's longtime tradition in verse.

Kathryn Stripling Byer has published four books of poetry, most recently *Wildwood Flower,* which won the Lamont Poetry Prize of the Academy of American Poets in 2002; *Black Shawl,* selected for both the Roanoke-Chowan Award and the Brockman-Campbell Award; and *Catching Light* that won the Southeastern Booksellers Book of the Year in Poetry in 2003. She has two collections: *Wake* (2003), a chapbook, and *Coming to Rest* (2006). She has received fellowships from both the National Endowment for the Arts and the North Carolina Arts Council, and in 2001 she received the North Carolina Award for Literature. She was Poet-in-Residence at Western Carolina University until 1998 and was recently named Poet Laureate for North Carolina. She also received the Hanes Poetry Award for 2007 from the Fellowship of Southern Writers.

Fred Chappell published 26 books of poetry, fiction, and critical commentary during his 40 years at the University of North Carolina–Greensboro where he was the Burlington Industries Excellence Professor of English. His latest books of poetry are *Family Gathering,*

Backsass, and *Companion Volume,* and his latest novel is *Look Back All the Green Valley.* He served for five years as Poet Laureate of North Carolina and has received many awards and honors including the 1985 Bollingen Prize in Poetry, an award in literature from the National Institute of Arts and Letters, and most recently, the Order of the Long Leaf Pine by the State of North Carolina as well as the Appalachian Heritage Writers Award by Shepherd University. He is a current faculty member emeritus of the university's MFA Writing Program.

Mark DeFoe is Chairman of the English Department at West Virginia Wesleyan College. Most recent chapbooks are *Air, Aviary, The Green Chair, Mark DeFoe's Greatest Hits,* and *The Rock and the Pebble.* A former Bread Loaf Scholar, DeFoe's poetry has received awards from *Appalachian Heritage, The Atlanta Review, Tulane Review, Black Warrior Review, A Smartish Pace, Nimrod, Chautauqua Literary Review,* and *Now and Then.* He has received two Artists Fellowships from the State of West Virginia.

Charles B. Dickson (1915–1991) published four collections of poetry—*A Touch of Wholeness* (traditional poetry), and three chapbooks of haiku: *fragrance of frost grapes, Out of Cassiopeia,* and *Taste of Summer.* For the last three years of his life he received an annual award from *The Lyric.* He was regarded as a master of haiku, having received many honors and awards for his work in this genre. A perfect-bound collection of his haiku, *A Moon in Each Eye,* was published posthumously. Also a volume of his haiku will be published in the fall of 2007 by Red Moon Press as part of the American Haiku Master Series.

Gregory Dykes has taught English and literature throughout the region: at Mars Hill College, Tusculum College, Western Carolina University, Brevard College, East Tennessee State University, and currently at Northeast State Community College. Poetry and prose pieces have been published in *The Asheville Poetry Review, The Walking Magazine,* and *Marquee Magazine.*

Marita Garin has poems appearing or forthcoming in *Zone 3, Southern Indiana Review, Borderlands, Literary Trails of the North Carolina Mountains: A Guidebook* (edited by Georgann Eubanks), and the anthology *Transform.* She has received writing fellowships from both the Tennessee Arts Commission and the North Carolina Arts Council and has been a Resident Fellow at MacDowell Colony.

Richard Hague has published *Ripening, Possible Debris, Lives of the Poem: Community & Connection in a Writing Life, The Time It Takes Light* (poems around and about physics), and *Alive in Hard Country,* which won the 2004 Poetry Book of the Year from the Appalachian Writers Association. In 1984 he received a Teacher's Award grant from the Greater Cincinnati Foundation and in 1990, a National Endowment for the Humanities grant to study literature and landscape at Oxford University, England. His *Milltown Natural: Essays and Stories from a Life* was nominated for a National Book Award in 1997.

Marc Harshman has published several collections of poetry including *Turning Out the Stones, Rose of Sharon,* and *Local Journeys.* His poems have appeared in *The Georgia Review, Southern Humanities Review, Christianity and Literature, Appalachian Heritage, Shenandoah,* and many other periodicals in the U.S. and Britain. His ten children's picture books have won recognition and many awards including a Smithsonian Notable Book for Children and Parent's Choice Award for *The Storm.* He holds degrees from Bethany College, Yale Divinity School, and the University of Pittsburgh.

Don Johnson has published two books of poetry, *The Importance of Visible Scars* and *Watauga Drawdown.* His poems have appeared in *Prairie Schooner, Iowa Review, The Georgia Review,* and *Shenandoah* among other periodicals. He has been editor of *Aethlon: The Journal of Sport Literature* since 1990. In 2002 his article on Seamus Heaney and sport was published in *The Southern Review*. A critical survey of poetry about sport, *The Sporting Muse*, was published in 2004 by McFarland. Twice he has been nominated for a Pushcart Prize. He served as Dean of the College of Arts and Sciences at East Tennessee State University from 1995 to 2002.

Stephen Knauth has published four poetry collections, most recently *Twenty Shadows* and *The River I Know You By*. His poems have appeared in *North American Review, Pacific Review, Prairie Schooner, Seneca Review, Virginia Quarterly Review, Poetry Daily*, and other national publications. He has received two fellowships from the National Endowment for the Arts and two Creative Writing Grants from the North Carolina Arts Council.

Mary Kratt most recently published *The Only Thing I Fear Is a Cow and a Drunken Man, Valley*, and *Small Potatoes* that won the Campbell-Brockman Poetry Book Award. An earlier collection of poems, *Spirit Going Barefoot*, won the Oscar Arnold Young Award for poetry. Her non-fiction books include stories of regional history, particularly of the Charlotte, North Carolina, area, two of which have won history book awards. She is a MacDowell Colony Fellow, her residency there funded by a North Carolina Arts Council award.

P.J. Laska has published eight collections of poetry, the most recent being *The Mason-Dixon Sutra* (with poems by Joseph Barrett and Bob Snyder, two poet friends who died in the 1990s). An earlier collection, *D.C. Images and other Poems*, was a National Book Award finalist. He is a former teacher of philosophy and has been a National Endowment for the Humanities fellow. Two years in Japan, extensive travel around the world, and the ancient wisdom of the Tao Te Ching have influenced his poetic sensibility toward Far Eastern philosophy. He writes from that perspective in poems which are placed in rural West Virginia, his birthplace.

George Ella Lyon has published two collections of poems, *Mountain* and *Catalpa*, that won the Appalachian Book of the Year award. She has also published numerous picture books, two of which have won a Publisher's Weekly Best Book of the Year Award and a Kentucky Bluegrass Award, five novels for young readers, an autobiography, and an adult novel, *With a Hammer for My Heart*, featured in Borders Bookstores "Original Voices" series and presented as a play at Georgetown College. Recently she edited the anthology *A Kentucky Christmas*.

Jeff Daniel Marion has published short stories, a children's book, and seven collections of poetry including *Vigils: Selected Poems, Lost & Found, The Chinese Poet Awakens, Letters Home*, and *Ebbing & Flowing Springs: New and Selected Poems and Prose, 1976–2001*, which won the 2003 Independent Publisher Award in Poetry and was named Appalachian Book of the Year by the Appalachian Writers Association. In 1978 he was awarded a Literary Arts Fellowship by the Tennessee Arts Commission. In 1993 he participated in the Distinguished Writers Reading Series jointly sponsored by the NEA and the University of Tennessee. He received the Appalachian Literature Award in 2002 and the Educational Service to Appalachia Award in 2005 from Carson-Newman College. For 33 years he taught creative writing at Carson-Newman College where he was poet-in-residence, director of the Appalachian Center, editor of *The Small Farm* from 1975 to 1980, and editor of *Mossy Creek Reader*. Currently he operates Mill Springs Press, producing chapbooks and broadsides printed by letterpress.

Michael McFee has published seven books of poetry including *Plain Air, Vanishing Acts, Sad Girl Sitting on a Running Board, Colander, Earthly*, and *Shinemaster*. He has edited two anthologies, *The Language They Speak Is Things to Eat: Poems by Fifteen Contemporary North Carolina Poets* and *This Is Where We Live: Stories by 25 Contemporary North Carolina Writers*, both from the University of North Carolina Press. *The Napkin Manuscripts: Selected Essays* *and an Interview,* a book of prose, was published in 2006 by the University of Tennessee Press. He has received numerous awards and honors for his poetry including Ingram-Merrill, North Carolina Arts Council, and NEA fellowships. He is professor of English in the creative writing program at UNC-Chapel Hill.

Llewellyn McKernan has published poetry and prose in 28 anthologies. She has received 11 fellowships including ones from the American Association of University Women and the West Virginia Commission on the Arts and has won 70 awards and prizes from state, regional, and national competitions. Poetry books include *Short and Simple Annals: Poems About Appalachia* and *Many Waters: Poems from West Virginia*. She has also published four books for children.

Irene McKinney has been an associate professor at West Virginia Wesleyan College as well as a visiting poet and teacher at Western Washington University, University of California–Santa Cruz, University of Utah, and other universities. She has also served as assistant editor of *Quarterly West*. In addition to four books of poetry that include *Six O'Clock Mine Report* and *Quick Fire and Slow Fire,* she recently published a new collection, *Vivid Companion,* and also edited the anthology *Backcountry: Contemporary Writing in West Virginia*. Her awards include an NEA fellowship, the Utah Arts Council Prize Award in Fiction, the Kentucky Foundation for Women Award, the Appalachian Mellon Fellowship from the University of Virginia, fellowships at both MacDowell Colony and the Virginia Center for the Arts, and a Bread Loaf Scholarship. She has been Poet Laureate of West Virginia since 1993. A documentary film on her life and poetry was shown on PBS.

Louise McNeill (1911–1993) published prose, fiction, essays, scholarly works, and five books of poetry including *Gauley Mountain, Paradox Hill: From Appalachia to Lunar Shore,* and *Hill Daughter: New and Selected Poems by Louise McNeill* (edited by Maggie Anderson). She also wrote *The Milkweed Ladies,* a memoir of her mountain girlhood, considered by many to be one of her most notable books. She earned her Ph.D. in History and English from West Virginia University and went on to teach until 1972. She was named West Virginian of the Year in 1985 and was appointed Poet Laureate of West Virginia in 1979, a position she held until her death in 1993. Her literary awards include *The Atlantic Monthly* Poetry Prize, the annual book award of the West Virginia Library Association, and the 1988 Appalachian Gold Medallion from the University of Charleston.

Jim Wayne Miller (1936–1996) published seven collections of poems, the most notable being *Dialogue with a Dead Man, The Mountains Have Come Closer,* and *Brier: His Book*. The last two were combined into one volume, *The Brier Poems* (Gnomon Press), after his death. His first novel, *Newfound,* was named "Editor's Choice" by *Booklist* and one of the "Best Books of the Year" by the American Library Association. *His First, Best Country,* a sequel to that novel, was also produced as a play. An editor and scholar of Southern Appalachian literature, he was the guiding spirit behind the Appalachian Writers Workshop at Hindman Settlement School in Hindman, Kentucky. He received numerous awards including the Thomas Wolfe Literary Award, the Zoe Kincaid Brockman Memorial Award for Poetry, and the Appalachian Writers Association's Book of the Year and Outstanding Contribution to Appalachian Literature awards. During his career he edited major collections of poems by James Still and Jesse Stuart and published two books of translations from the Austrian poet Emil Lerperger. He was a professor of German literature at Western Kentucky University for 33 years and taught writing workshops throughout the Appalachian region.

Robert Morgan has published eleven books of poetry, most recently *The Strange Attractor: New and Selected Poems;* five novels of which *Gap Creek* received the Southern Book

Critics Circle Award in 2000; and three books of short stories. He received the Appalachian Heritage Award from Shepherd College in 2003. A member of the Fellowship of Southern Writers, he currently teaches at Cornell University and has recently been visiting writer at both Duke University and East Carolina University. His latest project is a biography of Daniel Boone to be published in the fall of 2007.

Valerie Nieman has published a collection of short fiction, *Fidelities* (West Virginia University Press), and is the author of two novels and two chapbooks of poetry. Her short stories and poetry have appeared in *The Kenyon Review, Arts and Letters, Poetry, West Branch,* and various anthologies including *Racing Home: New Stories by Award-Winning North Carolina Writers*. Her awards include a fellowship from the National Endowment for the Arts, the Elizabeth Simpson Smith prize in fiction from the Charlotte Writers Club, and the Greg Grummer Prize in poetry from *Phoebe*. Having completed her MFA at Queens University of Charlotte, she now teaches both English and journalism at North Carolina A & T State University. A new collection of poetry, *Wake, Wake, Wake,* was published in 2006 by Press 53.

Lee Pennington is the author of 19 books, nine of which have been poetry. Two of his poetry collections, *I Knew a Woman* (1977) and *Thigmotropism* (1993), were nominated for the Pulitzer Prize. He has had nine plays produced. In 1984 he became Poet Laureate of Kentucky. In 1993 he received an Honorary Doctorate of Philosophy in Arts from the Academy of Southern Arts and Letters. He was professor of English at the University of Kentucky Jefferson Community College until retirement in 1999. He and his wife, Joy, owners of Jole Productions, produce cultural documentaries, among them *The Mound Builders* and *Easter Island: Eyes that Look at the Sky* (2001), and have traveled widely in the United States and in 68 foreign countries.

Ron Rash, whose family has lived in the Southern Appalachian mountains since the mid–1700s, writes primarily about the region in his two books of short stories, *The Night the New Jesus Fell to Earth* and *Casualties*; three books of poetry, *Eureka Mill, Among the Believers,* and *Raising the Dead*; and three novels, *One Foot in Eden, Saints at the River,* and *The World Made Straight*. He has published poems in *Southern Review, Georgia Review, Poetry, Shenandoah, Yale Review, Texas Review,* and many other periodicals. In 1994 he received a National Endowment for the Arts Fellowship. His many awards and honors include an O. Henry Award, the Sherwood Anderson Prize, and the Novella Festival Novel Award. In 2002 *One Foot in Eden* won *Foreword Magazine*'s Gold Medal in Literary Fiction as well as being named Appalachian Book of the Year. In 2005 he won the James Still Award from the Fellowship of Southern Writers and the Southern Book Critics Circle Award for *The World Made Straight*. He holds the John Parris Distinguished Professor Chair in Appalachian Cultural Studies at Western Carolina University.

George Scarbrough has had work published in 30 anthologies and reference volumes, including *History of Southern Literature* and *Encyclopedia of Eastern Tennessee*. He received the Bess Hokin Prize from *Poetry* in 2000 and the James Still Award from the Fellowship of Southern Writers in 2001. In 2004 he was awarded a Doctorate Degree in Letters from Lincoln Memorial University, Harrogate, Tennessee.

Bettie Sellers taught in the English Department at Young Harris College at Young Harris, Georgia, from 1965 to 1996, served as Chairperson of the Division of Humanities (1975–1985), and was Goolsby Professor of English from 1986 to 1996. She is the author of the following books of poetry: *Westward from Bald Mountain, Appalachian Carols, Spring Onions and Cornbread, Morning of the Red-Tailed Hawk, Liza's Monday and Other Poems, Wild Ginger,* and *Satan's Playhouse* (chapbook). She also published *The Bitter Berry: The Life of Byron*

Herbert Reece. She has received various awards from the Georgia State Poetry Society, Mid-South Poetry Society, the Atlanta Writers Club, and the New York Poetry Forum as well as other regional and national awards.

Vivian Shipley recently published *Gleanings: Old Poems, New Poems* that won the 2004 Paterson Prize for Sustained Literary Achievement and was also nominated for the Pulitzer Prize. *When There Is No Shore* won the 2002 Word Press Poetry Prize and the 2003 Connecticut Book Award for Poetry. She is the Connecticut State University Distinguished Professor and Editor of *Connecticut Review*. She has won the Hart Crane Poetry Prize from Kent State University and the Julia Peterkin Poetry Prize. She has also received a Connecticut Commission of the Arts Grant. A twelfth book of poems, *Hardboot: Poems New & Old,* was published in 2005.

Nancy Simpson has published poems in *The Georgia Review, Southern Poetry Review, Prairie Schooner,* and other magazines as well as having her work included in the anthology *Word and Witness, 100 Years of North Carolina Poetry*. She edited *Lights in the Mountains, Stories, Essays and Poems by Writers Living in and Inspired by the Southern Appalachian Mountains.* Currently she is a Resident Writer at John C. Campbell Folk School.

R.T. Smith received the 1981 John Masefield Award for Narrative Poetry and the 1986 Brockman Award for his book of poems *Birch-Light,* chosen by A.R. Ammons. In 1990 he won a National Endowment for the Arts Fellowship, and in 2000 he received a Virginia Arts Commission Fellowship. His books include *Faith: Stories; Trespasser; Split the Lark: Selected Poems; Messenger,* which won the Library of Virginia Book Award; *Brightwood;* and *The Hollow Log Lounge,* which won the Maurice English Prize for Poetry in 2003. He has also published a book of short stories, *Uke Rivers Delivers.* Currently he is editor of *Shenandoah: The Washington and Lee University Review* and Philips Family Distinguished Professor of Rhetoric and Composition at Virginia Military Institute. A new book of poems, *Outlaw Style,* is forthcoming from Arkansas University Press.

Bob Snyder (1937–1995) graduated from West Virginia University and went on to develop and direct Antioch College Appalachia in Huntington and Beckley, West Virginia, in the 1970s. A dedicated teacher, he entered Harvard's Graduate School of Education and completed his Ph.D. in 1991, his thesis topic being "Cognition and the Life of Feeling in Susanne K. Langer." He published widely in literary journals, and in 1977 his poetry collection *We'll See Who's a Peasant* appeared under the pen name "Billy Greenhorn." At the time of his death, he had completed a second collection of poems, *Milky Way Accent,* and a collection of witty short stories based on his experiences growing up in West Virginia.

Katherine Soniat has published *Cracking Eggs, Alluvial, The Fire Setters, Notes of Departure* that won the Camden Prize from the Walt Whitman Center for the Arts and Humanities, and *A Shared Life* that won the Iowa Poetry Prize and a Virginia Prize for Poetry. New poems are forthcoming in *Southern Review, Iowa Review, Shenandoah, Seneca Review, Prairie Schooner, The Virginia Quarterly Review, Crazyhorse,* and *Hotel Amerika*. She taught in the Master of Fine Arts program at Virginia Tech and is now emeritus professor of English. A new collection, *The Swing Girl,* is forthcoming from LSU Press.

James Still (1906–2001) published two volumes of poetry, *Hounds on the Mountain* and *The Wolfpen Poems*; two novels, one of which, *River of Earth,* won the Southern Authors Award; three short story collections, the most notable being *On Troublesome Creek*; and several books of fiction for young adults. He received awards for his writing from the American Academy of Arts and Letters and the National Institute of Arts and Letters, the O. Henry Prize, the Weatherford Award for Appalachian Writing, the Milner Award of the Kentucky

Arts Council, and many others. He also received honorary degrees from Berea College, University of Kentucky, Transylvania University, Morehead State University, and Lincoln Memorial University. In honor of his legacy, a James Still Award is given biennially by the Fellowship of Southern Writers to a writer for his or her achievement in writing about the Appalachian South.

John Foster West has had earlier novels, *The Summer People* and *Time Was*, and his researched study *The Ballad of Tom Dula* recently re-published by Parkway Publications. *Time Was* is now considered a "Southern classic." Collections of poetry include *Wry Wine* and *High Noon in Pompeii*. A fifth novel, *Going Home to Zion*, is now in print. He retired in 1990 as emeritus professor of English at Appalachian State University at which time he endowed the John Foster West Creative Writing Prize that is self-sustaining.

Charles Wright won the Ruth Lilly Poetry Prize in 1993. His collection *Black Zodiac* won the following awards: the National Book Critics Circle Prize and the Los Angeles Times Book Prize in 1997; the Pulitzer Prize and the Ambassador Book Award in 1998; and the Antico Fattore Prenio (Italy) in 1999. His book *Chicamauga* won the Lenore Marshall Prize in 1997. Other poetry collections include *Zone Journals, Appalachia, Negative Blue: Selected Later Poems, A Short History of the Shadow, Buffalo Yoga,* and *Scar Tissue*. He also has published translations of the Italian poet Eugenio Montales. Among many awards he has received Fulbright, Guggenheim and Ingram-Merrill fellowships and a National Book Award for Poetry.

Isabel Zuber has published poetry and short fiction in *The American Voice, Poetry, The Greensboro Review, Pembroke Magazine, Shenandoah,* and *Southern Review*. Prizes include the publication prize in the North Carolina Writers' Network poetry chapbook contest, the Lee Smith Award for Fiction from the Appalachian Writers Association, the University of Tennessee Press prize for short story, the Irene Leach Literary Contest, and a Forsyth County Arts Council grant. She has participated in many conferences, literary festivals, and visiting writers and readers series throughout the region, the most recent being the First Carolina Mountains Literary Festival in Burnsville, North Carolina, in 2006. Her poetry collections are *Oriflamb* and *Winter's Exile*. Her novel *Salt* was selected in 2003 for the Virginia Commonwealth University's First Novel Award.

Index of Poems and Poets

"Abandoned" (Miller) 155
"After an Image in Faulkner" (Smith) 208–209
"Afterwards, Far from the Church" (Byer) 29
"Almost" (Harshman) 80–82
"Ancestorial" (Laska) 107
"And All the Princes are Gone" (Sellers) 191–192
"And the River Gathered Around Us" (Johnson) 88–90
"The Anguish Lessons" (McKinney) 137–138
"Another Misty Morning" (Zuber) 245–246
"Appalachian Nativity" (West) 229–230
"Appalachian Parthenon" (Dickson) 48–49
"An April Exultation" (Barrett) 22–23
"Asa Gray on Cheat Mountain" (Laska) 107–108
"At the Edge of Town" (McKernan) 135
"At the Union Picnic" (Nieman) 166–167
"Aunt Orlena" (West) 230–231

Baber, Bob Henry 11–17
"Back to Bandana in Brown Season" (Downer) 54–55
"Banjo Bill Cornett" (Still) 225
"Baptism: Watauga River" (Johnson) 85–86
"The Barn" (Harshman) 79–80
Barrett, Joseph 18–23
"Before the Preacher Went Blind" (Zuber) 244
"Beneath the Mound" (Smith) 210–211
"Beyond the Two of Us" (Harshman) 83
"Billy Edd Wheeler" (Pennington) 173
"The Bird Carver" (Smith) 208
"Bittersweet" (Byer) 28–29
"Blackwater Mountain" (Wright) 235–236
"Blizzard" (McNeill) 144

"Blood of the Lamb" (Garin) 63–64
"Blue Ridge Moments: Nine Haiku" (Dickson) 49
"The Body of Elisha Mitchell" (Morgan) 160
"Bridge on the River Kwai" (Simpson) 205
"The Brier Breathing" (Miller) 153–154
"The Brier Losing Touch with His Traditions" (Miller) 151–152
"Broomsedge" (Morgan) 157–158
"Bull's Branch Revisited" (West) 232–233
"Bus perched on top of a mountain like a skull on a wedding cake" (Downer) 54
Byer, Kathryn Stripling 24–30

"The Call" (Smith) 207–208
Chappell, Fred 31–39
"Cold Quilt" (McFee) 127
"Comfort Me with Hyssop" (Snyder) 214
"Coming Back to West Virginia" (Kratt) 100–101
"Crab Orchard Prediction" (Garin) 66
"Crowded House" (Simpson) 202–203
"Cumulonimbus" (Knauth) 95

"Dark Lake" (West) 230
"Dark Smell" (Pennington) 172–173
"Death Crown" (Morgan) 159–160
"The Decrease of the Tribe" (Zuber) 243
"Deep Mining" (McKinney) 139–140
DeFoe, Mark 40–45
"Detour" (Barrett) 21
"Diamonds" (Byer) 27
Dickson, Charles B. 46–49
"Dog Creek Mainline" (Wright) 236–237
"Dogwood Farmstead" (Snyder) 217
Downer, Hilda 50–55

"Driving the Great Craggy Mountains" (Knauth) 97
"Drought" (Still) 224
"Dulcimer" (Still) 225
Dykes, Gregory 56–61

"Earth-Bread" (Still) 226
"Ebbing & Flowing Spring" (Marion) 119–120
"1836: In the Cherokee Overhills" (Knauth) 94
"Elopement" (Lyon) 112
"Emergency Re-pairs" (DeFoe) 43
"Expedition" (Nieman) 167–169

"Fall" (Marion) 121–122
"Family Reunion Near Grape Creek Church, Four Miles West of Murphy, N.C., 1880" (McFee) 126
"The Farm Tender" (DeFoe) 44–45
"Fencepost" (Miller) 150
"'15-Year-Old Mother Killed...'" (Garin) 64
"Firstborn" (Wright) 237–239
"The Flying Snake" (Morgan) 162–163
"For Women Who Have Been Patient All Their Lives" (McKinney) 138–139
"The Former Miner Returns from His First Day as a Service Worker" (DeFoe) 41–42
"From a Ridge in Eastern Kentucky" (Garin) 64–65

Garin, Marita 62–67
"The Gift of Tongues" (Morgan) 163–164
"Going Back the Hard Way" (Hague) 70–71
"Going Home" (Johnson) 90–91
"Good Friday, 1995, Driving Westward" (Rash) 182
"Greenbrier Portraits" (Hague) 72–74
"Guard Duty" (Snyder) 216–217

Hague, Richard 68–76
"Haiku-Senryu-Haiku" (Barrett) 20

"Hand-Me-Down Days" (Marion) 122
"Having Foreseen the Deaths of Others, the Old Mountain Woman Awaits Her Own" (Rash) 180–181
"Having Recovered His Sight After Being Struck by Lightning, the Old Farmer Quiets Those Who Would Question Him" (Rash) 181
"Her Words" (Lyon) 112–113
"Here" (Chappell) 39
"Hiding" (Snyder) 216
"The Hillbilly Odyssey" (Laska) 108–109
"Hill Daughter" (McNeill) 144
"Hill Woman" (Smith) 212
"Hills so beautiful, they sting" (Downer) 52–53
"Hiwassee River" (Scarbrough) 188–189
"The Hollow" (Morgan) 158
"Homecoming" (Wright) 239–240
"Homeward" (Barrett) 19
"Horse Breath Winter" (Shipley) 197
"The Hounds Are Restless" (Pennington) 172
"How America Came to the Mountains" (Miller) 150–151
"How the Letters Bloom Like a Catalpa Tree" (Lyon) 113–114

"I'd Have Waited a Lifetime for You, Greer Garson" (Kratt) 101
"Impossible Creek" (Knauth) 96–97
"In the Woods Beyond the Coal Fields" (Hague) 71–72
"The Inheritance" (Baber) 13–14
"It Is ..." (Dykes) 57–58
"Ivory Combs" (Byer) 26–27

"Jericho's" (Byer) 27–28
Johnson, Don 84–91
"July, 1947" (Rash) 178–179

"Kentucky Lucky" (Pennington) 174
Knauth, Stephen 92–98
Kratt, Mary 99–103

"Lady Sewing Songs" (Pennington) 173
Laska, P.J. 104–109
"The Last Man on Devil's Nose" (Marion) 117–118
"Leaving in the Dead of Winter" (Simpson) 204–205
"Lives in One Lifetime" (Simpson) 203–204
"Liza's Monday" (Sellers) 193–194
"Looking at a Photograph of My Mother, Age 3" (Lyon) 114–115
"Lost Flower" (Morgan) 159
Lyon, George Ella 110–115

"MacKenzie Gap's Namesake" (West) 232

"Made" (Zuber) 244
"Magnet" (Dickson) 48
"A Man Singing to Himself" (Still) 227
Marion, Jeff Daniel 116–123
"Mary Daugherty" (Hague) 71
"Mayapple Hill" (McNeill) 144–145
McFee, Michael 124–129
McKernan, Llwellyn 130–135
McKinney, Irene 136–141
McNeill, Louise 142–147
"Merle" (Snyder) 215–216
Miller, Jim Wayne 148–155
"Miracle at Raven Gap" (Sellers) 193
"Moonshiner" (McNeill) 145
Morgan, Robert 156–164
"A Mountain Fable of a Sort" (Marion) 118–119
"My Grandmother Speaks of the Early Years" (Rash) 178
"Mystistry" (Laska) 109

"Nail Bag" (Morgan) 158–159
"Naomi's Nerve" (Sellers) 192
"New Organ" (Morgan) 161–162
Nieman, Valerie 165–169
"Night-Fishing on Irish Buffalo Creek" (Knauth) 93
"Night in the Coal Camps" (Still) 226
"Night Student" (Simpson) 202
"The 1940s" (Kratt) 102–103
"1946" (Johnson) 87
"No More Hard Times" (Dickson) 47–48

"October" (Hague) 74–75
"Offerings of Light" (Zuber) 246
"On the Steep Side" (Kratt) 102
"On the Wings of a Dove" (Miller) 153
"Opossum Spring" (DeFoe) 44
"Our Lands and Fields, Mother" (Zuber) 242–243
"Outside Cecelia, Kentucky" (Shipley) 198–199
"Outmigration Time Again" (Laska) 105–106

"Panther" (Marion) 120
"Passenger Pigeons" (Still) 224–225
"Pattern for Death" (Still) 224
Pennington, Lee 170–176
"Picnic in Cherokee National Forest" (Garin) 65
"Pilgrim Number One" (Snyder) 214–215
"The Pine Figures" (Knauth) 97–98
"Pink" (Sellers) 192–193
"Pink Washborn" (West) 231
"Plain Air" (McFee) 128
"Poem for James Collins" (Baber) 14–15
"Poet of the Soil" (Pennington) 175–176
"A Prayer for Slowness" (Chappell) 39

"A Prayer for the Mountains" (Chappell) 32
"A Preacher Who Takes Up Serpents Laments the Presence of Skeptics in His Church" (Rash) 179–180
"Primer" (Harshman) 80

"Rain polka dots the sidewalk" (Downer) 53–54
"Raising the Dead" (Rash) 181–182
"Rambling Rose" (Marion) 120–121
Rash, Ron 177–182
"Raymond Pierce's Vietnamese Wife" (Johnson) 88
"Reclamation" (McFee) 125–126
"Reclamation: Washing Machine" (Nieman) 167
"Reflections During a Country Funeral"(Dykes) 59–61
"Remembering Wind Mountain at Sunset" (Chappell) 32–37
"Remodeling the Hermit's Cabin" (Chappell) 37–39
"Return" (Pennington) 172
"Richwood" (Baber) 13
"River Bed" (Byer) 29–30
"The Roads" (McNeill) 146–147

"Sailin' on to Hawaii" (Johnson) 86–87
Scarbrough, George 183–189
Sellers, Bettie 190–194
"Setting the Hook" (Harshman) 82–83
"The Shaker" (McKernan) 134–135
"A Shared Life" (Soniat) 220–221
"Shenandoah" (McFee) 128–129
Shipley, Vivian 195–199
"The Shoenatural Prophet" (Snyder) 215
Simpson, Nancy 200–205
Smith, R.T. 206–212
"Snowbird" (Byer) 28
Snyder, Bob 213–217
"So much has come and gone that the Appalachians never existed" (Downer) 52
"Solstice" (Zuber) 246–247
"Sometimes I Am Looking" (Hague) 75–76
Soniat, Katherine 218–221
"Spring" (Still) 223–224
Still, James 222–227
"Still Life" (Barrett) 22
"Street Dance: West Virginia" (DeFoe) 42–43
"The Strike: A Bird's Eye View" (McKernan) 131–134
"The Strikers" (Barrett) 19–20
"Summer Tea" (Soniat) 219–220
"Sunday Evening at Middlefork Creek Pentacostal Church" (Rash) 180

"Tenantry" (Scarbrough) 185–186
"A Testimony" (Lyon) 111–112
"Thriving to Fail" (Zuber) 245
"Timber Boom" (McNeill) 145–146

"Tinted Pictures" (McFee) 127–128
"To Be" (Pennington) 175
"Trail of the Lonesome Pine" (Baber) 15–16
"Trillium" (Byer) 25–26
"Truck at the Top of the Field" (Soniat) 219
"A Turning" (Miller) 152–153
"Twilight in West Virginia: Six O'Clock Mine Report" (McKinney) 140–141

"Vandalia" (Baber) 16–17
"Visiting My Gravesite: Talbott Churchyard, West Virginia" (McKinney) 140

"Weather Diviner" (Garin) 65
"Weave" (Smith) 210

"We Came" (Pennington) 175
West, John Foster 228–233
"What I Have Learned" (Dykes) 61
"What the Hunter Brings Home" (Zuber) 244–245
"Whiskey Tree" (Morgan) 160–161
"White Chickens" (Shipley) 197–198
"White Highways" (Still) 226–227
"White Lie" (Simpson) 203
"Widow Horvath on Coal Run Then and Now" (Laska) 105
"The Widow McDowell on Her Granddaughter's Divorce" (Laska) 106–107
"A Winter Baptism" (Barrett) 20
"Winter Bread" (Scarbrough) 186–187
"Winterfolk" (West) 231–232

"Winter Watch" (Marion) 122–123
"Wolfpen Creek" (Still) 227
"Woman Playing a Juke Box" (Barrett) 21
"Worms" (Shipley) 196–197
"The Wreck" (Simpson) 204
Wright, Charles 234–240

"A Yard Near Elizabethton, Tennessee" (Garin) 66–67
"Yonosa House" (Smith) 209–210
"You Must Teach the Student" (Dykes) 58–59
"Your Old Ways" (Zuber) 242

Zuber, Isabel 241–247

www.ingramcontent.com/pod-product-compliance
Ingram Content Group UK Ltd.
Pitfield, Milton Keynes, MK11 3LW, UK
UKHW050538150426
5217IPUK00026B/1988